KEGAN PAUL
A VICTORIAN IMPRINT

PUBLISHERS, BOOKS AND CULTURAL HISTORY

LESLIE HOWSAM

LONDON AND NEW YORK

First published 1998 by Kegan Paul International

2 Park Square, Milton Park, Abingdon, Oxon OX14 4RN
711 Third Avenue, New York, NY 10017, USA

Routledge is an imprint of the Taylor & Francis Group, an informa business

First issued in paperback 2016

Copyright © 1998 Leslie Howsam

All rights reserved. No part of this book may be reprinted or reproduced or utilised in any form or by any electronic, mechanical, or other means, now known or hereafter invented, including photocopying and recording, or in any information storage or retrieval system, without permission in writing from the publishers.

Notice:
Product or corporate names may be trademarks or registered trademarks, and are used only for identification and explanation without intent to infringe.

British Library Cataloguing in Publication Data
A catalogue record for this book is available from the British Library

ISBN 13: 978-0-7103-0605-0 (hbk)
ISBN 13: 978-1-138-97398-5 (pbk)

Publisher's Note
The publisher has gone to great lengths to ensure the quality of this reprint but points out that some imperfections in the original copies may be apparent. The publisher has made every effort to contact original copyright holders and would welcome correspondence from those they have been unable to trace.

KEGAN PAUL
A VICTORIAN IMPRINT

To Jessica

ACKNOWLEDGEMENTS

The research upon which this book was based was made possible by a postdoctoral fellowship granted in 1990 by the Social Sciences and Humanities Research Federation of Canada. The University of Toronto Department of History provided an institutional base for the project and supplemented the fellowship with opportunities for part-time teaching. The University of Toronto Library borrowed the all-important microfilm edition of the Kegan Paul archives for me from the Centre for Research Libraries. I spent the two years of the fellowship studying the archives, constructing a database, and writing three preliminary articles based on the research. The first three chapters of *Kegan Paul – A Victorian Imprint* were composed in the summer of 1993 in a cottage at Long Point, Ontario. That fall I joined the Department of History of the University of Windsor, and the fourth chapter was written there; I wrote chapter five in Toronto during the summer of 1994, while I was enjoying a Northrop Frye Visiting Fellowship at Victoria University.

Michael Collie supported the project from the beginning. I became aware of the Kegan Paul archives in our work as collaborators on a bibliography of the International Scientific Series, which was published by the King and Kegan Paul firms. As we worked to understand the company's ledgers for the Series, the possibility began to emerge of using them for a larger study. Michael supported the fellowship proposal, kept in touch as the research developed, and was the first person outside my family to read the completed manuscript. John M. Robson was my second indispensable supporter. From my first year as a Masters' student in Victorian Studies he encouraged me to become a historian of the book. That support continued through my dissertation and first book, and he, too, supported the postdoctoral fellowship proposal and remained interested in the Kegan Paul project as it emerged as a book manuscript. Jack became a good friend as well as colleague and counsellor, and his death in July of 1995 was a great loss.

Both Michael Collie and John Robson were members of the Toronto Bibliography Group; I want to acknowledge the collegiality and friendship of all members of the group, not least when I presented to them a paper on this project. Gillian Fenwick has co-ordinated the meetings of the group since it began in 1988, and she and I have been talking about bibliography and the history of the book since we were students together in 1981. Her friendship and counsel have been immensely valuable to my work and to this book.

I received assistance for which I am grateful from Robin Alston, Patricia Anderson, Bill Bell, Simon Eliot, Eric Griffin, Richard Landon, Laura McLeod, Jane Millgate, Michael Millgate, Jacqueline Murray, Mary Patton, Ann Robson and Albert Tucker. The University of Windsor Department of History secretaries, Sylvia Allison and Arlene Boudreau were always efficient and helpful with printouts and correspondence.

I read papers on this research at the following conferences: Canadian Historical Association, Ottawa, 1993; Society for the History of Authorship, Reading and Publishing, Washington, 1994; and the Midwest Conference on British Studies, Toronto, 1994. On each occasion I benefited from the responses of the audience. Three anonymous readers selected by the University of Toronto Press and the Canadian Federation for the Humanities wrote thoughtful comments that enabled me to revise the manuscript for publication. At the University of Toronto Press, the incomparable Suzanne Rancourt has been the best of editors, tactful, reassuring and shrewd. And Peter Hopkins of Kegan Paul International has been remarkably gracious to the Canadian scholar whose proposal for a book on the prehistory of his firm turned up at the 1993 Frankfurt book fair. Norman Franklin, former chairman of Routledge & Kegan Paul, very kindly read the manuscript, shared his long knowledge of the firm and suggested several useful revisions.

No bibliographical project can avoid a massive debt to libraries, and no historical one to archives and record offices. The staffs of

ACKNOWLEDGEMENTS

the University of Toronto libraries, of the British Library, and of Cambridge University Library were always helpful. At the Library of University College London I worked with the original manuscript archives of the Kegan Paul publishers, and had the opportunity to meet Gillian Furlong. The Public Record Office census rooms, the registry of wills at Somerset House and the Dorset County Record Office yielded information about the households and finances of some of my subjects. I found letters of Charles Kegan Paul in the Thomas Hardy collection in the Dorset County Museum, the University of London Library, Cambridge University Library, the Harry Ransom Humanities Research Center, the Tennyson Research Centre, Lincolnshire County Library and the Library of King's College, Cambridge. I examined the papers of Archbishop Trench in the Representative Church Body Library, Dublin.

Neil Campbell has read every work of this book at least once, and engaged in lengthy discussions and arguments about the relative merits of narrative and of bibliography in writing the history of an imprint. Our marriage has survived his preference for entrepreneurial Henry S. King, and his aversion to Charles Kegan Paul, whose enigmatic personality I continue to enjoy. Jessica Kamphorst receives the dedication for this book because she was my research assistant, and is my daughter. She spent the summer of 1992 suffering eye strain and reporting a boredom I cannot easily comprehend, as she worked her way from A to Z through the volumes of the *National Union Catalogue of Pre-1956 Imprints* to ascertain the correct title and publication date of every book the publishers brought out from 1871 to 1889.

Leslie Howsam
Department of History
University of Windsor

CONTENTS

Acknowledgements	vii
Tables	xii
Plate section	xiii
Introduction	1
Chapter 1: Henry S. King: businessman of letters	15
Chapter 2: Charles Kegan Paul, pastor to publisher	48
Chapter 3: Kegan Paul, Trench – the partnership with a reputation for serious and beautiful books, 1877–1888	84
Chapter 4: Kegan Paul, Trench, Trübner & Co. Ltd.: a financial crisis and a revolution in management, 1889–1911	138
Chapter 5: The Kegan Paul legacy: the making, consolidation and survival of a reputation for serious books	174
Notes	191
Chronology of Events	208
Who's Who	211
Index	213

TABLES

1. Henry and Ellen King: family and business; Henry and Harriet King: family, business and books — 25

2. Series published by Henry S. King & Co., 1871–7 — 33

3. Charles and Margaret Paul – family, business and books — 63

4. Genres of books published under the three imprints — 92

5. Series published by C. Kegan Paul & Co. and by Kegan Paul, Trench & Co., 1877–88 — 110

6. Types of contracts issued under the three imprints — 125

7. Gender of the author in the publication books — 135

8. Chronology of proprietorship and management of Kegan Paul, Trench, Trübner & Co. Ltd., 1888–1911 — 139

9. Series published by Kegan Paul, Trench, Trübner & Co. Ltd., 1888–1911 — 155

PLATE SECTION

1. Youthful portrait of Charles Kegan Paul
   from the collection of Kegan Paul International
2. Charles Kegan Paul
   from F.A. Mumby, *The House of Routledge, 1834–1934 with a History of Kegan Paul, Trench, Trübner and Other Associated Firms* (1934)
3. Alfred Chenevix Trench, November 1878
   from F.A. Mumby, *The House of Routledge, 1834–1934 with a History of Kegan Paul, Trench, Trübner and Other Associated Firms* (1934)
4. Portrait of the house at 65 Cornhill where the firm first did business
   from Leonard Huxley, *The House of Smith Elder* (London, 1923)
5. Paternoster house, Charing Cross Road, the new premises of Kegan Paul, Trench, Trübner & Co. Ltd.
6. Dryden street premises of Kegan Paul, Trench, Trübner & Co. Ltd.
7. 'Pleasure' yearbook
8. 'Arbor Scientiae Arbor Vitae' the firm's trademark
9. The International Scientific Series
10. The Parchment Library
    from *Living English Poets MDCCCLXXXII* (London, Kegan Paul, Trench & Co., 1883)
11a. The Westminster Biographies title-page
    from Arthur Waugh, *Robert Browning* (London, Kegan Paul, Trench, Trübner & Co. Ltd., 1899)
11b. The Beacon Biographies title-page
    from Annie Fields, *Nathaniel Hawthorne* (Boston, Small Maynard, 1899)

PLATE SECTION

Plate 1 Youthful portrait of Charles Kegan Paul
from the collection of Kegan Paul International

Plate 2 Charles Kegan Paul
from F.A. Mumby, *The House of Routledge, 1834–1934 with a History of Kegan Paul, Trench, Trübner and Other Associated Firms* (1934)

PLATE SECTION xvii

Plate 3 Alfred Chenevix Trench, November 1878
from F.A. Mumby, *The House of Routledge, 1834–1934 with a History of Kegan Paul, Trench, Trübner and Other Associated Firms* (1934)

Plate 4 Portrait of the house at 65 Cornhill where the firm first did business from Leonard Huxley, *The House of Smith Elder* (London, 1923)

Plate 5 Paternoster house, Charing Cross Road, the new premises of Kegan Paul, Trench, Trübner & Co. Ltd.

Plate 6 Dryden street premises of Kegan Paul, Trench, Trübner & Co. Ltd.

Plate 7   'Pleasure' yearbook

Plate 8 'Arbor Scientiae Arbor Vitae' the firm's trademark

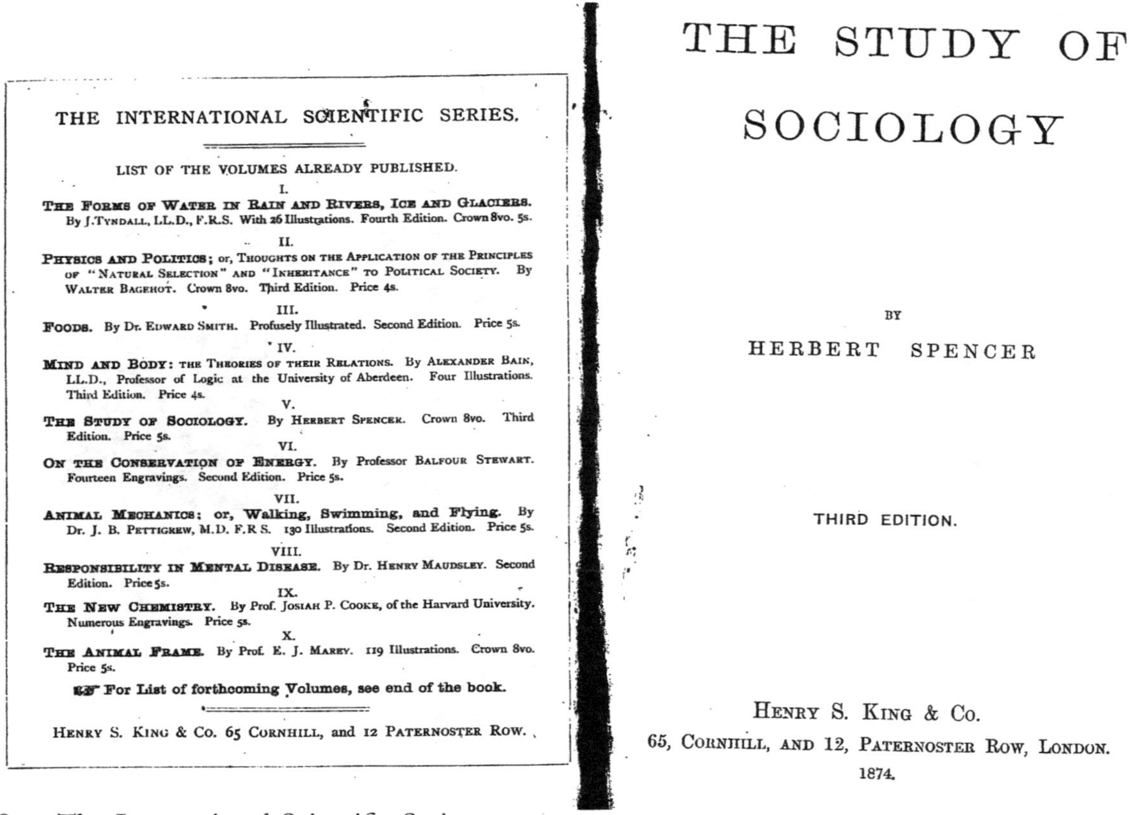

THE STUDY OF SOCIOLOGY

BY

HERBERT SPENCER

THIRD EDITION.

HENRY S. KING & CO.
65, CORNHILL, AND 12, PATERNOSTER ROW, LONDON.
1874.

THE INTERNATIONAL SCIENTIFIC SERIES.

LIST OF THE VOLUMES ALREADY PUBLISHED.

I.
THE FORMS OF WATER IN RAIN AND RIVERS, ICE AND GLACIERS. By J. TYNDALL, LL.D., F.R.S. With 26 Illustrations. Fourth Edition. Crown 8vo. 5s.

II.
PHYSICS AND POLITICS; or, THOUGHTS ON THE APPLICATION OF THE PRINCIPLES OF "NATURAL SELECTION" AND "INHERITANCE" TO POLITICAL SOCIETY. By WALTER BAGEHOT. Crown 8vo. Third Edition. Price 4s.

III.
FOODS. By Dr. EDWARD SMITH. Profusely Illustrated. Second Edition. Price 5s.

IV.
MIND AND BODY: THE THEORIES OF THEIR RELATIONS. By ALEXANDER BAIN, LL.D., Professor of Logic at the University of Aberdeen. Four Illustrations. Third Edition. Price 4s.

V.
THE STUDY OF SOCIOLOGY. By HERBERT SPENCER. Crown 8vo. Third Edition. Price 5s.

VI.
ON THE CONSERVATION OF ENERGY. By Professor BALFOUR STEWART. Fourteen Engravings. Second Edition. Price 5s.

VII.
ANIMAL MECHANICS; or, WALKING, SWIMMING, and FLYING. By Dr. J. B. PETTIGREW, M.D. F.R.S. 130 Illustrations. Second Edition. Price 5s.

VIII.
RESPONSIBILITY IN MENTAL DISEASE. By Dr. HENRY MAUDSLEY. Second Edition. Price 5s.

IX.
THE NEW CHEMISTRY. By Prof. JOSIAH P. COOKE, of the Harvard University. Numerous Engravings. Price 5s.

X.
THE ANIMAL FRAME. By Prof. E. J. MAREY. 119 Illustrations. Crown 8vo. Price 5s.

☞ For List of forthcoming Volumes, see end of the book.

HENRY S. KING & Co. 65, CORNHILL, and 12 PATERNOSTER ROW.

Plate 9   The International Scientific Series

MESSRS.

KEGAN PAUL, TRENCH & CO.'S

EDITIONS OF

SHAKSPERE'S WORKS.

THE PARCHMENT LIBRARY EDITION.

THE AVON EDITION.

The Text of these Editions is mainly that of Delius. Wherever a variant reading is adopted, some good and recognized Shaksperian Critic has been followed. In no case is a new rendering of the text proposed; nor has it been thought necessary to distract the reader's attention by notes or comments

1, PATERNOSTER SQUARE.

[P. T. O.

Plate 10 The Parchment Library
from *Living English Poets MDCCCLXXXII* (London, Kegan Paul, Trench & Co., 1883)

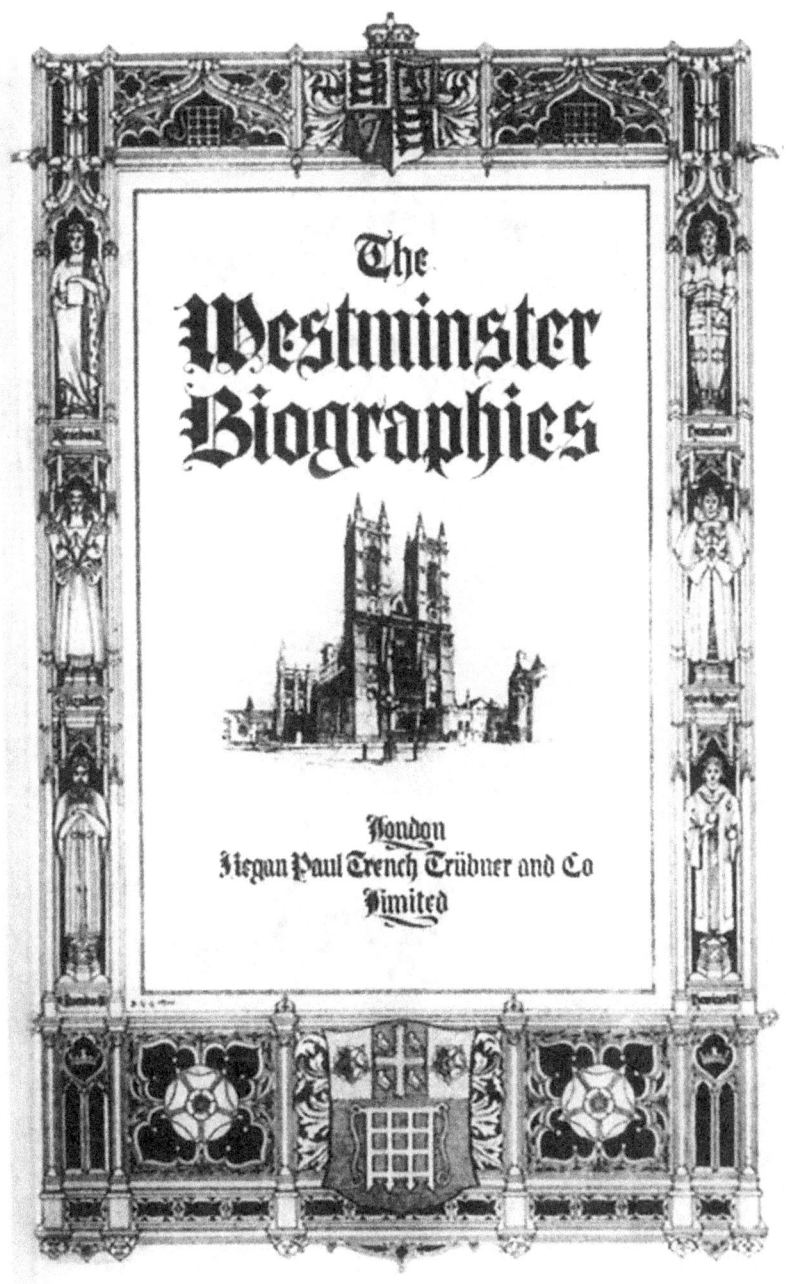

Plate 11a The Westminster Biographies title-page from Arthur Waugh, *Robert Browning* (London, Kegan Paul, Trench, Trübner & Co. Ltd, 1899)

Plate 11b The Beacon Biographies title-page from Annie Fields, *Nathaniel Hawthorne* (Boston, Small Maynard, 1899)

INTRODUCTION

This book, the history of a publisher's imprint, tells two connected stories: one about the personalities of a group of London publishers and the impression their characters made on the people who knew them: the other about a remarkable collection of books whose title pages bore those publishers' names over the course of four decades in the Victorian age. It is both a case study in nineteenth and early twentieth-century publishing and a contribution to the method and theory of the history of the book.[1] The intention is to demonstrate how that history, sometimes characterized as the study of authorship, reading and publishing,[2] can benefit from a focus on the publishers whose purpose it was to bring together the demands of readers with the preoccupations of authors.

Charles Kegan Paul is only the best-remembered of the publishers whose lives and work are chronicled in the pages that follow.[3] Paul's predecessor Henry S. King, his partner Alfred Chenevix Trench, and his successors George Redway and Spencer Blackett are also considered here, and so too are their wives, especially Margaret Agnes Paul, novelist, and Harriet Eleanor Hamilton King, poet. Although Nicholas Trübner was never directly involved in the firm, the managers during its last twenty years in business inherited his legacy of books on Asia and the Middle East. Influential figures like the stock promoter Horatio Bottomley and the journalist Alfred Sinnett moved behind the scenes to shape the firm's direction. The Kegan Paul imprint, given substance by all these people, has survived until the present day. The name is associated with the imprint Routledge & Kegan Paul, of London and later also of Boston. That distinguished list of works in the social sciences and philosophy has made a mark that is recognized not only by scholars but by all serious readers. However Routledge and Kegan Paul came into being in 1947, thirty-six years after Charles Kegan Paul's company died.

The imprint's history began in the spring of 1871, when Henry S. King set up as a publisher in Cornhill, London. Chapter one is an examination of King's life before and during that time. Besides his experience as a provincial bookseller and as a partner in a major London publishing house, King was an international entrepreneur, a banker and India agent. He published a number of specialized works along with a spate of novels and, among other coups, signed a five-year contract with Tennyson. King remained in business as a publisher from 1871 to 1877. About halfway through that time, he engaged Charles Kegan Paul as his manager and literary adviser. Chapter two picks up the story of Paul, who had been an Anglican clergyman in rural Dorset, lost his religious faith and consequently resigned his living, and was now a freethinker and Positivist. When King retired, his list, his contracts with authors, and his business headquarters were put into the hands of C. Kegan Paul & Co. From 1881 the imprint became Kegan Paul, Trench & Co., when Paul entered into partnership with a man twenty years younger than himself, Alfred Chenevix Trench. Paul and Trench worked together, developing a solid reputation in London for serious literature, especially poetry, for religious books and for science. The third chapter of this book is largely an analysis of the books they published, and the way in which they published them, during these years.

At the beginning of 1889 there was a financial crisis: the partners involved their firm with the affairs of Horatio Bottomley and his Hansard Union, and the firm was amalgamated with two other businesses. Chapter four sorts out the tangled narrative of the three companies that went to make up the new firm of Kegan Paul, Trench, Trübner & Co., Ltd., a limited company operating with staff managers under the control of a board of directors, its shares traded on the Stock Exchange. The Trübner part of the name came from the largest of the three lists now being amalgamated, namely the very large 'oriental' publisher, the late Nicholas Trübner, who specialized in books about India and Asia, and titles on Indian and Asian languages and cultures. The next largest list was that of Kegan Paul, Trench, and the smallest was the firm of George Redway, a youngish, rather esoteric, small publisher in Bloomsbury, who serviced the theosophist community. The managers of the new limited company, for the first five years, were Paul and Redway. Both Trench and the senior members of the Trübner staff immediately retired. Redway remained in office until 1895, when a crisis arose and both he and the board of directors lost the confidence of the shareholders. Paul retired, disabled by a traffic accident, a few months later. They were replaced by Spencer Blackett, reporting to a new board of directors. Blackett was yet another small publisher, initially trained for a military career. After ten years, in 1905, he too fell from grace with the board, and other managers were engaged. Finally in 1911 the firm of George Routledge and Son ended a decade of embarrassment that was financial as well as literary by taking over the business.

The narrative ends at that point, and chapter five, after concluding the biographical account for each individual associated with the Kegan Paul imprint, offers an analysis of the company's reputation as a serious publisher. It is important to note, however, that Routledge continued to operate Kegan Paul, Trench, Trübner as a separate business until 1947. When they changed the imprint to Routledge & Kegan Paul, the evocative name was still preserved, and since 1985 the newly revived imprint of Kegan Paul International continues to build on the reputation developed in the 1870s and 1880s by Charles Kegan Paul.

The theme of *Kegan Paul – A Victorian Imprint* is the duality of imprint: the publisher's imprint upon a list of books: and publishers' personalities, the imprint of their taste and judgement on the culture in which they lived. The sources and methods upon which this book is based therefore include both bibliography, the approach pertinent to a study of books, and biography, which is proper to a study of publishers.

Two broad approaches to biographical scholarship are used here. The first is a critical analysis of Charles Kegan Paul's influential memoir, including research to discover matters he omitted from that book. Charles Kegan Paul attempted to dictate to posterity the tenor of his personal reputation, and perhaps that of his firm, by writing *Memories*, the book he published in 1899 to record 'the somewhat varied life I have lived'. Paul's memoir, in the words of the editorial introduction to a 1971 reissue, is 'filled with entertaining stories of country and parish life, school and nursery in the high Victorian years'.[4] The narrative continues to late-Victorian London and a chapter on the author's career as a publisher. This part of his life is treated briefly and with circumspection, because Paul declined to comment on persons still living at the time. Now that there is a revival of scholarly interest in Victorian publishing, however, chapter nine of *Memories* is being explored and exploited.[5] Paul's *Memories* is used extensively in the chapters that follow, but always in the context of a critical reading, one that is attentive to silences and evasions.

The value of biographical research to the history of the book has recently been demonstrated by James L.W. West III, who argues that 'In book history the essential goal is the same as that for biography: to reconstruct human behavior from the past, using testimonial or archival evidence. . . . [A]ny reconstruction of the history of books will be an effort to recapture, in words, some part of the lives of those who wrote, made, published, sold, or read the books'.[6] In Paul's case we have an apparent wealth of material, spoken by a single voice. Scholars cannot, however, depend upon having a memoir, however evasive, as a source. The second approach is the detective work of biographical research, in genealogical, archival and literary sources. King, Trench, Redway and Blackett have been rather obscure names in the history of publishing. Now they are names to whom personalities, if not faces, have been attached. Henry S. King wrote no memoir and left no private papers. Much of what we know about him comes from Paul's *Memories*. King's wife, the poet Harriet Eleanor Hamilton King, provides another point of view in her *Letters and Recollections of Mazzini*. In addition, fragmentary evidence can be obtained from the memoirs and biographies of people with whom King was associated. The same kind of research is required to trace Alfred Chenevix Trench, Paul's partner, and his successors George Redway and Spencer Blackett. The wives of King and Paul were writers, and each contributed in significant ways to the family business. Snatches of evidence about these men and women are to be found in trade journals and other contemporary publications. Such documents would be of little use, however, without the large body of evidence also available

INTRODUCTION

to illuminate the personalities of the publishers: the books they offered to the London trade and to British and international readers.

Together with the archival records documenting the details of their production, the King and Kegan Paul books constitute the bibliographical evidence required to write the history of an imprint. The archival records begin with Henry S. King & Co. (1871–7), and continue through Paul's proprietorship in partnership with Trench (1877–89) and on to the management of Redway, Blackett and others in the operation from 1889 to 1911 of an amalgamated limited company. These records have not only survived a fire in 1883 as well as the London blitz and other vicissitudes in a fair measure of completeness, but they have been published on microfilm by Chadwyck-Healey, thus making them reasonably accessible to scholars outside England.[7] Accessible but initially frustrating, because the Kegan Paul archives contain virtually no correspondence that might illuminate author-publisher relationships, and nothing from readers. Although they published novels by Thomas Hardy and George Meredith, politics by Walter Bagehot and Henry George, science by T.H. Huxley and social and political thought by Herbert Spencer, no revealing document from any of these giants is to be discovered in the tin trunk where contracts were kept. Instead, the records consist mostly of publication books and publication account books, profit-and-loss ledgers for the 2,000-odd titles published from 1871 to 1889, and further titles until 1911.

The account books and ledgers of a publishing house are of great use to the historian interested in Victorian culture. Taken together with analysis and description of the books they represent, and supplemented by a thorough knowledge of the personalities of the publishers, these records can be approached the way a historian approaches pollbooks or a census: we can count the titles, categorize them according to the genre of the text, the gender of the author, and the type of contract involved, and produce a database susceptible to analysis. This approach avoids the problem often encountered in publishing history, that of focusing on the well-known books on the publisher's list and ignoring the rest. To build such a database is in itself a significant bibliographical task. The author-title records in the Chadwyck-

Healey index do not indicate how many books were published each year, what literary genres they fell into, or whether the authors were men or women. These sparse facts have to be determined by a careful examination of the titles, looking at many books directly, and assessing others on the basis of records in library catalogues. Further information is derived from an analysis of the Publication Books, records that include information about what kind of contract was made between the author and the publisher. It makes sense to start with King, most of whose books were new when he was new to publishing, and to continue through the years of Paul–Trench, since they were constituted as 'successors' to the King business. However, although the narrative goes on to 1911, the detailed analysis of authors, titles and contracts is not carried beyond the 1889 amalgamation, since the incorporation into the list of books that had their own history earlier, within the history of Trübner's or Redway, transformed its character.

In the substantial database that emerged, each title was coded for genre, for type of contract, and for the gender of the author. This database forms the general framework for a history of the imprint interweaving the intellectual and business interests of King, Paul and their successors with the record of the books their firms published. These data are discussed throughout the book and summarized in tabular form in Tables 4, 6 and 7. They demonstrate that the Kegan Paul publishers, and King before them, concentrated on theology and poetry, while bringing out a great many novels; more than 80% of the authors were men, fewer than 20% women; and nearly half the contracts were commission agreements, wherein authors, not publishers, undertook the financial risk of publication.

The creation and analysis of a database was done in combination with more orthodox bibliographical research: large numbers of books have been examined and described, read and enjoyed. Their title-pages, texts and especially their prefaces, often yield clues to the terms under which they came into being. This is particularly so in the case of books in series, a form at which King and Kegan Paul excelled. The publishers' advertisements bound in with the text add further to a recreation of the contemporary experience of handling and reading the book. And on the rare occasions when a letter from the author has survived, either in the 'contracts' section of the archive or in some other repository, it can further illuminate the moment of publication.

It is important to note that this is the history of an imprint, not a bibliography of a publishing house. The database does not include every book published between 1871 and 1889. It includes all the titles recorded in the archives, with their contracts, plus a tentative assignment of genre based on an analysis of the title; and a tentative assignment of author's gender based on her name or title. King and Kegan Paul advertisements would yield a handful more titles, for which records were never made. The meticulous labour of a bibliographer would likely produce others, but the results would not justify the time and expense that would be necessary to locate, examine and describe every title, in each reissue and new edition, and correlate the evidence of the book as artefact with that of the book registered in the ledgers. A thorough bibliography would be of use to collectors of the Kegan Paul imprint, but there are few if any bibliophiles whose interest is delimited that way. The present book, rather, is intended for the reader who seeks an accurate and detailed account of an important group of Victorian publishers, of the wide range of significant books they brought out, and of their changing business practices as the book trade went through a major transformation. It is also intended for the student of the history of the book who seeks guidance on how to proceed with the sometimes bewildering combination of evidence and methodologies that field encompasses.

Kegan Paul – A Victorian Imprint is a historian's contribution to the broad field known as the history of the book: the study of books in the past, and the scholarly investigation of books as those material objects which, in particular and culturally specific ways, record and transmit literary and other texts.[8] Although it builds in important ways upon the traditions of analytical bibliography, this is a field of study in which the posing and answering of questions about people – readers and writers – is just as important as questions about books. The field has expanded dramatically in the past fifteen years. Conferences have been held, graduate and undergraduate courses taught, new journals launched and essays on the history of the book appeared in established journals. Centres for the Book in countries and cities around the world are engaged in celebrating the tradition of the book, and advocating the preservation of surviving artefacts of print culture. National histories of the book are in print, in France, or in various stages of planning and production, in Australia, Britain, Canada, Germany, Scotland and the United States. Most of all, as is only appropriate, a number of important monographs have been published on the history of the book, and several publishers have launched series which bring together the work of active scholars. In a brief review of some of this literature, designed to place the present work in a burgeoning field, the research can be categorized according to the approach it takes: some scholars focus on books as books, writing the histories of important single works; others engage in enquiries into the book trade. The majority of research, however, is directed to studies of authors, of readers and of publishers.

It is perhaps surprising how seldom the history of the book takes the form of the history of *a* book. Perhaps the best-known example here is Robert Darnton's *The Business of Enlightenment: A Publishing History of the Encyclopédie* (1979). My own *Cheap Bibles* (1991), although limited to scriptures published by the British and Foreign Bible Society, demonstrated how the publishing history of a single influential work can answer questions about the history of social class relations and changing gender roles in the past. The method required to study the history of a single really influential work is both innovative and interdisciplinary: for Victorian Britain, wide-reaching scholarly studies of the authorship, publication and reception of books like John Stuart Mill's *On Liberty*, Darwin's *On the Origin of Species*, Leslie Stephen's and later Sydney Lee's *Dictionary of National Biography*, or Isabella Beeton's *Book of Household Management* would be welcome.[9] Not all books, however, lend themselves to such intensive scholarly treatment.

More conventional literary and business history has focused on significant events within the book trade. The development of serial publication in the nineteenth century, for example, and its effect on the composition and reception of novels by Dickens and others is well documented in John Sutherland's *Victorian Novelists and Publishers* (1976). Sutherland also explicates the transition from a convention of publishing small numbers of books in the cumbersome three-volume format and at very high prices at the beginning of the century, to a practice of producing cheap books in large quantities but slighter formats at the end. Similarly the commercial circulating library made famous by Charles Edward Mudie shaped the experience of readers as well as of writers. Mudie, with his censorious views on respectable literature, advertised that 'Novels of objectionable character or inferior ability are almost invariably excluded'.[10] When the libraries began to decline as commercial enterprises in the 1890s, they took the 3-volume novel with them. The reforms in copyright legislation in the nineteenth century were changes that protected and enhanced the author's livelihood: after 1842, authors' property in their texts extended for 42 years or seven years after their deaths, but not until 1891 were British authors legally protected in the United States, and then not unless their works were manufactured there. Similarly there was much energy devoted by the book trade to the question of whether the price of books should be fixed, or should be managed under the principles of free trade.[11] Changes of these kinds determined, to a large extent, the form of the books experienced by contemporary readers. A knowledge of the history of the book trade and of its major turning points is an essential starting-point for understanding the history of an individual book, author, or publishing house.

A new and important contribution to book trade history is Simon Eliot's *Some Patterns and Trends in British Publishing 1800–1919* (London: The Bibliographical Society, 1994). By collecting and assessing the statistics of trade changes, Eliot has been able to correct the accepted narrative in some places and to confirm it in others. Along with his publication with John Sutherland of *The Comprehensive Microform Edition of The Publishers' Circular and The English Catalogue 1837–1900* (1988), Eliot's book puts the history of the British book trade on much firmer ground than before. He is also associated with some encouraging work recently completed in Cambridge, as one part of the commitment of Cambridge University Press to publish *A History of the Book in Britain* and of the Leverhulme Foundation to sponsor some of the extensive primary research necessary before the task can be undertaken. Under the title of 'Productivity and profit: A quantitative survey of publishing and authorship 1839–1939', the scholars involved aimed 'to establish a database of book production information which can be used for detailed studies of the publishing industry through the period'.[12]

The third possible approach to the history of the book is to focus on its author, and the great bulk of scholarship about the publishing history of Victorian books has been located in literary studies.[13] That is, it concerns the ways that publishers contributed to the creation of the great Victorian novels. In John Sutherland's words, 'no Victorian novel . . . was not materially influenced by the publishing system'. Dickens, Thackeray, Trollope, Gaskell and George Eliot were published by substantial and powerful publishers; in some cases, as with Dickens and Chapman & Hall, the author's popularity made his publisher substantial, powerful and wealthy. In his *Victorian Novelists and Publishers*, Sutherland was content to consider seven selected publishers, what he called the 'leviathans'. They were enough for him to 'generalize fairly confidently about the production of the "literary novel"'. Even a more comprehensive book like John Feather's *A History of British Publishing* concentrates, in its nineteenth-century chapters, on the period's explosion of literary talent and its parallel expansion of literate readership. Feather observes of 'the general trade publisher' that 'They dealt in both fiction and non-fiction, never too specialized, but never wholly devoted to the popular best-seller while not despising the books which sold well.'[14] That a commentator can categorize the whole range of essays and economics, sermons and science, politics and polemic, in terms of what it is not (fiction) says a good deal about the literary bias of much of publishing history. We have studies of Scott and his publishers, of Tennyson and Dickens and theirs, among many others.[15] A particularly innovative new book on Victorian publishing and a novelist is Peter L. Shillingsburg's *Pegasus in Harness*. Shillingsburg uses publishers' archives and rigorous bibliographical analysis to write an analysis of Thackeray as a professional writer, and a discussion of 'how the trade of book publishing impinged on the writer and how that might affect our approaches as readers and editors to Thackeray's texts'.[16]

A fourth area where historical attention has been paid to the book trade has been in studies of the reading public. As long ago as the 1950s, R.K. Webb gave us a historian's account of *The British Working Class Reader*, and Richard Altick a literary scholar's analysis of *The English Common Reader*.[17] In both these works, the shift of focus away from writers and towards what Sutherland called 'their shadowy accomplices, the Victorian reading public' permitted an expansion of scholarly interest. Researchers examined a variety of projects mounted by people of the educated classes, who tried to use printed texts as a way to influence the newly literate, and newly menacing, 'mass reading public' that had been brought into being by population increase, industrialization, popular education, and urbanization. Religious publishers on the one hand, and the promoters of political economy on the other, competed with the indigenous working-class press to 'engage the minds and imaginations' of 'the English millions'. Altick and Webb performed an important service to the history of publishing. Their work, generalizing as it does over a whole century and a wide range of social and institutional subjects, demonstrates the need, however, for more detailed studies. One such study is David Vincent's work on working-class autobiography, *Bread, Knowledge and Freedom* in which the importance of books, material artefacts, in the developing consciousness of working-class writers, ranks just below the importance of religion, self-education, and radical politics. 'There emerged a tradition of reading, of pursuing knowledge, which had at its centre, quite simply, a love of books.'[18]

Despite recent arguments that the analysis of diaries and autobiographies can produce direct evidence of reader response, Victorian readers remain the 'shadowy accomplices' of authors and publishers.[19] Scholars have found it notoriously difficult reliably to attribute motives and intentions to readers in the past, and even more difficult to make explicit the connection between the transmitted text of the author's manuscript, and the received text of the reader's experience. The literature of reader response criticism does not really satisfy the scholar looking for documentary evidence of a particular reader's response to one specific text, and even less does it provide evidence of the response of a class of readers to a genre of books. Direct evidence of readership, while not impossible to find, is often fragmentary and problematic.[20] Neither the report of a publisher's professional reader on the manuscript, nor the formal review that appears in print, is equivalent to documentation of the fleeting response to a text of the contemporary browsing a bookshop, or settled before the fire with a fresh volume of poetry, or perhaps perched on an omnibus engrossed in a shilling shocker. And even when documentation of such responses survives, the document is itself a text, subject to interpretation. Reading is such a private act, the connection between reader and author so evanescent and intimate, that a satisfactory history of readership may never be possible. A preferable way of making that connection is to focus on the publishers, the men and women who had it in their power to accept manuscripts, transform them into books, and offer them to the marketplace – and to handle the process in ways that evidence their understanding of the culture in which they lived and worked, thought and read, and did business.

The genre in which much of the history of publishing has been written is the house history. The best of these books are grounded firmly in the archival records of the house in question, such as Royal Gettman's *A Victorian Publisher*, which was not 'a full-dress history of the House of Bentley', but rather 'a study of the problems of nineteenth-century publishing as they are embedded in the records of Richard Bentley and Son'.[21] When the records are incomplete, authors must depend upon their own memories and those of others, as Michael S. Howard does in *Jonathan Cape, Publisher*. Howard admits that: 'No one should expect a commemorative work of this kind to be objective', and refers to 'the obvious effects of *pietas* and pride'. Similarly J.E. Morpurgo, in his biography of *Allen Lane King Penguin* addresses the problem that a house history is normally commissioned by the firm that constitutes its subject, so that 'with very few exceptions, publishing histories are bland, uncritical paeans to the shrewdness and benevolence of a race of men unhampered by the frailties and avarice commonplace among lesser beings'. Gettman, Howard and Morpurgo are sensitive to the charge of bias, and all of them make extensive use of surviving archival records.[22]

Another type of house history, however, is based on selective memory rather than objective scholarship, and exists primarily as a promotional vehicle, to celebrate the survival and the successes of a firm, usually on the occasion of an anniversary, rather than analyse its place in the trade or in the contemporary culture. A particularly unsatisfactory one is F.A. Mumby's *The House of Routledge, 1834–1934, with a History of Kegan Paul, Trench, Trübner and*

Other Associated Firms (1934). In this type of chronicle, only the successful books by well-known authors are mentioned, along with any business relationships that generated amusing anecdotes about the publisher. Failed books and forgotten authors are suppressed, as are events and practices that might reflect to the discredit of the firm's management. House histories not based on rigorous scholarship often contain useful information, but they need to be analysed and verified against independent sources, as part of a modern reappraisal of their subjects. Such a reappraisal will recognize that the publishing decisions of the house being documented were a significant expression of the contemporary culture.

One of the purposes of the present book is to demonstrate that books and publishers can fruitfully be used as the focal point for writing about cultural history. Publishers, because they selected some manuscripts, rejected some, and revised others, might be regarded as canaries in the coal-mines of the contemporary culture, testing the atmosphere in which they were doing business. Those who prospered, like John Blackwood of Edinburgh who could afford to take a chance on the unknown supposed parson 'George Eliot', were astute interpreters of at least the elite part of their society. Those whose business insight was obscured by their ideology, such as Tweedie, who promoted temperance, reveal in their careers the extent to which their readers shared their passions, and the point where sympathy and enthusiasm broke off. Someone like Samuel Beeton could exploit the new prosperity of the middle classes, and their new interest in domestic comfort, by publishing *The Book of Household Management*, popularly known as Mrs Beeton's (1861), and all the better if the publisher was the author's husband. And someone like Emily Faithfull, who expressed her support for expanded educational and employment opportunities for women by engaging women as compositors at her Victoria Press, brings together, in her own person and her own list of books, an important shift in contemporary mores, and part of the material evidence for that transition.

The business decisions that publishers made are part of the evidence for their sense of what contemporary readers were looking for. The King and Kegan Paul Publication Books include lists of the periodicals to which review copies were sent, and the pages of the reviewing journals reflect the results of that policy, as the men and women of Victorian letters pronounced on the quality of individual titles and of books in series. The publishers' expenditures for advertising, and their decisions about producing new editions and reissues, also provide some insight into how they sought to attract readers. If an astute publisher like Henry S. King or Charles Kegan Paul felt confident enough to spend a couple of hundred pounds on an advertisement in *The Athenaeum*, then he expected the book to sell. And if a book remained in print in a fifth or sixth edition, two or three decades after its first publication, or if the verso of a title-page imprint showed ten reprintings within a two-year period, that book was finding a significant readership.

In the history of the book and publishing much attention is paid to books as books: the imprints on the title-pages are essential primary evidence about the company and the people that produced them. But the student of cultural history is also interested in the imprint of the personalities of the publishers, on the sensibilities of the culture in which they lived, and of that culture on their own characters. *Kegan Paul – A Victorian Imprint* incorporates the lives of the publishers together with the statistics that identify the kinds of books they were choosing. What emerges from this dual analysis is the reputation for seriousness that the firm had established by the late 1880s, a reputation that survived even the financial rigours of the 1890s, and the frivolous attitudes of the last generation of managers. In terms of lives, the emphasis is on the publishers' ideological, especially religious and intellectual, interests, but the chapters below also take a hard look at their finances. This approach is based on the notion that the publishers were gatekeepers, or perhaps mediators – no metaphor is quite right – for the culture they lived in. That is, that within financial constraints, market constraints, they had the power to select one text and reject another, and to frame the way that manuscripts appeared in published form. When that power is isolated and examined critically, it becomes apparent that one of the better ways to get to know about the experience of the Victorians as readers, is to get to know about the ways that Victorian publishers make their decisions.

CHAPTER I
HENRY S. KING: BUSINESSMAN OF LETTERS

I

When Charles Kegan Paul took over Henry King's business in 1877, Tennyson was alarmed. Trusting King, disliking Paul, and dubious about any change to existing arrangements, the poet laureate insisted that the company's advertisements and letterhead bear henceforth the words 'Successors to the Publishing Department of Henry S. King & Co.'. The long-lived Kegan Paul imprint was very much a successor to King's, and never altogether lost the tone and flavour imparted to it by the man who founded the list and managed the business for the first seven years. In November 1872 the trade newspaper *The Publishers' Circular* had called his company 'that most enterprising of modern firms'. King was an energetic and entrepreneurial publisher. But he was also an energetic and entrepreneurial banker and East India agent; and as a young man he had displayed identical qualities of energy and entrepreneurship, first as a clerk, and later as a bookseller.

The King list was a general one: ephemeral novels and new books of poetry jostled guides to Indian currency and self-help works on Hindustani. One year the publisher embarked on an ambitious and controversial new scientific series; the next he persuaded a popular writer of juvenile stories to desert her regular publisher. He invested in Stopford Brooke's broad-church theology and in Walter Bagehot's about-to-become-classic political work *The English Constitution*. He purchased copyrights from North America, commissioned translations from Europe, and sold books and periodicals around the globe. He behaved more like the financier he was than like the man of letters he had recently become.

King was described by his successor, Charles Kegan Paul, as 'a man of no ordinary force of character'.

> He exhibited great urbanity to all who were first introduced to him, unwearied attention to business, a large power of generalisation combined with extraordinary attention to details, an almost unexampled memory, and an iron will. And under the urbanity this iron force was very apparent: not all were able to penetrate below it. Those who did so found an extremely tender heart, a most loving and loveable nature, a high and stern sense of duty for himself and others, with great toleration bursting through a seeming and impatient intolerance.[1]

One who did, presumably, penetrate to the second and third levels of King's character was his second wife, Harriet Eleanor Hamilton King. But she knew the 'urbanity', too, once telling a correspondent that her husband 'had a peculiar gift, not the affectation of one, of being able to talk fluently about anything and to any one without having the slightest acquaintance with either'. His politics were as conservative as his religious views were liberal, Paul remembered, but neither creed was particularly orthodox.[2]

Born on 15 November 1817, King was 54 in 1871 when his London business opened in Cornhill. He came from one of those nineteenth-century families that swung from great wealth to poverty and back to wealth. His grandfather had been a prosperous banker in Lewes, in Sussex, where Henry was born. His father, Daniel King, lost his own inheritance and had no other means of support, and Henry set out, with the traditional shilling in his pocket but with no formal education, to work as a clerk at the age of thirteen. He saved enough from his earnings to 'help his family, educate himself, and get on in the world'. In 1830, this was no easy task; poverty and unemployment were common, and there was a real possibility of social unrest or political upheaval. Charles Kegan Paul, himself from a much more secure and comfortable background, observed that 'the tale seemed to the hearer at once romantic and heroic, though to the narrator it was the record of mere duty, and, as it appeared to him, within the reach of all'.

In 1838 the twenty-year-old Henry and his elder brother Richard together started a bookselling business at Brighton, the fashionable seaside resort. An abundance of reading material has traditionally been an important advantage for self-education of even the most menial worker in the book trades, and young Henry King (Richard resigned to take holy orders) took advantage of it. He developed a 'wide and accurate' knowledge of English literature, a habit of careful reading, and a 'singularly retentive memory'. Paul, writing the story as he interpreted, selectively, King's own reminiscences, also selective, may have underestimated the business side and over-romanticized the literary: he stated that

> for books – the shrines of literature – [King] had a real passion and a sort of personal affection. Hence he became a bookseller of a type which is getting rarer each day – one who rises far above the mere tradesman, the friend and literary associate of his customers, who look to him as, in some sense, the judge and critic of his wares.

Paul's account is the only one we have of Henry S. King the over-the-counter bookseller. The evidence of the friends he made in Brighton, and books he published there, suggests a keener interest in the politics of religion than in the 'shrines of literature'.

Two friends were Frederick W. Robertson, an elderly and influential preacher, and Stopford Brooke, a young and ambitious one. Both were associated with what later became known as the Broad Church, a movement within the Church of England that sought to minimize the doctrinal and ecclesiastical issues that tended to cause dissension, and instead to stress that a national church was, and should be, inclusive in character, even opening itself to modern and controversial ideas, and particularly to biblical criticism. Some of the better-known names in Broad Church circles were F.D. Maurice and Charles Kingsley, the Christian socialists, and Benjamin Jowett, the classical scholar and philosopher. (A later adherent, obscure but passionately involved, was Charles Kegan Paul.) Robertson preached at Trinity Chapel, Brighton, to enthusiastic congregations, and when he died in 1853, his friends and associates were eager that his sermons be published and his life and letters written. 'The Broad Church party,' writes Brooke scholar Fred Standley, 'was anxious to obtain a competent individual, who shared its general views, to undertake the project of a biography which by its inherent nature would be an *apologia* for the movement.'[3] Henry S. King undertook the editing of the sermons, and was influential in securing Stopford Brooke to write the life.[4] The Broad Church party had not only a biographer, but also a bookseller actively promoting its interests.

In the mid-nineteenth century, the term 'bookselling' was ambiguous: it meant not only retailing books, but could also incorporate the literary and financial commitments involved in publishing them. King was both kinds of bookseller: his Brighton imprint appears on the title-pages of sermons and religious meditations in 1842, 1843 and 1850. These title-pages also suggest that he was developing social connections in Brighton, as well as business connections in London. In 1842–3 he was styling himself 'Bookseller to the Queen Dowager' (Queen Adelaide, widow since 1837 of William IV, lived quietly at Brighton until her own death in 1849). And his books were distributed in London by Hamilton and Adams and by Hatchard and Son, both major retailers.[5]

But it was marriage, not business, that propelled Henry King into the exhilarating and competitive centre of mid-century London book publishing. He married into the Smith, Elder firm that was publishing Ruskin and Browning, Matthew Arnold, Thackeray, and Charlotte Brontë, under the management of George Smith. Two sisters, Ellen and Elizabeth Blakeway, Quakers, daughters of a London wine merchant, married two publishers.[6] Ellen and Henry King were married in 1850, settling down in East Street, Brighton, and producing two sons;[7] Elizabeth and George Smith were married in 1854. Meanwhile another partnership had been instituted: King purchased in 1853 a quarter-share in his prospective brother-in-law's historic London publishing house of Smith, Elder, located at 65 Cornhill in the heart of the book trade. Henry was thirty-five in 1853, and Ellen twenty-nine.

The Kings made a dramatic move up in the world, from the Brighton over-the-shop premises to The Manor House, Chigwell, Essex. The village near Epping Forest had by that time become absorbed in the complex of residential suburbs of Greater London, and Henry was able to commute to and from his office by train each day. A third child, a daughter, was born about 1858, and then Ellen King died in childbirth on 18 February 1860, only 37 years of age. The family remained in Chigwell, where Henry King later became a magistrate.[8]

His company was not like other publishing businesses, being involved in alternative and more lucrative activities than bookselling. The literary side of Smith, Elder, located in Waterloo Place, was operated in parallel with an East India agency and banking concern, which was based in the original headquarters at 65 Cornhill. And although King's edition of Robertson's sermons was first published by the firm in 1855, he was most likely occupied primarily with the financial and commercial side of the operation.[9] This part had evolved out of bookselling: the export of books and stationery to East India Company officers, posted far from home and anxious to keep up with current events in the capital. But the firm soon discovered a market for providing money drafts and other banking services to their customers, and stepped in to supply it. Similarly, they exported a wide variety of consumer goods, realizing more substantial and secure profits here than from their activities as literary publishers. They also published newspapers for their customers, *The Overland Mail* (from 1855), conveyed home news to India; and the *Homeward Mail* (from 1857) relayed the Indian news to England. The Indian Mutiny in 1857 was costly for the Smith, Elder partners: in one weekend of rebellion and repression in Bengal, many of the firm's customers (and debtors) were killed, and afterwards the old East India Company was replaced by a government department. Business, however, continued to flourish. In 1866 there was a turnover of £627,129.[10]

The overseas trade subsidized the literary side of Smith, Elder's business, and provided much of the capital for the large payments they were able to make to popular authors. George Smith's journal, *The Cornhill Magazine*, and the firm's newspaper, the *Pall Mall Gazette* also benefited from the infusion of funds. The *Cornhill*, begun in 1860, was initially edited by Thackeray. King seems not to have been involved in the editing or publication of the magazine. The *Pall Mall Gazette* was founded by Smith in 1865; the title was an allusion to a newspaper in Thackeray's *Pendennis*, a 'paper written by gentlemen for gentlemen'. Smith turned the editorship over to Frederick Greenwood. Under the terms of the partnership agreement, King had to approve the enterprise; he did so, with the proviso that he would have the right at any time to discontinue it. This right was exercised after the first number appeared. In King's opinion the editorial tone was supportive of Palmerston's Liberal government, which 'placed him in a somewhat false position, for he had always belonged to the opposite party'. As Leonard Huxley put it, the newspaper was too Liberal for King's 'stout Conservative' politics.[11] That was the end of the firm's connection with the newspaper, and Smith now became sole owner.

The King–Smith partnership lasted fifteen years, then came apart in 1868. Smith admitted that 'partnerships have their disadvantages as well as their advantages. I had been always accustomed to determine matters without reference to any other judgement than my own; to be, in a word, the "captain of my own quarterdeck" and had the fault of being not too patient with opinions that differed from my own.'[12] King, as we have seen, was equally stubborn and independent. Charles Kegan Paul revealed to a colleague what he was too discreet to record in his memoir of King, a story of how

> on alternate Wednesdays Smith would go to Cornhill and King would come to Waterloo Place to settle their partnership affairs. ... The brothers-in-law, who detested each other, would meet in the parlour and stiffly bow, take chairs, discuss the business of Smith, Elder & Co., rise and, again bowing solemnly, would re-enter their respective spheres.[13]

By this time, Ellen Blakeway King was dead, and Henry had been remarried for five years. The two partners shared neither political convictions nor family connections.

By the terms of the agreement to separate in 1868, the disparate activities of Smith, Elder were permanently divided. George Smith took the imprint, the firm's name and its publishing business; Henry King took the East India agency and banking operation, including the Cornhill house and the office at 45 Pall Mall, which incorporated living quarters. He agreed to refrain from entering the publishing trade for at least three years, that is, until 1871. The moment the time was up, he brought out the first book under his own name and Cornhill imprint, Stopford Brooke's controversial piece of theological politics, *Freedom in the Church of England*.

King's first marriage had provided him with a business partner; his second union gave him a promising writer of poetry to publish on the Smith, Elder list, as well as entrée into a partisan London literary circle and ultimately, as we shall see, another business associate, when Charles Kegan Paul wrote a favourable review of the poetry of 'Mrs Hamilton King'. On 22 September 1863, the 46-year-old father of three married 23-year-old Harriet Eleanor Baillie-Hamilton.[14] She was the daughter of Admiral W.A. and Lady Harriet Baillie-Hamilton and a niece of Lord Aberdeen and of the Duke of Abercorn; a later admirer described her as 'a delicate woman . . . noble-minded, red-haired and pre-Raphaelite-looking': quite a catch for an ex-Brighton bookseller who was double her age.[15] The bride's family may, however, have been pleased to accept almost any husband for their wayward daughter, while she must have been anxious to escape her parents' surveillance for the cosmopolitan lifestyle promised by her new husband. Harriet had been obsessed since the age of seventeen with the cause of independence for Italy, and was engaged in an ardent correspondence with Giuseppe Mazzini.

The Italian nationalist spent thirty years in England, in exile from his native country, and many English men and women were devoted to him and to the cause of Italian liberty. Mazzini was the subject of poetry by both Elizabeth and Robert Browning, as well as by Algernon Swinburne. In a novel, *Clara Hopgood*, published in 1896, the heroine died for the cause of Italian freedom.[16] She might have been modelled on Harriet Eleanor Hamilton.

In her *Letters and Recollections of Mazzini*, Harriet Eleanor Hamilton King records how between the ages of fourteen and seventeen she read through seventeen volumes of Sismondi's *Républiques Italiennes*, (still only covering events up to the close of the fifteenth century): 'All the history and all the poetry I read imbued and confirmed me in ideas of patriotism and deliverance from foreign oppressors, and of the value of conspiracies.' At seventeen, she read Gladstone's translation of Farini's *History of the Roman State*: 'it gave me for the first time an intelligible and connected view of Italian politics up to the present time'. Now she became interested in Mazzini, whose 'actual actions and words . . . formed an image of the ideal patriot, hero, and saint in my mind. From that moment I recognised Mazzini as the master-mind of the century, and the master and responsive note of my own mind'. On the morning of 16 February 1858, her eighteenth birthday, 'I received permission henceforth to read *The Times* regularly. This was unusual at that time, and at my age.' The same day, walking with her father in Regent Street she saw a portrait of Mazzini's comrade Felice Orsini. 'Upon me, at the most impressionable age, the most impressionable moment, the effect was instantaneous and indelible. I came away dazed, and with the image of Felice Orsini paramount in my mind.' It remained so until long after she read in *The Times* of Orsini's execution a month later.[17]

Harriet Hamilton had been writing poetry since the age of six, influenced by Felicia Hemans and Walter Scott; now 'a new and sudden influx of poetic inspiration came to me, accompanied by original form as well as thought'. She wrote *The Execution of Felice Orsini* in 1859 and 1860, years when 'the passion for Italy so completely absorbed me that my own life was of no importance to me in comparison; I only longed to be able to sacrifice it. But I had no idea of the horrors of war.' As the obsession developed, 'I found that my health suffered greatly from dwelling so intensely on such a painful topic; and I had the sensation strongly that I was being dragged down to the grave by Orsini, to be beside him. . . . I resolved, to save my life, as I thought, to banish Orsini at once and completely out of my mind.' She succeeded only by transferring her attention to Garibaldi, 'grieving all the while that I was still too young to act independently and be with him'. There matters remained during 1861, and up until August of 1862, when she wrote her first letter to Mazzini.

Hamilton was now over twenty-one, 'I was free now; I might go to him – the way of Death was open to me; I might die a Martyr, I might die young – for the thought of old age had always been a terror to me.' Addressing the Italian patriot as 'the mild father of my spiritual life', she told him 'I am a woman, fearless, of tender hands and heart. I have nursed the sick and dying; let me offer relief and consolation to the Martyrs of the Holy War. I am a poet too, and could record the exploits of God's heroes, might I accompany them.' She sent him copies of her poems as well as a donation and a photograph, informing him with respect to the Orsini poem that 'A high literary authority has assured me that this poem merits attention; and I am now in negotiation for its publication.' The authority may have been Henry S. King; he was certainly the publisher, still under the Smith, Elder imprint at Cornhill. 'Though young,' she continued, 'my life has been strange and sad already, and I am loose to those ties which bind to home.' Her family, as it turned out, was not quite so loose, and she not quite so free: they whisked her off to the north of Scotland.

Although Harriet Hamilton eventually returned to London, and saw her poem through the press (on 5 November King sent her twelve copies, 'They were beautifully printed and bound, six in black cloth with red edges, six in black morocco with gilt edges.'), her family did not relent. The next spring, in May 1863, 'I was positively compelled, by pressure which I had no means to resist, to break off all correspondence with Mazzini, hitherto permitted, and to promise in writing not to renew it – at least for the present.' She noted, however, that her forthcoming marriage would remove her from the authority of her parents: 'and I was no longer bound by the promise I had made. [In mid-September] I wrote again to Mazzini . . . '. Harriet Eleanor Baillie-Hamilton and Henry Samuel King were married 22 September 1863.

Not surprisingly, she told Mazzini about how she came to know her husband:

> My life has been romantic hitherto, and it was strangely that we came together. First, through some poems which I sent to the *Cornhill Magazine*, his thoughts were drawn towards me; and afterwards it was through my poem on Orsini that we were brought into closer sympathy. And now I am very happy, and my heart is at rest, and at home. My future husband is widely known, and by all beloved and esteemed. He is the friend of your friend, Mr Shaen.[18] He unites with me in sympathy with the cause of Italy, and in admiration for your character. His political views are not on all points identical with yours, but in those feelings and truths which meet above the range of temporary questions, he is one with all noble souls.

Mazzini could now write to Harriet, not at her new home in Chigwell but care of Smith, Elder.

If the speculation is correct that King represented to the Hamilton family the lesser of two evils, and the salvation of their daughter from certain disgrace and possible death in the cause of Italian independence, then they achieved their objective: 'My marriage created a new relationship, which, in a manner, placed a barrier between Mazzini and myself, only removed by his death. I had no longer a *single* life; entering into a double one, I lost my independence of mind. Moreover, the claims upon me of the life I entered into were so engrossing and overwhelming as to leave no room for any exterior interest. My past in Mazzini was not killed, but overlaid and buried for many years: only rising to the surface in an occasional pause.'

The 'engrossing and overwhelming' new claims included six children, Violet (born 1864), Arthur (1866), Margaret (1868), Katherine (1869), Honoria (1870) and Samuel (1871), as well as some responsibility for her step-children, Henry Seymour (born 1852), Harold (1854) and Ellen (1858). The family remained at The Manor House, Chigwell, enlarging it in 1865. At the time of the 1871 census the two parents and nine children lived there with ten servants. But domestic responsibilities did not altogether stifle the poet's obsession.

In January 1864 while she was pregnant with Violet and under her husband's chaperonage, Harriet finally met Mazzini: neither of them said much; 'It was my husband who principally sustained the conversation. I do not think he had ever read anything of Mazzini's, nor had any but a vague idea about him, but he had accepted him wholly as my friend, and as a man of distinction: he met him with the greatest cordiality, and being himself a great speaker, he mainly did the talking. Mazzini and I gazed at one another.' The relationship continued in this cordial fashion for several years, King sending cigars and the occasional financial contribution to his wife's idol, and Mazzini responding with blessings to little Violet. In 1865 Smith, Elder published an English translation of Mazzini's works in six volumes, by Harriet King's friend Emilie Ashurst Venturi. Mazzini visited the family in Chigwell in December 1866 and again in June 1867 and May 1868, occasions that were a combination of pleasure and frustration for Harriet: her

Table 1 Henry and Ellen King: family and business; Henry and Harriet King: family, business and books

Henry Samuel King (1817–78)
1817 born 15 November

Ellen Blakeway (ca 1824–50)
born about 1824

1838, with Richard, started publishing and bookselling business at Brighton

married 1850
1852 Henry Samuel

1853: purchased partnership in business of George Smith, of Smith Elder, who married Ellen's sister Elizabeth Blakeway the following year

1853 moved to Chigwell, Essex
1854 Harold
1858 Ellen

1860 died 18 February

Harriet Eleanor Baillie-Hamilton (1840–1920)
1862 Orsini poem published

married 1863
1864 Violet
1866 Arthur
1868 Margaret

1868: end of partnership with Smith

1869 Katherine
1870 Honoria

1871: opened publishing business in Cornhill

1871 Samuel

1872: alliance with Stranhan

1873: *The Disciples*

1874: engaged Charles Kegan Paul as manager
1875: beginning of illness
1877: sold business to Charles Kegan Paul
1878: died 17 November (age 60)

many more books after 1878
died 1920

housewifely duties and the hubbub of a very large household interfered with her rapturous communion with her idol. When Mazzini died on 10 March 1872, Harriet King wore deepest mourning for a year, but

> My sorrow was, however, lightened by the wave of poetic inspiration which had swelled up within me, and by the sense that I was at last really serving him and working for him. I was now putting into execution the work which I had vaguely planned in 1857, and for which I had all along been preparing and collecting materials, though these were but scanty owing to want of leisure and opportunities. The work now sprang full-grown from my brain. It seems to me, referring to my Diary, reinforced by my own recollections, inconceivable how I could have written anything at all, in the midst of domestic harass and disturbance past recounting, and in constant suffering, sometimes agony. All I can say is, it was an irresistible force; it hardly took up any time, the words flowed straight out of my mind, generally without after-correction.

This was *The Disciples*, published by H.S. King & Co. in 1873; Samuel, her youngest, was two years old. The long career in poetry now begun by 'Mrs Hamilton King', as she liked to style herself, emerged out of Mazzini's inspiration, but it was inexorably shaped by another factor. She wrote within the limits imposed by King's notion of how to be a good husband to a passionate woman obsessed not only with another man, but also with a cause for which he had little or no personal sympathy.

Meanwhile, the financial and commercial services of Henry S. King & Co. were greatly expanded. Their letterhead proclaimed them 'East India Army, Civil Service, and Colonial Agents and Bankers'. The shipping and supply departments were located in Cornhill, the banking and India agency at 45 Pall Mall. They opened branch offices in Calcutta (King, Hamilton & Co.), Bombay (King, King & Co.), Southampton and Portsmouth (King, Seymour & Co.), and Liverpool (King, Baillie & Co.).[19] In June 1869 King expanded an old Smith, Elder newspaper as *The Homeward Mail from India, China and the East, and the Official Gazette*. It was still oriented to the comings and goings of English officers in

India and their families, published on the arrival of each overland mail, and providing news of returning passengers, of deaths in the Indian service, and of events in the various parts of colonial India. It was also a vehicle for advertising the firm's financial services: 'The Business comprises Departments for Banking, Monetary and Personal Agency; for Passages and Outfitting, Shipping and Warehousing Goods, and for General Supplies, including Stationery, Books, Magazines, Newspapers, and Miscellaneous Goods of all kinds.' For readers in India there was *The Overland Mail*, carrying political, military and commercial news, reviews of new works, announcements of inventions and 'a chapter of Literary, Artistic, and Social Chit-chat, embodying the current *on-dits* and varied Gossip of Society and the Clubs'.[20] And when the colonial community required the services of a banker, King's was available to purchase and sell government stock, East India, colonial and foreign bonds and other securities, and to undertake the custody and receipt of interest and dividends; they would also receive pay, pensions and allowances of naval, military and civil officers and handle the payment of family remittances; they offered drawing accounts, deposit accounts, and letters of credit issued on their branch firms in Calcutta and Bombay.[21]

Beginning in January 1871 King also published *The Week's News: A London Newspaper for English Readers at Home and Abroad*, providing for threepence 'an accurate and agreeable epitome of the news of the world'. The paper was later advertised as 'the best and lowest-priced Summary for Family Reading, for Libraries or to Post Abroad', especially designed for those who were in the habit of forwarding their copy of a newspaper to the Colonies, as well as for English residents on the Continent. It listed births, marriages and deaths, eschewed politics, and published 'leading articles . . . written mainly to elucidate facts – to be a trustworthy Guide to the comprehension of Passing Events'.[22] King was developing a successful and profitable global business, accruing profits, gaining experience, and developing or reinforcing routines and attitudes that would be habitual by the time he returned to publishing books.

Henry King worked hard. According to Paul's memoir, 'summer and winter he breakfasted at half-past seven, and was at work in the City soon after nine. He rarely left his office before six, and the Saturday half-holiday was often his busiest time.' He also served as a Justice of the Peace in the county of Essex, and later on the boards of the London Life Assurance Company and the Union Steamship Company. He may have travelled to India on business; we know he went to Switzerland for pleasure, and to Egypt and to Italy for his health. Harriet, Ellen, Violet and a maid accompanied him to Italy in 1876. (It was Harriet's first journey out of England.) A glimpse of the home life at Chigwell is afforded by her record of Mazzini's visit in 1867:

> There was a heterogeneous party staying at the house: – my two sisters-in-law – both antagonistic, two of my stepsons, schoolboys – quite indifferent, a lady and gentlemen with few ideas, and a cousin of my own, gentle and amiable, but quite unable to counterpoise the others. All, with the exception of my cousin, were loud and voluble talkers, so that Mazzini and I had little chance; and I had no private sitting-room to retire to except a little room inside my bedroom, to which I could not take him. . . . When my husband came home to dinner . . . things were more agreeable; for he was always most warm and friendly to Mazzini, and he was able to dominate the conversation.

Certainly Henry King had no lack of confidence. He was forceful, energetic, apparently thriving on stress that would flatten most other people. It is perhaps not surprising that he also developed a heart condition that would kill him two days after his sixty-first birthday.

II

On 16 May 1871, the *Publishers' Circular* announced that 'Messrs Henry S. King & Co. of 65 Cornhill, who succeeded to the East India Agency and Home and Export Bookselling business of Messrs Smith, Elder & Co., have now commenced publishing.' They had already produced *Freedom in the Church of England*, by Stopford Brooke, and were announcing three more titles 'for immediate publication', *The Nile without a Dragoman*, by Frederic Eden, 'A Journal Kept in France [in] 1848' by the late Nassau Senior (eventually published as *Correspondence and conversations of de*

Toqueville with N.W. Senior (1872), edited by Senior's widow, now Mary Simpson), and *The European in India* by E.C.P. Hull and R.S. Mair, subtitled *Anglo-Indian's Vade Mecum: A handbook of useful and practical information . . . to which is added a medical guide for Anglo-Indians*. A travel guide, a political memoir, and a medical handbook: perhaps the new firm was merely adding specialty book-publishing to its extensive services to the colonial community. However, the announcement went on, 'They have also in the press new novels entitled *Half a Dozen Daughters* by J. Masterman and *Her Title of Honour*, by Holme Lee.' These were the pseudonyms of Victoria Rybot and Harriet Parr. Clearly, a new literary publisher had appeared to compete with Smith, Elder and the other 'leviathans' of the 1870s; it remained to be seen how long he would last.

King invested heavily in copyrights during his first year; the firm's archives reveal that he paid £50 to £100 for each of the five titles first advertised. And he was repaid, at least in terms of attention from the book trades. In a review of *Her Title of Honour* (which they judged to be not very good), the *Publishers' Circular* remarked that 'Messrs King seem to be taking vigorous strides in the direction of rendering the famous "Sixty-five Cornhill" as celebrated as in the days of Thackeray and the Misses Brontë.'

At Christmas the firm embarked on an ambitious annual entitled *Pleasure: a holiday book of prose and verse*. It contained a new poem by Algernon Swinburne, and prose contributions by Caroline Norton, Charles Kingsley, Amelia Edwards, Countess von Bothmer, Hain Friswell, Holme Lee and others. King secured Swinburne's contribution by getting Emilie Venturi, Harriet's friend and with her part of the circle around Mazzini and Garibaldi, to ask the poet, another sympathizer, to contribute to an anthology.[23] According to King's advertisement, *Pleasure* could be obtained either 'elegantly bound in ornamental cloth cover, with gilt edges and illuminated frontispiece', for 2s 6d, or with an illuminated cover, merely sewn, at 1s. The *Athenaeum* observed that 'From a literary point of view Mr Swinburne's new poem is the most notable of its contents'; the *Standard* was more enthusiastic: 'An extraordinary shilling's worth. [Swinburne's] "Tristram and Iseult" is alone worth far more than the price of the publication, which is a very good annual, and very creditable both to the editor and publisher.' The firm's records reveal that almost £200 was paid to authors, ranging from Swinburne's £30 to Countess von Bothmer's 8 guineas, Kingsley's 5 guineas and 1 guinea to Thomas Hood. James Hain Friswell received £45.15.0 for editing the book (anonymously) as well as for his contribution. It is not known how many copies were printed, but 5,000 were sold, possibly remaindered, at 7d to Appleton's in New York, and 10,800 at 2d to the Strand bookseller W.H. Smith & Son. The Christmas 'annual' turned out to be a one-off, however. It was not repeated in 1872.

King published about twenty-five books in 1871, from Stopford Brooke's *Freedom in the Church of England* in May, to *Pleasure* in time for Christmas. Nine were novels, three poetry; there were four works on travel, four on religion and five in a miscellaneous category. In fiction, potboilers like *Cruel as the Grave* by Countess Mary von Bothmer vied with Fanny Bunnett's *Linked at Last*. Harriet King's *Aspromonte and other poems* led the list for verse, along with *Songs of Two Worlds, by a new writer*. This turned out to be Lewis Morris, a Welsh poet who was later a contender for the laureateship. All these writers were compensated either by purchase of copyright or by an agreement to share profits between author and publisher. In addition, King offered his imprint on a commission basis to specialty writers. G.S. Drew's *Scripture Lands*, based on his journal of an Eastern tour in 1856–7 was published at the author's expense, and King's deducted a commission of 10% on all copies sold, agreeing to advertise the book. Moreover, Drew had to pay interest after two years on any monies he owed the firm, at 2% above the bank rate.

King was not bound by the constraints of custom in the trade; he had plenty of money and was prepared to spend it on promising projects; he was equally prepared to accept an author's subsidy to bring out 'on commission' a book that did not look like making a profit. Although the term 'vanity publishing' had not yet been invented, most serious publishers stayed away from accepting books on commission. King wanted to be taken seriously, and was, but commission payments were as welcome as any other source of income in his balance sheet.

In 1872, his first full year of operations, about eighty books appeared under King's new imprint. He continued to favour ephemeral novels, but began to package them in an attractive series, The Cornhill Library of Fiction. A second series, of Lives of English Popular Leaders, amounted to only two titles, *Stephen Langton* and *Tyler, Bell and Oldcastle*, both by Charles E. Maurice. But the third series that emerged in 1872, the International Scientific Series, continued for forty years. The general shape of the King list was now clear: two- and three-volume novels for the circulating library market; books in series, where sets of related titles could be marketed together; and a line of sermons and other religious works, headed by Stopford Brooke and leaning in the direction of Broad Church theology.

As we shall see, King favoured fiction considerably more than did his successors. The statistics summarized in Table 4 show that during his tenure as head of the firm, 16.5% of the books were novels, a figure that dropped to about 5% when Paul and Trench took over. New novels of 1872 included *Sir Edward's Wife*, by Hamilton Marshall, which earned its author £25 and *Too Late*, published anonymously for £20 by a Mrs Newman. Another anonymous novelist was Margaret Agnes Paul, whose other occupation was keeping house for her husband, the Rev. Charles Kegan Paul of Sturminster Marshall, Dorset. *Thomasina: a biography* was her ninth novel. The first seven, beginning in 1856 with *Dorothy: a tale* had been published by J.W. Parker and Son. Parker had already printed second editions of some of her earlier books and sold some titles to Tauchnitz for publication in Germany. Parkers had been sold in 1863 to Longmans and Margaret Agnes Paul's *Three Weddings* was published by that historic firm in 1870; possibly her move to King's in 1872 had something to do with her husband's developing association with the publisher. In any case, King must have been happy to draw up a contract with this proven writer, for £100 for a two-volume novel.[24]

For publishers, the series of reprint fiction was less risky than the original novel. So-called 'standard works', especially standard novels, were the books that publishers and booksellers identified as likely to remain in print for some years, and to command a steady readership. King's flagship series of standard works was the Cornhill Library of Fiction, named, of course, for his business address but perhaps also intended to evoke the image of the distinguished review, *The Cornhill*. The series was marketed initially under the stodgy title of 'Approved Fiction: the Library of Cheap Reprints.' King's advertising for the series stressed its design and physical quality: 'It is intended . . . to produce books of such merit that readers will care to preserve them on their shelves. They are well printed on good paper, handsomely bound, with a Frontispiece, and are sold at the moderate price of 3s 6d each.' They were elegant little volumes, in their uniform bindings of dark blue cloth, with black lettering and gilt on the spines.[25] The Cornhill Library was much admired in trade circles. The *Publishers' Circular* on 1 June 1872 called it a 'very handsome series of reprints . . . eminently worthy' of booksellers' patronage.

Much more dramatic and difficult than instituting a series of reprints was to plan a series of scientific works, as yet unwritten, on controversial subjects, entering into agreements with some of the most prominent characters in London scientific circles as well as with publishers in New York and in the capitals of Europe. The International Scientific Series would require all of King's urbanity. On 14 August 1871 a dinner was held at the St James Hotel to settle plans that had been developing informally for the past few months. There were four Englishmen present, and two Americans: King was the choice as publisher of the three prominent members of the London intellectual community who were looking for a vehicle to circulate advanced ideas in an accessible form. These were John Tyndall, the physicist and popular lecturer, T.H. Huxley, the biologist and palaeontologist whose reputation as a proponent for science was already well established, and Herbert Spencer, the philosopher who applied the idea of evolution to social contexts. These three were also concerned that English scientific authors be remunerated appropriately for their literary work, not only in England, but in the United States, where the lack of a copyright law made it possible for publishers to reprint English books and distribute them in the huge American market without compensating the authors. The first American visitor, with whom originated the idea of the series, represented both science and publishing in one person. He was Edward Livingston Youmans, writer of works on popular science and representative of D. Appleton & Co., the New York firm whose list already included Darwin, Tyndall, Spencer and others, and which was held in high regard by English scientific authors because it was scrupulous about paying them a

Table 2 Series published by Henry S. King & Co., 1871–7

Cornhill Library of Fiction (11 titles, 1872–5)

Lives of English Popular Leaders (2 titles, 1872)

International Scientific Series (98 titles, 1872–1911)

---

royalty on American sales.[26] W.H. Appleton had come over to London to support his agent in the negotiations with King, whom Youmans described as 'a wide-awake, wholehearted fellow'.[27]

The St James Hotel agreement, initially for an 'Anglo-American Series of Scientific Works', called for payments of £50 for each edition of 1,250 copies in London (equivalent to 20%), and a royalty of 10% on copies printed in New York. The two publishers, the venerable American Appleton's and the newcomer H.S. King, would share the cost of stereotype plates and the blocks necessary to print illustrations. Professors Tyndall and Huxley, and Mr Herbert Spencer not only 'professed their warm sympathy with the plan and promised all possible assistance in furthering it', they also agreed to act as a consulting committee. At a subsequent meeting it was agreed that 'neither publisher shall introduce into the series issued by him any book that has not also been published in the same series in the other country'.[28] A printed prospectus, dated 28 December 1871, was later circulated by King 'to British Scientific Authors', and John Tyndall undertook to prepare the first book in the series, based on his work on glaciers, *The Forms of Water*.

King and Youmans marketed the Series as 'an elegant and valuable library of popular science, fresh in treatment, attractive in form, strong in character, moderate in price, and indispensable to all who care for the acquisition of solid and serviceable knowledge'. Its purpose was 'to provide the public with popular scientific books of a superior character'. These were not, however, to be vulgar simplifications or hack work: 'Their preparation has been confided only to men of eminent ability, and who are recognized authorities in their several departments.' These men (there were no women contributors) were 'pledged to the utmost simplicity of exposition that is possible consistently with clear and accurate representation'.[29]

King's new and expensive commitment to science and to secular ideas did not interfere with his line of religious books. He brought out a 'People's Edition' of Brooke's *Life and Letters of F. W. Robertson*, as well as capturing Robertson's sermons from their former publisher, Smith, Elder and adding Brooke's own sermons. Another well-known Broad-Church clergyman was Hugh Reginald Haweis, whose *Music and Morals* (published 1871 by Strahan) had introduced the intriguing and, as it turned out, influential idea that the experience of music influences the listener's moral character. King profited from Haweis's popularity by bringing out his *Thoughts for the Times*, sharing profits half-and-half with the author on the first edition and paying him a £50 lump sum for the copyright on the second, in 1874.

The year 1873 saw five books added to the International Scientific Series and four to the Cornhill Library of Fiction. This was the year when King's association with Charles Kegan Paul began, and the year when he started to experiment with juvenile fiction, most notably in an association with 'Hesba Stretton', the author of the enormously popular *Jessica's First Prayer*. As we have seen, King had already been in touch with Margaret Agnes Paul the previous year, and it is possible that their business was transacted through her husband. If this was so, Charles suppressed the fact in his *Memories*, merely remarking that he 'assisted Mr King for a few years as his literary adviser'. He claimed that the occasion of their 'literary connection' was his favourable review, in *The Examiner* (17 January 1874), of Harriet Eleanor Hamilton King's *The Disciples*, a tribute to Mazzini's followers. Whatever was the case, it is important to note that the two publishers were brought together, and the link in the firm's history forged, by one or other of those two formidable literary women who were their wives.

Charles Kegan Paul (still the Rev. Mr Charles Kegan Paul, Vicar of Sturminster Marshall in rural Dorset) was a King author in 1873. He entered into a two-thirds to the author, one-third to the publisher share agreement for his verse translation of Goethe's *Faust*, and also published his edition of William Godwin's essays entitled *The Genius of Christianity Unveiled*. Paul was a devotee of

Godwin and, more particularly, of the philosopher's first wife Mary Wollstonecraft, and was entrusted with the editorship of these unpublished essays by their grandson, Percy Shelley. Later, in 1876, the firm published his biography *William Godwin: His Friends and Contemporaries*. For the essays, however, King required a contribution of £85 towards the publication, plus £20 for advertising, although part of this would be repaid by royalties of 3 shillings per copy sold during the first three years. It appears that Shelley, not Paul, provided the necessary sponsorship and of course collected the small rewards.

By 1873 Paul was anxious to escape from his Dorset vicarage, unhappy with Anglican doctrine and discipline, in financial trouble, quite likely bored with his parochial duties, and beginning to turn his mind towards London. Other metropolitan publishers engaged educated London men and, frequently, women, to vet the manuscripts submitted to them.[30] This country clergyman, former Eton master, Oxford-educated and friendly with Kingsley and Maurice, was the ideal 'publisher's reader' for Henry King. There is no clear documentation in the company's records of when the reading arrangement began. Paul read the manuscripts of *Two Girls* by Frederick Wedmore (1873) and *Socialism; its nature, its dangers, and its remedies considered* by the Rev. Mauritz Kaufman (1874). It was not until some time in 1874 that he moved to London and commenced full-time work as King's 'literary adviser' or 'manager', and October 1877 that King sold him the firm.[31]

Henry King's publishing coup of 1873 was to lure away from the Religious Tract Society (RTS) their most prolific and popular author. Founded in 1799, the RTS was by the mid-nineteenth century committed to circulating not only improving tracts, but religious works more broadly defined. The writing of Sarah Smith, under her pseudonym of 'Hesba Stretton' was always 'improving' as well as being intensely poignant and engagingly entertaining; it was among the best written of what the RTS published, as well as the most popular. Sarah Smith had been an author since 1859 and aspired to be known as a serious writer of novels for adults. Instead, to the RTS, she was 'the author of *Jessica's First Prayer*', for which they had paid a flat fee of less than £50 in 1867 and collected the astronomical profits ever since.[32] Best known for sentimental tales of London streetwaifs, Stretton was also a skilled stylist who used vivid characterization, complex plotting and engaging humour to construct her powerful narratives; politically, she was a vehement polemicist who used her stories to call for the redress of social injustice. She was also concerned with justice to herself as an author, and remarked of the RTS that 'truly all men are cheats, especially publishers'. King offered her royalties of 1½d per copy (25%) on *Jessica* and other popular stories. He also published her full-length adult novels on the same terms: first the story that was her own personal favourite, *Michel Lorio's Cross* (1873) and later *David Lloyd's Last Will* and *The Crew of the Dolphin* (1876). Paul's literary judgement concurred with King's commercial sense: he rated Hesba Stretton on a par with Newman, Walter Pater and Hardy among the best of contemporary stylists.[33]

At the same time that H.S. King & Co. were advertising and profiting from Hesba Stretton's stories, they were contracting, more cautiously, for two texts by another juvenile writer, Charles Camden. These books are distinguished not only by their absolute obscurity, but also by a tone that identifies them as books of their period and, therefore, part of the evidence for the mores of the high-Victorian years. Both were commission books, and neither remained long in the firm's financial records. One was *The Travelling Menagerie*. The other, *Hoity Toity, the Good Little Fellow* (1873), was 195 pages of text and illustrations enclosed in a brown cloth binding with an illustration in black and gilt. It had originally been published in the journal *Good Words for the Young*. The expression 'hoity toity' describes riotous or giddy behaviour, or characterizes a hoyden or romp. Camden's 'Hoity Toity' is a creature unidentified to the reader except by negatives: he was 'no fool'; nor was he, although people called him so, 'a playful little toad'. He kept a stick with two horns, Easum and Stoppum, the one for nudging good people, or needy people and the other for prodding bad or ungrateful people, especially children.

King's third full year of operation, 1874, surpassed his earlier commercial exploits of securing both the International Scientific Series and Hesba Stretton. Now he put his imprint on the works of the Poet Laureate: Alfred, Lord Tennyson. Tennyson was at the height of his fame, the laureate since 1850. His lyric poetry was widely read; Queen Victoria had used *In Memoriam* to help her deal with the grief of Prince Albert's death; *Maud* and *Idylls of the King* had sold very well, and made a profit both for Tennyson and for his several publishers.[34] From 1869 to 1874, Tennyson had a contract with Alexander Strahan. Unfortunately, from the laureate's point of view (he hated to change publishers and feared that he would be criticized for frivolous transfers), Strahan's business faltered in the early seventies and he turned for financial help to Henry S. King. King lent money to Strahan and became joint-owner with him of several periodicals (see below). In the words of a letter from Tennyson to his wife in October 1872, Strahan had 'joined himself to King'.

King dined with Tennyson in November, graciously remembering an earlier visit to the poet's country home, at Farringford on the Isle of Wight. The following spring, with the help of Strahan and another colleague, James Knowles, the two men worked out a contract to begin in January 1874. King would pay £25,000, broken into five annual instalments, for the right to reprint Tennyson's earlier work, either from existing stereotype plates or from new settings of type, and would also have the privilege of publishing new works on a commission basis, at 5%. Having made the deal, King turned over the day-to-day management of the Tennyson account to Charles Kegan Paul. This should have worked out well, since Paul had tutored young Hallam and Lionel Tennyson in 1865–6 at Sturminster, and had written kindly to their mother about the boys' religious development. But the neophyte publisher's assistant managed to offend the firm's illustrious and expensive client, not just once but over and over again.

In August 1874, Tennyson wrote to Paul (whom he referred to as King's head-man of business) to put a stop to plans for illustrations (portraits of houses associated with Tennyson) to accompany a new edition of the collected works. He expressed his

> utter disapproval of the kind of illustrations you wish to prefix to my volumes. I had thought you would be satisfied with my photograph in the first, and that the other illustrations would be on subjects drawn from the poems themselves: but it seems now that I am to be Americanized and vulgarised: both my houses and my birthplace etc. are to be exhibited as if I were a dead man.

'Moreover,' he was certain, 'all the world will impute these Yankeeisms to me not to my publishers.' Then he invoked a higher authority: 'I am sure that if you were to state my feelings to Mr King he would pay some respect to them.' Paul replied, not directly but via young Hallam Tennyson, by now serving as his father's manager. The plans were not his personal responsibility, but had been made before his arrival in Cornhill. He had consulted King, and found that his principal remembered the matter of illustrations having been discussed. Paul disagreed with the view that readers would blame the author, and also with the theory that such illustrations were a modern vulgarity:

> While I dislike as much as any one, anything like over curiosity about a man's private life, and would resent for my friends as for myself anything like impertinence, I must say that a desire to possess the *ipsissima verba*, or as near them as may be of one we love and respect seems to me a blameless little bit of the instinctive worship we pay to those we love. It would be much if your father could concede this point.

The conflict simmered down with a compromise, but it was not long before Paul and Tennyson came again to epistolary blows.

In the new twelve-volume Cabinet edition, published in 1874, Tennyson took advantage of re-publication to add some lines to 'Vivien'. Paul seized immediately upon the marketing potential of the expanded text, and again ran into Tennyson's tender sensibilities. He wrote directly to the poet in October 1874:

> We are of course always anxious to comply with any request you may make, especially one made with such urgency, but I confess I am quite unable to understand *why* we should not say that Vivien has in it additional lines. Having written them and consented to their publication, it is to be presumed that you wish them to be known. There are hundreds, I may say thousands of people, who having already the Idylls of the King will not buy another edition of them, unless they know that there is in them something new, but who it may be hoped will do so if they have that knowledge. And advertising is simply the way of stating a fact, which we suppose you as well as ourselves wish to be

known. While we endeavour as far as possible to put ourselves in your position, and look on these matters as you do, in which we have not always succeeded, I am sure you will forgive our asking you to remember that the success of literature has two sides, and that the trade element is an important one, nor if rightly considered is it, I think, a wholly prosaic one.

Paul, however, was not the final authority: 'I have read your letter to Mr King, who says that since you put it on the ground you do, there is not a word more to be said.'

The underlying problem of the ten years during which Tennyson was dealing with King (and later directly with Paul) was that the poet laureate did not write enough in that time to justify their huge expenditures. The two dramas, *Queen Mary* (1875) and *Harold* (1876) were not as popular as the lyric poetry, and the market for reprints, however skilfully 'got up' with illustrations and revisions, was limited. In August 1876 Paul wrote rather plaintively to Hallam Tennyson, 'Are you aware that Harold will make only 160–170 pp as against 276 pp in Queen Mary? The few lines which may here and there be inserted will increase it a little, but it will be difficult to get the same price for it as for Queen Mary. Could your father introduce more of those lyrics of which he is so inimitable a master.' But Tennyson was adamant. He also refused to entertain Paul's proposal that an Annotated Edition of the poems, with notes, would find a scholarly market.

Tennyson was outraged in October 1877 to find that his books had been transferred, without his knowledge or approval, to the imprint of C. Kegan Paul and Co. In vain, Paul told the poet's lawyer that the arrangements had been kept secret for business reasons, that he was in fact the first of the authors to be informed:

> It is a matter of great disappointment to me considering my long and intimate relations with Mr Tennyson that he is the only person who has taken any but a cordial line on the subject. I have a drawer full of letters expressing the most friendly co-operation with the new Firm – yours is the only one to the contrary.

Despite this beginning, as we shall see, the two men agreed in 1879 to work together for a further five years. But it was King, not Paul, who earned the poet's respect.

King's 'alliance' with Alexander Strahan brought him more authors than Tennyson. As we have seen, King had funds generated from other sources available to invest in publishing; Strahan, on the other hand, had to borrow money to finance his periodicals and books, and King was a major creditor. Strahan had begun in Edinburgh as a 'Scottish Presbyterian' publisher; he moved to London in 1862 and widened his interests to include what his modern biographer Patricia Srebrnik identifies as the literature of Christian social reform.[35] This literature included books by politicians (Gladstone), by novelists and essayists (Robert Buchanan and Edward Jenkins), by writers for children (George MacDonald and Jean Ingelow) and by poets (Tennyson and Buchanan). Although Strahan published many important books, his main interest was in the several periodicals by which he hoped to persuade the 'chief authors' of the time to 'descend to the magazines', in order to provide 'the people' with inexpensive literature. The most notable of these periodicals was the *Contemporary Review*, established in 1866 as a Christian competitor to the secular reviews, and containing articles on theology, philosophy, literature, and social problems. James Thomas Knowles was involved with editing the *Contemporary*; he was founder of the Metaphysical Society and in touch with serious-minded people in London's political as well as literary and philosophical circles. *Good Words*, and its juvenile co-publication *Good Words for the Young*, both including fiction as well as articles on issues of contemporary interest, were aimed at a more narrowly religious market, and *Saint Paul's Magazine* was a vehicle for serialized fiction, including novels by Trollope.

All this activity, particularly the expensive arrangement with Tennyson, pushed Strahan towards bankruptcy. His major creditors (a printer and a stationer) forced him to resign in March of 1872, although he retained control of some of his books and of the *Contemporary*, *Good Words for the Young* (retitled *Good Things for the Young*) and *Saint Paul's Magazine*. The firm continued as Strahan and Co., and Strahan himself was therefore forbidden to use his own name in business until December 1873. During those awkward twenty months, King bought his way into control of Strahan's lucrative and prestigious, if ill-managed publications. Strahan set himself up in Paternoster Row and used King's imprint on the title pages of his periodicals; King's wholesale network handled their distribution. The two men even joined forces to publish a new penny weekly, the *Day of Rest*, beginning in December 1872. And as popular books by Strahan's authors came up for reprinting, the imprint on their title-pages was that of H.S. King & Co.

One of the Strahan authors whose names appeared and remained on King's lists was George MacDonald, now remembered chiefly for his children's stories but in his own time regarded as an important poet, preacher and lecturer, as well as prolific novelist. Many of his books were set in Scotland. The first of MacDonald's works on the King list was *Gutta-Percha Willie, the Working Genius* (1873); during the eighties Kegan Paul, Trench published many of his novels in various formats, including their Colonial Library. Another Strahan author was Jean Ingelow, poet and juvenile writer, whose *Off the Skelligs* (1873) and other children's books cost King a total of £362 5s 6d in the transfer. She, too, survived into the nineties with the firm. Robert Williams Buchanan was more of a problem. His books of essays and poetry (*A Child of Nature* (1872); *Master-Spirits* (1873)) were not particularly profitable. But the transfer of his books from Strahan cost King the services of an important poet.

Buchanan is now remembered primarily for his attacks on Algernon Charles Swinburne. Despite some questions about the morality of his verse, and despite (or because of) his association with Rossetti and the Pre-Raphaelites, Swinburne was a celebrated writer. It was a coup for King to get him to contribute to *Pleasure* in 1871, and he hoped to use the association, opened up by Emilie Venturi and the Mazzini circle, to secure further contracts. But Swinburne refused to appear under the same imprint with Buchanan. The latter had attacked him on moral grounds along with the Pre-Raphaelites, whom Buchanan labelled 'The Fleshly School of Poetry' in a *Contemporary Review* article (1871). When King brought out a collected edition of Buchanan's poetry, Swinburne wrote: 'Faugh – it will be impossible for men of honour and character to publish with him afterwards.'[36]

Perhaps the most profitable author King acquired from Strahan was Edward Jenkins, who combined the production of sensational literature with legal practice and investigative journalism. His fictional *Ginx's Baby* was the hit of 1870, a satire on the administration of charities in England's urban slums and how they were hampered by religious sectarianism. The King–Jenkins agreement for reprints of Jenkins's works, dated November 1872, allowed for an illustrated edition of *Ginx's Baby*. Although Jenkins is now obscure, while Tennyson is part of the literary canon, this reissue of the former's popular novel would, from the point of view of their publisher, have been as valuable a property as the contract for the latter's poems.

Even after Strahan reappeared under his own imprint and with fresh financial sponsorship in December 1873, he continued to mortgage his literary properties to King and others. The *Contemporary Review*, meanwhile, had developed under Knowles's editorship into a journal of debate and a vehicle for controversial essays; it was becoming the mouthpiece of the Metaphysical Society. Strahan's newest backers, however, disapproved of its increasingly secular, even anti-Christian tone, and forced him to dismiss Knowles early in 1877. They were a group of evangelical investors who wished to return the *Contemporary* to its original agenda. Knowles, not surprisingly, took his skills and his contacts with the most important writers of the day with him when he started a new journal, *The Nineteenth Century*, in March of 1877. Contributors to the inaugural issue included Tennyson, Gladstone, Cardinal Manning and Matthew Arnold. The publisher was Henry S. King.[37]

King was only 'publisher' of *The Nineteenth Century* in the sense of printing and distribution; Knowles was, and remained, the sole proprietor. But King, and later the Kegan Paul company under its various imprints, remained the publisher until June 1891.[38] Although the success of *The Nineteenth Century* in competition with the *Contemporary* has been attributed, correctly, to its more exciting and cosmopolitan contents, it is important to note that King used Strahan's debt to him to protect the fledgling publication. At the end of 1872, King had received from Strahan the copyright of the *CR*, as well as that of their joint publication *The Day of Rest* in return for the management of the latter periodical. When Strahan offered in September 1874 to repay his debt, and thus release the copyrights back into his possession, King refused, presumably because he wished to continue collecting the £1,200 per year commission as publisher. Thus matters stood in February 1876, when it was announced that the planned *Nineteenth Century* would be published by King, not by Longmans as originally suggested. Strahan claimed that King was using his 'unwarrantable retention of his hold over these properties' to destroy the *Contemporary* and promote its new rival. A judge agreed, and in February 1877 Strahan was granted permission to pay King and regain control over his (and his new creditors') property.[39]

The tangled business dealings of Henry Samuel King with Alexander Strahan may never be completely unravelled. Clearly, though, the man at 12 Paternoster Row (the Cornhill address was now reserved for non-book business) was continuing the old Smith, Elder policy of financing books and journals from the profits of other commercial operations, to the discomfiture of his competitors in the publishing business. And, in what was to be his last year as a publisher, he was exercising his own talent for identifying and fostering authors who would be popular, and books that would sell.

III

Charles Kegan Paul later turned up his fastidious literary nose at some of King's acquisitions. 'It must . . . be admitted', he wrote

> that a more critical literary judgment would have peremptorily rejected many books, which, interspersed with some of permanent value, swelled the earlier lists. There was little time for criticism remaining to a man who was extending a large mercantile trade, and some trivial books introduced at first were difficult to eliminate when better material flowed in, and some small part of the last six years was to undo the mistakes of the first two.

'Yet,' continues the man whose arrival coincided with the elimination of trivial books, 'the undertaking was steadily prosperous. It could scarcely be otherwise when it was the darling occupation of the head of the firm.' But as we have seen, King brought to his publishing business more than mere time, or an affection (however vulgar) for books as 'the shrines of literature'. He brought capital, and an entrepreneurial approach. If Countess von Bothmer's or 'Holme Lee's' novels failed to sell, they simply remained on the warehouse shelves while the publisher went ahead with his buccaneering attack on the Strahan list.

In the history of the book trade, Charles Kegan Paul is justly celebrated for his attention to aesthetic matters of design and to the details of typography, print production and binding.[40] What has not been acknowledged is that he learned his craft from King. Paul praised King's attention to 'every minutest detail of the production of a book, [where] the smallest deviation from his ideal was a serious trouble to him'. The evidence exists, although it may now be difficult to find examples outside a rare-book collection: the Cornhill Library; two editions of Tennyson's works; the slick red-and-black design emphasizing the global character of the International Scientific Series; and altogether about 650 new titles issued under his imprint between May 1871 and October 1877.

Henry S. King's company published about 100 works per year over a six-and-a-half-year period, and these were all unique titles. To add reprints and subsequent editions to the list would make the achievement even greater, and more impressive. They set a high standard for their successor companies, and we shall see that this standard was met at an even greater rate of productivity. It would be useful to know how large an editorial and clerical staff was involved in preparing these books for publication, but unfortunately the surviving records do not provide much insight into business arrangements of this kind. One exception is the name of Charles Welsh, who worked for Henry King 'from the publication of the first book with his imprint', in 1871 until 1877, when he joined the St Paul's Churchyard firm of Griffith and Farran.[41] As with most London publishers, the composing, printing and binding of H.S. King books were not handled in-house, but were contracted out to a number of local businesses. The printers William Clowes & Son and Messrs Spottiswoode were used frequently, as were the bookbinders Burn: all of these were firms that offered book-production services to houses throughout the London publishing trade.

King fell ill about 1875, with the heart disease that killed him a year after he gave up the concern to Paul. The transfer occurred in October of 1877, announced by the firm in the *Publishers' Circular* on the sixteenth:

> The great and increasing extension of our banking and agency business requiring all our time and attention, necessitates the disposal of our publication department, which also has become much enlarged. We beg to inform you therefore, that we have sold this branch of our business to Messrs C. KEGAN PAUL & CO. ... Mr Paul has been connected with our business for some years, and is thus personally known to nearly all the constituents of our publishing branch, with which he has been intimately associated.

How was the sale accomplished? There is nothing in the company's records to indicate how much King received for the goodwill, the copyrights and stock and contracts with authors, that comprised his valuable establishment. His style in other business matters suggests that Henry King would have driven a hard bargain. And yet Charles Kegan Paul was, as we shall see, a clergyman of modest means and large family, whose inheritance from his own father had long since been devoted to his mother's needs. Chapter two will take up again the question of this puzzling financial transaction. The transition was smooth, once Tennyson was mollified, and the 'Successors to the Publishing Department of Henry S. King & Co.' continued in business at 1 Paternoster Square, in the square mile of the City of London, at the heart of the publishing district.

Like many Victorians, King had been advised by his doctors to travel abroad in search of better health. They also suggested that he decrease his workload, but, as Paul reports, this was difficult. 'He parted [from the firm] to take still the keenest interest in it, and greet the issue of every new work as though it had been the birth of a fresh child of his own.' (Harriet King, coping with a large family and an ailing husband, might have had something to say about this.) Nevertheless when King retired it was not from all his business interests, but only from the publishing. He remained involved with the India agency and banking operations until the day of his death. He even considered entering politics, but his physician vetoed a plan to stand for Alderman in municipal elections. He underwent surgery in early November 1878, just before he turned sixty-one, and on his birthday wrote a letter to his son Henry Seymour King, which Paul piously quoted in the *Academy* obituary: 'We talk of going to Pall Mall to-morrow, leaving here [Chigwell] about twelve. I am, indeed, thankful for such progress, after such a severe operation. I shall hope there is in me yet some power that may come out usefully for others before I lay the burden finally down.' Instead he died, at the Pall Mall apartments above his bank, on 17 November 1878. Harriet King moved away, with her children and her poetry, and lived until 1920.

In his will, King disposed of an estate of some £45,000. There were bequests to a maiden sister, Frances, and a smaller one to his married sister, Eliza Coveney, and a bequest, later withdrawn by codicil, to the clergyman brother Richard ('having secured under the provisions of an infamous will made more than 30 years since all the property of our aunt Miss Sarah King to the exclusion of our two sisters he has no need of more'). Harriet was left half the residue of the estate as well as £2,000 and the household effects (furniture, plate, linen, china, books, pictures, wine, horses, carriages, live and dead stock); the children inherited the other half in equal shares. This was not all of King's wealth: he arranged for the business to carry on uninterrupted, in the hands of his eldest son. Henry Seymour King, later Sir Henry, not only continued his father's career as a banker but fulfilled his political ambitions, sitting as MP (Conservative) for Central Hull from 1885 to 1911. The banking and India agency business was amalgamated in 1923 with Lloyd's bank. He died in 1933.[42]

King's urbane and cosmopolitan character was remembered by Hallam Tennyson, who observed that 'With none of the publishers into whose hands circumstances had thrown my father, was the connection so uninterruptedly pleasant as with Messrs Macmillan, unless perhaps that with Mr Henry King.' Charles Kegan Paul, who knew him better, summed up his character this way:

> In business matters he was strict, even to hardness; away from business tender, at times to the verge of weakness, but never beyond the verge. He was a Tory and a Churchman, but had his one great ambition for political life been fulfilled, his party

would have found him far from manageable, and his creed, if closely examined, was deficient in more than one orthodox article.

Very little documentation has survived to delineate Henry King's personality, and most of it comes from a singularly prejudiced contemporary. Fortunately, Paul's comments can be supplemented by an analysis of the books King published and the contracts he drew up. Taken together, the evidence on Henry S. King illuminates for modern readers some of the character of the Victorian age. He was no stereotypical Victorian businessman, narrowly correct in his dealings and stifled by propriety; but nor was he the autodidact bibliophile portrayed by Paul. He was a global entrepreneur, prepared to bar Strahan from the market for quality periodicals, to undercut the Religious Tract Society's understanding with Hesba Stretton, to publish science at high prices in collaboration with Appleton's in New York and other publishers in Europe, and to imprint his name on some of the characteristic books of his age.

CHAPTER 2
CHARLES KEGAN PAUL, PASTOR TO PUBLISHER

I

Charles Kegan Paul's family did not share the double-barrelled surname affected by their husband and father. They were plain Mrs Paul, the three Misses Paul and young Louis and Maurice Paul. 'Kegan' was the maiden name of the publisher's grandmother and his own second given name. But 'Kegan Paul' was, almost invariably, the name by which the publisher was known to his contemporaries, and the name that outlasted both him and the business he took over from Henry S. King, as the imprint upon thousands of title-pages. (It may be noted parenthetically that Paul disliked the term 'contemporaries', preferring 'men of his time', as much as he disliked parentheses, the mark, in his opinion, of a bad stylist.)[1]

The men and women of Paul's time were struck not only by his strong opinions about literary matters, but also by the paradoxical nature of his personality. This must have been especially apparent when he first left his Dorset vicarage and, in the words of 'one who knew him', Wilfrid Meynell, 'unexpectedly found himself one of the chief publishers in London'.[2] In that world of cosmopolitans like Henry King, many of whom enjoyed to the full the 'paraphernalia of gentility', the carriages and dining clubs, the connoisseurship of good wine and fine spirits, Paul was an ascetic: a vegetarian and a teetotaller, who preferred to travel third-class on the Underground. And although Paul had made such literary reputation as he possessed in 1877 by contributions to the latitudinarian *Theological Review*, he was now involved with Comtist Positivism; despite this heterodoxy he used his old contacts to secure the publication in King's list of sermons and of essays on religious questions. Finally, this passionate upholder of the rights of agricultural labourers, who regarded himself as 'a liberal of the liberals', in some moods even a socialist, was also the editor and designer of the *Parchment Library*, a series of volumes that 'set the fashion', among bibliophiles in the London of the eighties, 'for really beautiful books'. Robert Louis Stevenson expressed this duality in his remark: 'Oh yes, Kegan is an excellent good fellow, but Paul is a [damned] publisher'. This chapter explores the man behind the name on the long-lived and celebrated imprint.[3]

Paul was the eldest son of a clergyman, at the time of his birth (8 March 1828) curate in sole charge of the village of White Lackington, in Somerset near the market town of Ilminster. His mother, Frances Kegan Horne, had grown up in Bath, but she was born in St Vincent, in the West Indies. In *Memories*, the autobiography published in 1899, he recalled that she 'was considered to have done well for herself in a worldly sense', by her marriage to a young man (they were both twenty-five) who 'had an ample, even a large income'. Both of Charles Kegan Paul's parents derived from the British colonial community in the West Indies, where the Pauls owned an estate in St Vincent and had earlier been West Indies merchants as well, and the Hornes were 'old Colonial', having come to St Vincent originally from The Netherlands. The couple's families had never met in the West Indies, and both were raised largely in England. Paul's father was educated at the Charterhouse and later at Gonville and Caius College, Cambridge, and took holy orders in order to establish himself in 'a fixed profession . . . with, no doubt, a determination to do his duty, but without the high ideas of self-devotion which all men are supposed to have, and many really have, in these days'. Paul's memoir displays little sympathy with his father. His 'considerable means from West Indian property' diminished rapidly in the course of Paul's childhood, as the abolition of slavery in 1833 was followed by bankruptcies and financial losses for the British planters. Sixty years later, Paul observed that 'We all know the ruin and disaster which fell on West Indian properties, perhaps justly, in punishment for slavery, extravagance, absenteeism, and racial contempt, but the ruin was hard to bear at the time.'

Paul's early childhood was spent not at White Lackington but at another village, nearer to Bath, where his father took two curacies in 1830. These were Writhlington, where they lived, and Foxcote. Both were coalmining villages, and the young Pauls were acquainted with colliers: 'a pleasant, kindly set of men, and on the best terms with us children'. Charles was the eldest of ten, and the only surviving son. It was an idyllic country childhood, untouched by the political upheavals that were happening both in England and in St Vincent, the stuff of nostalgia:

> I still seem to see a hedge of Roses de Meaux (do such roses exist now?) which formed a fence to our field, and to smell the syringa in the shrubbery, to taste the peppermint bull's-eyes, which our neighbour the farmer, whose suitable name was Mattick, used always to produce from his breeches-pocket, and am sure there were never such fruit-trees as the quince, the medlar, and the Siberian crab which grew upon the lawn.

The family had 'a very old green parrot, allowed to wander at will about the house and garden'. During a funeral, he was apt to sit on a tree-top and say 'O Lord, what fun! what fun! O my eyes, what fun!'

Paul began his literary and intellectual education with intensive reading during his early childhood, reading *Camilla*, *Gulliver's Travels* and the *Arabian Nights* in unexpurgated editions that, as he later observed, he was too young fully to understand: at that age, 'all that is improper passes by with the harder words'. The publisher John Murray's pioneer series of reprint fiction, the Family Library, found a place in Paul's early reading, along with Walter Scott and 'a good deal of Theology'. Paul discovered Shakespeare (he preferred the spelling Shakspere) at the age of twelve, from which point he dated 'my real awakening to the meaning of literature, my intellectual "conversion", so to speak', and became 'a diligent reader and student of the greatest English poet'. He also read the Bible, closely and thoroughly, every evening at bedtime with his mother.

As soon as Paul could read himself, he taught a class in the village Sunday school: 'The smell of Sunday corduroys, onions eaten for breakfast, peppermints to be sucked in church during the sermon, and "boys' love" stuck between the leaves of prayer-books, is never to be forgotten.' The Church of England clergyman and his family had to compete for the religious patronage of the local colliers and farmers with Primitive Methodists, or 'Ranters', who were more fervent and energetic than Anglicans about their preaching, prayer and singing. But to a sensitive child, because of his reading already conscious that experience takes many forms, the religious enthusiasm of his neighbours was material to be observed almost in an anthropological way, and to be remembered.

The idyll ended in 1836, when Paul was eight years old and had to go away to school. Oddly enough, he returned almost to his birthplace, to Ilminster School. Under the direction of the Rev. Mr John Allen it was 'a school which was, to me at least, a hell, and where life was one long misery'. Looking back after working for many years in education, and in the light of the reforms of the second half of the nineteenth century, Paul recalled that 'the textbooks used were bad, the facilities for private preparation of lessons were non-existent; we children were never helped to learn for ourselves; we never heard a word of kindness or encouragement; furious flogging for the majority, the grossest favouritism for a few, appeared to be the only discipline known or imagined'. Throughout Paul's memoir he pauses at each stage of life to remember the friends he made; even at Ilminster ('friendship rarely exists among bullied boys') there were a few.

By 1840 'the final and complete failure of the West Indian property' occurred and the Rev. Mr Paul was forced to take pupils, boys who lived in the vicarage and read classics and other subjects before going to school. It was common in the nineteenth century for clergyman to supplement their incomes in this way, and for clergy wives to provide the necessary domestic services, serving as surrogate school matrons. George Eliot described Tom Tulliver's experience of this kind of situation in *The Mill on the Floss*. She remarked that 'there are two expensive forms of education, either of which a parent may procure for his son by sending him as solitary pupil to a clergyman: one is, the enjoyment of the reverend gentleman's undivided neglect; the other is, the endurance of the reverend gentleman's undivided attention'.[4] Paul's recollection suggests that the second approach was favoured by his father: 'it was not a pleasant experiment, my mother never liked it, and her health was very unfit to cope with the situation'. As we shall see, Paul himself took pupils in his turn, and his wife objected just as his mother had. 'My father, though he taught fairly well, as I believe, had not the smallest sympathy for or understanding of boy nature, and pupils had the effect, as is generally the case, of breaking up our home life.' Paul left Ilminster at Christmas of 1839 because of a knee injury, and therefore spent a year or so at home, which was now situated at Wellow, yet another village about four miles from Writhlington.

At thirteen, in the spring of 1841, he went away again for five years, to a much more congenial, as well as more celebrated school, Eton. It was Paul's first railway journey, from rural Shropshire to Slough near Windsor, just west of London. He boarded in the house of his beloved tutor, C.O. Goodford. The household was managed initially by a housekeeper, the 'fussy and tiresome' Miss Edgar, and later by Goodford's wife, who 'presided . . . with charm and dignity'. His friends were not among the school's intellectuals but Paul himself 'read omnivorously; my tutor most kindly giving me the run of his library'. It was during those Eton years that Paul first became acquainted with Tennyson's poems, 'learning by heart the greater part of the original volumes, and thinking . . . that for subtle workmanship no one had at all approached the same perfection since Milton'. This adolescent passion for Tennyson's verse may have coloured the later business relationship between the two men: the literary idol had feet of commercial clay. Paul enjoyed punting and walking, but was not among the school's serious athletes. As for religious influences, although with the exception of his mother 'no one ever said one word to me', during those five years, 'about my religious life', nevertheless 'at Eton I learned to be a High Churchman'. He was not to remain one.

Paul's own father was an 'orthodox', as opposed to an 'evangelical' clergyman, that is he tended to be 'high' rather than 'low' in his churchmanship, but he also tried not to associate himself with parties in the Church (although in secular politics he was a 'Tory of the highest kind'). At Eton in the forties it was impossible to avoid taking a position with respect to ecclesiastical politics.

'The wave of the Oxford movement had affected Eton, and . . . in 1841 such of us boys who were inclined to think and read the newspapers became conscious of the great stir which was going on at Oxford; a few of our masters were falling under the influence of the new theology, and this could not be without its effect on the boys.' The great stir was the publication of *Tracts for the Times* (1833–41). The Tractarians, the Oxford clergymen and dons who wished to return the Church of England to what they believed to be its sacramental and authoritarian traditions, expressed their view that the Church should not be controlled in any way by the state. The new theology of the *Tracts* was inspired by John Henry Newman, a fellow of Oriel College, whose writings and sermons were intensely moving and significant to Paul, as well as to numerous other people. For some at Oxford, and in the fears of many more critics outside the movement, the logical extension of Tractarianism was adherence to the Roman Catholic Church, from which the English bishops had originally derived their authority until the merely political break of the Reformation. Newman initially regarded the Church of England as the *via media*, the middle way between Roman Catholicism on the one side and Protestantism on the other. Nevertheless in Tract 90 (1841) he argued that the Anglicans' regulations for clergymen, the Thirty-Nine Articles, were compatible with many doctrines of the Roman Catholic Church. And in 1845 he himself submitted to Rome and later became a Cardinal. Paul's own admiration for Newman began at Eton, and the fascination with Roman Catholicism that would lead to his own submission nearly half a century later, although it had tentative earlier roots, was strengthened and made articulate.[5]

It was his studies, though, not his religious beliefs, that most engaged Paul's attention during his late adolescence at Eton. In those unreformed days, the only training in history, geography, and modern languages (French was regarded as an *objet de luxe*) was outside the main curriculum; no science was offered. 'That which in old days was mainly taught at Eton was how to learn.' And the method by which learning was taught was the Greek and Latin classics. 'Education at Eton in those days was thoroughly haphazard, though it must be said that if a boy chose to work in the way of true scholarship he found every possible aid from some of the masters, nor was there any discouragement in the way of miscellaneous reading.' Fortunately for Paul, Goodford offered him this kind of encouragement and help. When the time came to go to Oxford, he was well prepared.

The eighteen-year-old Paul went up to Exeter College, Oxford in October 1846. Although at one time the family's fortune would have made this kind of launch in life a benefit to be taken for granted, he was warned not to expect much more: 'My father, who went to start me, put into my hands a long and kind letter, in which he explained his circumstances, how little likely it was that I should ever inherit anything from him, and that a small amount settled on me from my mother's fortune was all I could ever expect, and this only at her death.' At an age when Henry King was making his own living and learning the customs of the book trade as a publisher–bookseller in Brighton, his successor, although not much more secure financially, continued to absorb the classical education begun at Eton. It made sense, or seemed to, because the family had already decided that Charles Kegan Paul, their eldest, should take holy orders.

Paul's three years at Oxford as an undergraduate did not strengthen his ties with the Tractarian movement. Newman had departed, and Paul resisted the influence of Edward Pusey and regarded tolerantly the enthusiasm of friends like Hopkins of Balliol. The rooms of this old Eton acquaintance 'were decorated in the most ecclesiastical manner'. One day Paul

> found him stripping texts from the walls in wild haste, and appealing to those of his friends who had arrived to help him to shove under the bed a large crowned figure of the Blessed Virgin. It appeared that he had just heard that his father, a Berkshire squire, whose contempt for ecclesiastical millinery, &c., was most pronounced, was in Oxford, and even then on his way to Balliol. The transformation was effected, and the meeting between father and son was unbroken by storms.

Of his University life and of his many friends, Paul remembers that 'We read – far less than we should have done – in the mornings, we rode and boated in the afternoons, or took long pleasant walks, pouring out all our souls to each other, before life taught us the need of reticence, and that daws peck at hearts worn upon the sleeve.' His tutor, William Sewell, was unhelpful and Paul 'turned to a great deal of private reading . . . making great use of the Union library. At the Union I also became a debater, and learned considerable fluency in speech, which has since proved very useful.' The Oxford Union was the training ground for many of the great Parliamentary debaters of the age. The reading was largely devoted to Robert Browning's poetry and to Carlyle's history and philosophy.

Paul's Oxford years were marked by a great sorrow, the death of his mother in August 1848, and a great shock, his father's remarriage in 1851. In *Memories* he extolled Frances Paul's 'grace, beauty, wisdom, strength of character, and charm of manner'. As for his stepmother, he 'admitted her boldness in marrying a man of fifty with next to no means and with eight children; but this audacity was her only good quality'. It was not the custom for the father of a large family to remain a widower, and especially unusual for a clergyman, because the contribution of the rector's wife was important to the management of a parish. Paul's unsympathetic assessment of a man from whose authority he had largely escaped, suggests that he blamed his father too heavily for the family's misfortunes, whether it was the abolition of slavery in St Vincent or the loss of his mother and of the intimacy of family life.

In the spring of 1849 Paul found a new friend and mentor in Charles Kingsley. At that time the future author of *Westward Ho!*, and *The Water Babies* was thirty years old and well-established as the rector of Eversley in Hampshire. He had just published *Yeast*, his first novel. Its themes were issues that had been important to Paul, and would become more so: the conditions of agricultural labourers, and Tractarianism. The clergyman's personality was 'characterized by a sunny joyousness, an abounding vitality, and a contagious energy which were most attractive'. Bereft of his mother and, to all intents and purposes, of his father, Paul responded ardently to Kingsley: 'To young men still in the course of formation this coruscating person, ten years older than ourselves, but young in mind, and a born leader of men, came as a kind of revelation. We had never met anyone like him, nor indeed have I ever since encountered any one so impressive to the young.' Not to the young, perhaps, but thirty years later Paul would offer the same kind of intense admiration to Henry King, and later again, in the 1890s, to the publishing entrepreneur Horatio Bottomley. Kingsley's charisma, though, was spiritual: 'this man, so varied in knowledge and so brilliant in talk, athletic in habits and frame, a first-rate horseman, keen sportsman, good quoit player, was also a man of prayer and piety, filled with a personal, even passionate, love to Christ, whom he realized as his Friend and Brother in a fashion almost peculiar to the Saints'.

The Pauls had always intended that their eldest son enter the Church of England. But this young man who took life so seriously was not inclined to follow his father's unambitious example, and considered as alternatives a career at the bar or in medicine. 'As I grew older I disliked my father's humdrum life, and believed, as I still believe, that a country clergyman's life in the Anglican Church is either idle or fussy. He has next to nothing to do *as clergyman*, or he worries his people to death. . . . Kingsley showed me a different ideal.' A further alternative was the High Church 'vision of constant services and sacraments'. But at Oxford, under Kingsley's influence, Paul 'became dissatisfied with the Tractarian theory, and such biblical criticism as I had read was inclining me to those notions which were afterwards called "Broad", and of these Kingsley was the incarnation'. Paul was still profoundly moved, in spiritual and aesthetic terms, by 'the High Church vision' but his intellectual training required him to make room for critical readings of the scriptures, and his admiration for Kingsley quelled for many years the persistent hankering after Rome.

Like Henry S. King's clerical friends Brooke and Robertson, Kingsley was a leader in the nascent 'Broad Church' movement. Apart from the doctrinal appeal, Paul discovered in him a model for a workable form of life as a clergyman: 'A man always at work, treating his literary gifts, his schemes for social, sanitary, and political reform, as part of his priestly work; he took a large view of things, and gave me larger ones than I had ever had before.' Both men came to share the belief that the Anglican Church, in many ways so unsatisfactory, 'could and would be widened from within'. Paul's theological position at this juncture, while perhaps not unique, was by no means commonplace. He regarded himself as 'a very broad High Churchman, broad that is in doctrine, but with a strong feeling for pomp of ritual, for music in church, paintings and symbolism of all kinds'. Not many of those who shared his wish to widen the Church of England's theology, to include even modern scientific thought about evolution and the non-divine origin of species, also shared his aesthetic vision. 'Politically,' he continues, 'I became an extreme Radical . . . a Republican and a Socialist, so far as these things can be carried out without breach of public order.' An odd combination, but the Church of England had found room before for eccentrics among its clergy. What Paul needed was to find a parish where he would have the power and the time at his disposal to shape this unorthodox combination of beliefs into a satisfactory career. He was to discover, however, that the right kind of parish was difficult to find, and even more difficult to secure.

Paul took his Oxford BA degree in October 1849, and then spent a year and a half waiting until he came of age for ordination at twenty-three. 'This was a very unsatisfactory time, for I had nothing at all to do, and no particular home.' His father's vicarage was no longer congenial, and he spent months with Charles and Frances Kingsley, occasionally staying with other friends or at Bath, where his sisters lodged with an aunt. In the spring of 1851 Charles Kegan Paul reluctantly attended his father's marriage ceremony and then returned to Oxford for his own ordination as deacon: 'Never a man took Orders with more sincere desire than I to do his duty in the Anglican Church to the souls that should be given to my charge.' His first post was the curacy of Great Tew, a rural village parish in the Oxford diocese.

Paul's duties at Great Tew were not onerous, and his life had an unsettled quality. The landlord of the whole parish, who was also patron of the ecclesiastical living, renovated and furnished for him a labourer's cottage, and a village woman provided meals and housework. His solitude was broken by occasional visits from his sisters and from other friends. Subordinate to the rector in charge, he preached on alternate Sunday mornings, and took evening services every week in the neighbouring village of Little Tew. Not being responsible for visiting the parishioners, the curate was in no danger of 'worrying his people to death'. In the winter he discovered a new interest, when he inaugurated a night-school. He began to discover his 'deep sympathy' with the agricultural labourers of rural England and came to believe that as an unmarried clergyman he had a unique opportunity to exert a spiritual influence upon young men. He was not impressed, then or later, with Samuel Wilberforce, his 'astute and insincere' bishop. Wilberforce nevertheless offered him a difficult and challenging assignment after a year's service at Tew, sole charge of the village of Bloxham, about six miles away.

Bloxham required more of the young curate's energy and commitment. His predecessor was over ninety years of age and had neglected the services to the point of open scandal: on one occasion, the communion wine bottle was put on the table still unbroached, and the vicar had to ask his kneeling parishioners, reverently prepared for Holy Communion, 'Has any lady or gentleman a corkscrew?' Paul had the duty of presiding at the vicar's funeral, but his arrangement with Bishop Wilberforce for a curacy did not guarantee him a permanent right to the living, which was in the gift of the Provost of Eton College. He spent only six months there, in 1852, living comfortably in his own small house, while the presentation remained unsettled. Paul recalled that 'My work at Bloxham was singularly happy. . . . My preaching, for I wrote my sermons with care, was at any rate fresher and more intelligible than that to which the people had been accustomed.'

In one of these sermons, at a School Festival, Paul spoke of a subject near his heart, the problem that 'the clergy find most difficulty in their parishes with the young men after they have left school'. He regarded himself as particularly fit for this kind of ministry, because of his own school experiences at Ilminster: 'Those who have passed through the furnace, which nearly all schools were, who have handled pitch and happily not been defiled . . . are fain, both in village and in higher schools, to keep Christian boyhood what it should be, what it may be.'[6] This sermon, printed as a pamphlet and dedicated to the boys of All Saints Grammar School, Bloxham, was Paul's first piece of published writing.

His pews began to fill up, and he was ordained priest, still very close to Kingsley, and hoping that Bloxham might be the parish in which to set about emulating his friend and mentor. But in the arbitrary nature of the Anglican system of preferment, another vicar was appointed to the living, and Paul found himself 'in great doubt what was to be my next move'. His opinions, to himself so highminded, seemed to others unduly radical, and he missed being offered one possible post because he had attended a meeting presided over by Frederick Dennison Maurice, at which Kingsley had spoken. Confused and fatigued, Paul temporarily abandoned parish work and went to Germany and Switzerland in the autumn of 1852 in the post of tutor to two young Englishmen who were living abroad with their family. It was the first of many visits abroad for Paul, and he seized on the opportunity to learn German, but otherwise he found the experience 'terribly dull' and 'extremely dreary'. In the summer he fell ill with typhoid and resigned his tutorship. He now heard from his own old tutor that there was a post for him at Eton, where Goodford had been appointed headmaster.

II

This was a crucial time. Paul was still only twenty-five, but his hopes for a career of pastoral work at Bloxham had been thwarted, and whatever notions he may have had about making a profession of tutoring abroad had foundered on the limitations of his pupils and the pomposity of their father. He had alienated himself from his own father, who might otherwise have been able to help.[7] The Eton post was a initially a 'conductship', or chaplaincy, which included the curacy of the local parish. Paul and one other 'conduct' were responsible for the parish work (visiting, and the occasional marriage, baptism or funeral) and for services in local churches and in the College Chapel. He started in November 1853, moving into a small house with his sister Fanny as housekeeper. The stipend was very small, £120 a year, and Paul's inheritance from his mother was now dissipated, partly on his own maintenance in recent years, and partly as a loan, never repaid, to his father. Nevertheless, Paul was now comfortably settled, and happy to be back at Eton among congenial friends. Even Kingsley was at hand, a near neighbour at Eversley in Hampshire.

Here he discovered his vocation for teaching, or at least for counselling and advising the adolescent boys to whom Eton stood, however inadequately, *in loco parentis*. His mentor Goodford, with the consent of the College Provost, offered Paul the relatively new post of 'master in College'. In the complex network of Eton posts, this was neither a tutorship nor a mastership. It had been inaugurated as part of College reform, in order to promote discipline among the unruly students, where the tradition of control by the sixth-form boys over their juniors had got altogether out of hand. Paul's predecessors in the post had used it as a stepping-stone to tutorships; what Goodford had in mind was that Paul would make a proper job of it. In this he succeeded, with some difficulties, declining in *Memories* to 'go into the means by which after a time discipline was restored and many grave abuses rectified'. With memories of his own happy years as an Eton boy still fresh, and his frustrated zeal to build a useful career even fresher, Paul hurled himself into the work: 'It is impossible to speak too gratefully of all that the boys were to me. I lived for them and with them, and thought of them only, and as a rule they were to me like younger brothers and dear friends. I made some mistakes in character, but on the whole am glad to have trusted even bad boys as I did; they were the better for being trusted, and but few abused the confidence I placed in them.' Now he could be to others what Kingsley had been to him.

The financial situation, however, was still critical, and the master in college still celibate. Paul is discreetly silent in *Memories* about any women to whom he may have been attracted during the past few years. No sensible young man of the upper middle class would dream of asking a wife to set up house with him on £120 a year. A bride might bring money with her, but wealthy fathers who could provide their daughters with dowries would have been apt to wonder about the effect on Paul's professional prospects of his controversial opinions.[8] There was in fact no extra remuneration, when he took it on, for the arduous post of master in college. But he was permitted to augment his income by taking two private pupils, and it was by this arrangement that Paul became acquainted with the woman who was to become his wife, Margaret Agnes Colvile. Her widowed sister, Isabella Marindin, was the mother of one of Paul's two 'boys in college'. Their marriage took place some years after their first meeting, in London on 11 December 1856. The groom was twenty-eight, the bride a year younger; her uncle, the third Lord Auckland, who was also Bishop of Bath and Wells, performed the ceremony.[9] Like

Henry S. King, Charles Kegan Paul married a woman well above his social station.

Paul gives no hint in *Memories* that the two Colvile women came of a wealthy family with a country seat in Scotland. In fact he mentions explicitly that Mrs Marindin wished to keep her boys at home, in order to give them a cheaper education, which arrangement necessitated the services of a special tutor. It is necessary to turn to the genealogies of the Colvile (formerly Wedderburn) and Eden families, to discover with what a distinguished clan Charles Kegan Paul had allied himself.[10] And he is equally silent on his wife's literary career, just nicely established in 1856 with Parker's publication of her first two novels, *Dorothy: a tale* and *DeCressy*.

Margaret Agnes Paul was the daughter of Andrew Colvile and the Hon. Mary Louisa Eden. Her father, who had died a few months before his daughter's wedding, was the eldest surviving son of James Wedderburn-Colvile of Inveresk (near Musselburgh) in Scotland. He had been in London since 1799, as a partner in the family West Indian business; on the death of his own father, Andrew had sold Inveresk Lodge and acquired the estate of Craigflower in Fifeshire; at the same time he adopted the surname and arms of Colvile of Ochiltree, instead of Wedderburn. Margaret's mother was a daughter of William Eden, the first Lord Auckland, who had been a minister in several eighteenth-century governments, with special responsibility for colonial matters. Andrew and Mary Louisa Colvile had sixteen children. Margaret's eldest brother was James William Colvile, a distinguished judge with a career in Calcutta as well as in England. James died in 1880 and was succeeded as head of the family by his brother Eden. Eden's early experience was in business and in colonial government in Canada (where he joined the Hudson's Bay Company), followed by succession to his father's directorships and to the West India business carried on at 35 Leadenhall Street in the City of London. He died in 1893.[11] Two other sons died young. Margaret was tenth of the twelve daughters, of whom six others were still living at the time of her wedding, four of them unmarried. Like the Paul and Horne families, the Colviles derived their fortune from West Indian sugar plantations and from the institution of slavery; but unlike Paul's own father, they retained considerable capital after the 1840s. Similar, in another way, to Henry

S. King, they developed new ways to tap the colonial wealth when their old plantations ceased to be profitable. They lived partly at Craigflower, partly in Devonshire at a house called Lustleigh, and partly at the Eden estate of Langley Farm, Beckenham, located near Bromley in Kent. Their London home was near Moorgate in the City, at Milton Court.

Margaret Agnes Colvile's first novel, *Dorothy* was a romantic story, but it included plot elements which may have been autobiographical. Dorothy is a serious young woman who loves 'to wander in the mazes of metaphysics', and is impatient with the social constraints that shape women's roles. Her family wealth interferes with the development of a love affair with her cousin Lancelot, who goes away to India rather than accepting his vocation for the priesthood. An ill-fated character who may be modelled on Charles Kegan Paul, the Rev. Arthur Vaughan, suffers for being a man of high-church views who engages in social work with the poor people of his parish. Dorothy assists him in this work: 'The frank and winning courtesy, which did not always mark her intercourse with her equals, was now prompt to gain the confidence of those untamed spirits, which had . . . something in common with her own independence of control.' She herself, after many vicissitudes including Vaughan's death among others, marries Lancelot, and settles down to life in a country parsonage.

Margaret brought a marriage settlement to Eton with her, prudently established by her family as a trust fund.[12] It may have been the income from interest on this money, as much as the stipend that was finally attached to Paul's mastership in college that enabled him to give up private pupils. He observed that

> Our house was most unfit for a married man's residence, especially as my wife's health proved far from strong; but we made it do for five years, and three children were born to us there. Margaret's life was not a cheerful one at Eton; she did not like the boys to whom my thought and life were so much devoted, and a wife in such a position was necessarily left much alone. . . . Our house was more and more unfit for a family residence as children came.

Table 3 Charles and Margaret Paul – family, business and books

Charles Kegan Paul (1828–1902)	Margaret Agnes Colvile (1829–1905)
1828 born 8 March	
	1829 born 18 July
1846 matriculated at Oxford	
1851 ordained deacon	
1853 Chaplain at Eton; *The Communion of Saints*.	
married 11 December 1856	
	1856: *Dorothy* and *DeCressy*
	1857 *Still Waters*
Andrew Louis born Eton 1858	
	1858 *Maiden Sisters* and *Uncle Ralph*
Nancy Margaret born Eton 1860	
	1860 *Herbert's Holidays*
	1861 *Martha Brown*
1861: 'On the Terms of Communion'	
Ruth Frances born Eton 1862	
1862: Vicar of Sturminster Marshall, Dorsetshire	
Rose Mary born Dorset 1863	
1864: *A Reading Book for Evening Schools*	
Maurice Eden born Dorset 1865	
1869: *What the Rising From the Dead should Mean*	
	1870: *Three Weddings*
	1872: *Thomasina*
1873: translation of Faust and edition of Godwin	
moved to London 1874	
	1875: *Vanessa*
1876: *William Godwin: His Friends and Contemporaries*	
1877 purchase of firm from King	
	1878: *Gentle & Simple*
1879: edition of Wollstonecraft	
1881: partnership with Trench	
1883: *Biographical Sketches*	
	1886: *Kintail Place*
1888 began to go to mass	
1889 amalgamation of firm with Trübner and Redway	

1890 joined Roman Catholic Church
1891: *Faith and Unfaith, and Other Essays*;
Confessio Viatoris; several pamphlets for Catholic Truth Society

1895 road accident

1899: *Memories*; *On the Way Side: Verses and Translations*

1902 died 19 July (age 74)

1905 died 30 March (age 75)

Her sister Isabella Marindin no longer lived near Eton and this may have contributed to her loneliness.

The three children were Andrew Louis, born two years after the wedding in 1858, Nancy Margaret (1860) and Ruth Frances (1862). What Paul does not mention is that his wife's not-very-cheerful life also included the conception and birth of four more novels, *Still Waters* (1857), *Maiden Sisters* and *Uncle Ralph* (both 1858), and *Martha Brown, the Heiress* (1861). All published by Parker and Son, with authorship attributed to the anonymous 'author of Dorothy', these were conventional romantic novels. Like their two predecessors they were competent, well-plotted and well-written, peopled with engaging characters set in a variety of domestic situations, mostly in the rural south of England. A recurring theme was the problem of the wealthy young woman engaged or married to, or in love with, a young man whose own prospects were uncertain and career precarious. A gentle and persistent feminism pervades these novels, as the heroines assert their intellectual independence. The author's familiarity with European settings, as well as the French and German languages is also obvious. In addition there was *Herbert's Holidays: A Tale for Children*, published by Derby in 1860, which featured the tribulations of an Eton boy.

There is no real evidence about whether or not the marriage was a happy one. Paul's remarks about the difficulty of combining family life with his devotion to the Eton boys seems to suggest some matrimonial tension. However it must be remembered that while writing *Memories*, after his conversion in 1899, he was at pains to promote the notion that only celibates, as in the Catholic tradition, can really manage an educational facility properly. At a time much closer to the Eton years he told a friend that he had come to believe in day schools, where a boy could return every night to the 'pure influence of his own home', and that 'our whole system of making boys into men is wrong'.[13] The preoccupation with celibacy came later. Indeed, if Paul took the Kingsley household as a model for married life, he would then have acknowledged something he later preferred to suppress, that he shared in those days the hostility to celibacy which was the corollary to Kingsley's stress on the importance of sexuality to human development.[14] Margaret's novels, with their recurring theme of the problems attendant on marriages between wealthy women and poor men might be taken as autobiographical. But it is a dangerous and unsupportable assumption, even when much more is known about a novelist's life than we can ever hope to learn about hers, to read her life experience directly through her work. Unfortunately no private papers of Margaret's have survived, but her husband's letters to friends refer over and over again to his wife's and his children's travels, illnesses and activities, and imply his affectionate regard for them. His memory of the crowded discomfort at Eton can be corroborated independently: at the time of the 1861 census the family's lodgings in the school buildings housed Margaret and Charles, the two-year-old Louis and infant Nancy, a nursemaid, a cook, a housemaid, two college servants (a married couple) and five 'boys' maids' whose duty was to attend to the needs of Paul's charges.

The family left Eton in 1862, and Paul, after nine years at the school, finally secured an Anglican living where he could serve as the country clergyman he had been trained to be. The circumstances of the transition, however, reveal that time and marriage had made his religious and intellectual opinions no less eccentric or unacceptable. *Essays and Reviews* had been published in 1860: this was a series of signed essays in which the Broad Church leadership at Oxford promoted modern critical analysis of the biblical texts, and called upon the Church of England to make room for such criticism. In Paul's words, some of the ideas 'were alarming the orthodox mind not a little' and legal proceedings were taken within the ecclesiastical courts against two of the essayists. Most of the clergymen-masters at Eton registered a protest at the book; Paul not only failed to join them, but purchased his own copy in the flagrant publicity of the Eton book-club. Around the same time, he contributed a tract on the 'Boundaries of the Church of England' to a series of *Tracts for Priests and People*, signed only with his 'somewhat distinctive initials', and arguing 'that the very minimum of dogma was required from lay members of the Church of England, that on them the Apostles' Creed only was binding, and that as interpreted by themselves'. In other words, an Anglican layperson could believe as much or as little as he or she pleased.[15] Although Paul protested that his personal creed exceeded the minimum, and that clergymen ought to be required to profess more than the minimum, the Provost of Eton, Stephen Hawtrey, initiated proceedings to have him dismissed. The College found a way to ease Paul out without destroying his livelihood, although this solution involved some complicated Eton politics and the intervention of Bishop Wilberforce. They found him a parish, or in Anglican parlance 'presented him to a living in the gift of the college', one that had conveniently fallen open in 1862, Sturminster Marshall in rural Dorsetshire.

The family moved at Easter. Paul records that Sturminster Marshall was 'a living of but small value' – less than £300 in fact.[16] The church was St Mary's; the vicarage was called Bailie House. Its history went back to Elizabethan times, and so did some of its appointments. As Paul described the house it 'was a very rickety structure; with the exception of two or three rooms at the east end, it was thatched, a costly covering, and had large and expensive gardens. But it was a roomy and comfortable house, in which many previous vicars had taken pupils, and it was clear that I must do so too.' It is difficult to understand just how comfortable the 'rickety structure' could have been, even after the expensive repairs that Paul undertook when he arrived. A document dating from shortly after his tenure describes the house as 'damp and cold in winter'. Furthermore it was a mile from the church, which added greatly to the rector's work. 'The parish,' he admits, 'on a nearer inspection, had not much to recommend it.' The population of some 850 was nearly all made up of agricultural labourers, engaged in growing wheat, barley and turnips. Paul's political sympathy with the labourers, which did not of course extend to social relations with them, was an impediment to social relations with people of his own class. 'The squire and the farmers were good souls in their way and after their lights, but they were narrow and bigoted in Tory opinions.' The neighbours were 'very humdrum folk as a rule'. London was 117 miles away, and the Pauls must have missed the intellectually congenial company they had taken for granted at Oxford and at Eton. They spent 'every possible holiday on the Continent'.[17]

The objective conditions of Sturminster Marshall and of Bailie House, in terms of social isolation and damp, have been stressed here to counter Paul's frequently expressed love for Dorset, the pleasure he took in working with the agricultural labourers, particularly the young men, and his fascination with the rural dialect. All these things were certainly part of his experience, but the discomfort and the monotony, less fully documented, were equally real. This argument will become important when the question arises of Paul's loss of faith and departure from Dorsetshire, twelve years later.

Meanwhile there were the pupils, the parish work (which included an evening school), Paul's contributions to religious periodicals and his involvement, as usual, in theological and political upheavals. Two more children were born at Sturminster and baptized by their father, a daughter, Rose Mary (1863) and a son, Maurice Eden (1865). They must have been a lively family, reading widely, learning the modern languages that both parents valued,[18] and enjoying a country childhood something like what their father had experienced in rural Somerset. But the presence of unrelated young people in the house, the pupils, 'destroyed family life sadly'.

Paul specialized, in his role as tutor, in boys who had left school and were preparing to enter college or the army. They were not particularly intelligent, interesting or disciplined. 'With a few exceptions, my boys were not vicious, but they were idle and for the most part dull . . . Pupils enabled us to live, and to live in comfort when we could not have existed on the income of the living, but I saved nothing.' The pupils, otherwise nameless, included Lionel and Hallam Tennyson, the sons of the poet, in 1865–6.[19] In a letter to a friend Paul demonstrated what a dramatic effect the pupils had on the family income. At £100 each per year, a full complement of six would triple the basic value of the living.[20]

Perhaps a more compelling interest, although alluded to only indirectly in *Memories*, was an evening school he started on the model of the one at Bloxham. This led to Paul's first non-ecclesiastical publication, *The Evening School Reading-Book for Adults*, which he selected and edited. Longmans published it in February 1864 at 1s 6d and advertised it in their in-house periodical, *Notes on Books*. Paul explained in the preface that this was

> an attempt to supply a want felt by all those who have had the charge of evening schools in country parishes. Reading books for day schools are, for the most part, too childish for the use of older lads, and, since attendance at evening schools is apt to be desultory, it is difficult to keep up interest in a book on one continuous subject. . . . The extracts [from Goldsmith, Dickens, De Foe, Bunyan, Shakespeare, Smiles and others] are such as an ordinary village boy, from twelve to sixteen years of age, can understand.

Deprived of his loyal and loveable Eton boys, Paul preferred to let his pedagogical interests follow his political ones and teach working-class youths.

Paul was also a scholar, in his own eccentric way. He was fascinated with Mary Wollstonecraft, identifying not with her feminism but with her struggle to find a way to live, holding as she did radical ideas and involved as she was in unconventional relationships, while trapped in a social position that dictated conservatism and propriety. In her case it was being a woman, in his, an Anglican priest. The initial product of his work was a book not on Wollstonecraft but, as we have seen, a book of essays and later a life and times of her husband, William Godwin, published by Henry S. King in 1873 and 1876. A Dorset neighbour made possible the edition of essays. This was Sir Percy Shelley; his father was the poet and his mother Mary Shelley, daughter of the Godwins. Shelley provided the Godwin manuscripts that were the basis of the book.[21]

Paul found an outlet for his Broad Church views, now broadening to the brink of Unitarianism, in the *Theological Review*. Unitarians are Christians who deny the Trinity and affirm instead the unitary nature of God. Their nineteenth-century theologians had been among the first to embrace biblical criticism.[22] Here was a chance for Paul to stretch his intellectual muscles. The *Wellesley Index of Victorian Periodicals* records twenty-three contributions to the *Theological Review* from January 1865 to January 1876. In a review of *Études Critiques sur la Bible* by Michel Nicolas (January 1865), he argued that the Bible is 'a record of spiritual progress, of aspirations and revelations to the spirit of man: whatever of history, or geology, or chronology is therein, is beside the main purpose of the book'. Besides being doctrinally radical in a way that Kingsley would have understood, this statement is evidence of Paul's preoccupation with matters of the spirit. As for miracles, because of Christ's position as a superior example of humanity, he was 'able to do what progress has not yet advanced enough to let us do'. Scientific knowledge was the harbinger of that progress, and as such the clergy should welcome it. And in 'The Influence of the Church of England on Theology' (*Theological Review* September 1865), he had reached the point that 'We do not think the reaction begun by High-churchmen can stop; for they have, as it seems to us, no true logical stand-point; those may stay there who can accept a compromise; who cannot, must go back to Rome, or onwards with the Liberals wherever the winds and currents of God may bear them.' Paul himself was eventually to go both ways, but not until after he had tried to grapple with the problems of his Sturminster Marshall flock.

In 'The Influence of the Church of England on Society', (*Theological Review* May 1865) he held forth on a country clergyman's potential to influence his congregation, particularly by using evening schools to 'gather round him the young men of his parish'. He returned to the latter theme in a much more radical vein, in 'The Condition of the Agricultural Labourer' (January 1868). No class of men, he argued, 'are known so little by their fellow-countrymen as are the Agricultural Labourers'. Even George Eliot, the English writer he admired most, had got Adam Bede wrong. (He was later to except Hardy's portrayal of Dorset labourers.) Paul identified drunkenness and debt as 'the curse of our villages', where the public house offered 'light, warmth, conversation, tobacco, beer', and the village shop the doubtful service of long credit. In his article he recommended social reform, not moral chastisement of the labourers' customs. Schooling must no longer be 'withheld' from village children by the demands created by their parents' poverty. Instead, compulsory education would replace the 'inadequate palliatives' of night and Sunday schools in labouring boys' lives. Cottages must be improved and village co-operative stores put in place, requiring payments in ready money that would otherwise go to the public house. Machines might make it possible for women to work in agriculture without 'making them brutal and unfeminine'. There was nothing intrinsically immoral about the village practice of postponing marriage until after the bride was pregnant: Paul's young men were faithful partners, who for historical and financial reasons were unconcerned with what they regarded as mere formalities. Furthermore, Broad Church doctrine (that is, its lack of doctrine) made more sense in this stratum of society than anywhere: 'Any one who has seen how in country places a High-Church rector may succeed a High Calvinist, and the people remain unconscious of the change, or if conscious adapt themselves almost at once to the new state of things, will understand . . . that dogmatic differences have . . . no meaning whatever to the poor.' Finally he arrived at contemporary concerns: 'the present depression of wages'. There was no way for an agricultural labourer to save for his future; every clergyman knew that every labourer found his way to the Union workhouse or the parish relieving officer when he was too old to work. Finally, stronger words, from the man who had called himself a socialist and republican 'so far as these things can be carried out without breach of public order'. 'If . . . there ever come in England a strife of classes, the starvation minimum of out-door relief, the foul abominations of many country workhouses, the almost enforced neglect of many sick by the underpaid Union doctor, will not and cannot, we may almost say ought not, to be forgotten by the poor.' In the absence of more difficult-to-manage reforms, he coolly suggested that one of the two Guardians elected to control poor relief in each parish should be elected by the recipients of relief. Paul predicted, no doubt accurately, that his article would be called 'irreligious, immoral, dreamy, revolutionary, unpractical, utopian'.

Four years later he threw himself 'with all [his] heart' into Joseph Arch's 1872 movement for a trade union among agricultural workers, when that remarkable agitation made its way to Dorset.

Another route to reform appealed to Paul at a deeply personal level: the campaign for total abstinence from alcohol known as teetotalism. The temperance movement was then gathering strength at all levels of Victorian society. Teetotalism, particularly, was a working-class movement.[23] In *Memories* he recalled how Mrs Sullivan, a recent addition to the upper reaches of Sturminster society, challenged his ability to deal with drunkenness among his parishioners: '"You do not think they would tell you, who are not an abstainer, their trouble; they tell me because I am!".' Paul says he then left off drinking alcohol and never started again. The Sturminster Marshall *Parish Magazine* tells a more vivid and moving, perhaps a more accurate story. One parishioner, George Dicker, recalled that 'There were no half measures with the Rev. Kegan Paul. I remember that one of the villagers pointed out to him that if he gave up drink, he had plenty of meat etc., whilst the villagers took drink to make up for a lack of meat. To meet this case Mr Paul gave up meat entirely, and I think got the man to give up drink.'[24] Paul explains in *Memories* that it was impossible for him to abstain totally from meat ('the difficulties of carrying out such a mode of life in a flesh-eating community, unless one live a hermit life, are great'), but he preferred a vegetarian diet if it were possible 'to get anything to eat without discomposing the habits of all around me'.

Margaret Paul, whose habits were presumably the most subject to discomposition, managed the household with the assistance of a footman, a housemaid, a cook and a kitchen maid.[25] It must still have been difficult for her to find the time and solitude for literary work, but she wrote two more novels. *Three Weddings* was published by Longmans in 1870, but two years later the historical novel *Thomasina. A Biography* went to H.S. King and Co. And her *DeCressy* was translated into French and appeared in Paris in 1874 as *Miss Mortimer* (Roman traduit de l'anglais). She may also have developed in the Bailie House grounds her interest in gardening, later recorded in a *Nineteenth Century* article, 'Old fashioned gardening'. But there is no evidence of whether she participated in or withheld herself from the conventional parish duties of the rector's wife, visiting the sick, teaching Sunday School and so on, or how often she took the children to London or to the homes of the extensive Colvile connection for a respite.

She must have been as exasperated as were many of Paul's friends. It was Richard Strachey who finally asked him 'When are you coming out?' It took Paul years to acknowledge the obvious fact that his opinions were no longer compatible with the Thirty-Nine Articles of belief stipulated by the Anglican church, or even with the Apostle's Creed, however liberally interpreted, and 'to recognize that the place I filled ought to be mine no longer'.

So much for the philosophical side of the question: the practical problem of how to support a large family might still have forestalled any breach with the Church, had Paul not immersed himself in yet another public controversy. The Free Christian Union was a society that may be said to have extended the Broad Church principle even beyond the limits of Anglicanism. It was a Unitarian body, the intention of which was, in Paul's words, 'to promote . . . a general union of all persons holding Unitarian theology within the various orthodox churches and sects'. He preached a sermon in London under the auspices of this society, a sermon which was reported in the *Pall Mall Gazette*.[26] Its heterodoxy is evident in the following excerpt: ' . . . louder and louder swells the assertion that God has written His word in Creation, and in Humanity, that Science has a canon which never closes, by it must be tried the canon which has closed – by it and the voice of conscience in the heart'.

Paul wrote to a close friend, J.M. Ludlow, the Christian Socialist and social reformer:

> I was able satisfactorily and completely to arrange the difficulty I named to you, and was going on as it seemed most securely and full of pupils, when the Pall Mall Gazette, like Goldsmith's mad dog, 'to gain its private ends' chose to misrepresent most wantonly, and I fear most wilfully a sermon I preached before the Free Christian Mission [*sic*]. This so frightened some good people whose sons were coming to fill my vacancies, that they did not send them, thus I have three pupils instead of six from Septr. till Christmas, making a difference of £200 in my receipts for this time. . . . I have no doubt the tide will turn, but at present things look very black for me.[27]

Paul's congregation was not disturbed by the news, having, presumably, survived years of increasingly heterodox sermons unscathed, but neighbouring clergymen, like his pupils' parents, were outraged.

Even so, four years went by, between the publicity, early in 1870, over the Free Christian Union sermon and the move to London in 1874. The memoirist recalls only that 'I resigned my living and came up to London,' and then, 'almost coincidentally with my quitting Sturminster, [Mr Henry S. King] offered me a more intimate post in his business in London.'

Memories does not mention any introduction that Paul may have had to King, whose manager he became in 1874, only that he 'had been engaged in reading books' for the Cornhill publisher for some years. As we have seen, Margaret Paul's novels were published by King's firm, and Harriet King's poetry was reviewed by Paul. Henry King's poor health, the growth of the Cornhill imprint and the demands of his other businesses, and perhaps family pressures, may have made him decide to engage a responsible editor-manager. Certainly the two men had many acquaintances in common, and Kingsley and Stopford Brooke, for example, might have combined to find a post for their friend and colleague at his moment of crisis; Rowland Williams, the 'essayist and reviewer', was a King author as well as a close friend of Paul's in Dorset. There may have been others. James or Eden Colvile, Margaret's brothers, might well have had business connections with King, and mutual obligations, within the London network of colonial agencies and services. Although no link can conclusively be demonstrated, it is important to remember that Paul tells in *Memories* less than the full story. He had learned, since Oxford, 'the need of reticence', and life had taught him 'that daws peck at hearts worn upon the sleeve'.

Finally, the philosophical and financial issues attendant on the move from Dorset to London should be seen in the context of how disagreeable and monotonous rural life had become, in contrast to the excitement and attraction of the metropolis. In Sturminster, the Rev. Mr Paul found the neighbours of his own social class uncongenial, and many, at least, of his parochial duties irksome: not even the fees of pupils could be depended upon. In London, 'C. Kegan Paul' took a house in the suburbs and joined a bookish gentlemen's club, the Savile.[28] At forty-four, he had escaped his father's profession at last, and been absorbed instead into 'the hurry of our London life, that London which, as a sponge draws water, seems to gather to itself the life-blood of the country'.[29]

III

In London, as King's manager and literary adviser, Charles Kegan Paul no longer merely read Tennyson and Browning, the literary heroes of his school and university years, he was now in a position to dictate terms to Tennyson, or at least so he thought, and to invite Robert Browning to dinner. Instead of writing about his admiration for George Eliot, he and Margaret were regular Sunday afternoon visitors at her home.[30] And he could act as a mentor to younger writers, encouraging the work of Wilfrid Scawen Blunt and Austin Dobson.

Soon after his arrival in the metropolis, Paul shook off the last vestiges of the Church of England, whose services now 'seemed distasteful and untrue'. But he could not manage without a formal structure of belief, and allied himself with Comtist Positivism. Positivism is the philosophical system developed by the French thinker August Comte; it was particularly influential in England in the 1880s and 1890s. The English movement was created and led by the intellectual and former Anglican clergyman, Richard Congreve. Comte's theory of the historical development of human knowledge incorporated three stages of development, from theological to metaphysical to positive, each of which occurred not only in world history, the final stage having been attained with industrialization in the nineteenth century, but in the progress of each individual. For the Comtist, a complete system of scientifically verifiable knowledge replaced the revealed religion of Christianity, and the 'religion of humanity', rigorously empirical, aimed at improving social conditions for humanity. Its adherents were attracted by the notion that the moral authority implicit in religious belief can exist without the belief itself. Christopher Kent has demonstrated that Comtism in mid-Victorian England was 'a comprehensive ideology remarkably harmonious with certain established English currents of thought and remarkably well suited to the needs of a middle-class intellectual élite'.[31] A notable feature of this élite was 'the Victorian tragedy of the intellectual choked by the clerical collar', such as Congreve; a less celebrated example would be Charles Kegan Paul.

Paul had read Comte twenty years earlier, while still at Eton, and been impressed by the philosopher's teaching, at least 'in politics and in social matters'. Now, finally a mere layman in the Anglican communion, 'with no external obligation to use words in which it was necessary to find some meaning consistent with my opinions . . . the outward scaffolding on which I had striven to climb to God, every sacramental sign under which I had sought to find him, had crumbled into nothingness'. Without quite using Huxley's word, Paul declared himself an agnostic: 'I was content not to know, and to wait.' Meanwhile he attended Positivist Sunday services, and found that it 'gives order and regularity to life, inculcates simplicity of manners, aims at a certain amount of discipline, and caricatures, unconsciously, and with some effect, the sacraments, the *cultus* of Saints, the place of our Lady in worship, making of humanity the ideal woman, the great mother and mistress of all'. Positivism, in short, was 'Catholicism without God'. These remarkable rationalizations are the voice of the elderly Paul, written after his reception into the Catholic fold.

He was still a Positivist, and still delighting in encouraging and making friends with young men, in 1886 when the architect and designer, C.R. Ashbee, reflected in his diary on the friendship of 'Kegan Paul', whom he called 'a good and wise man – endowed with the quality of sympathy'.

> Met Kegan Paul by appointment at the Positivist service in Lambs Conduit Street . . . No I repeat it Positivism won't do for me however much my good Kegan Paul and our dear dull old Dr Congreve . . . would like me into the little flock that worships the plaster cast of August Comte on the sham marble pedestal in the Church of St Humanity! . . . If she turns out such men as Kegan Paul however one has a good mind to woo humanity in the abstract.

Ashbee's mother, with her eighteen-year-old son by the elbow, had made the round of London publishers in 1881, looking for career contacts. Ashbee remembered it as 'a wild goose chase. Kegan Paul was the last of our wild geese and a rare catch too!' Paul suggested he go to university, and helped Ashbee get into King's College, Cambridge. Later, in London, he introduced Ashbee to architects and took him to visit houses, to which he had the social entrée, so that the young architect might study their design.[32] Paul remained involved with the Positivist circle, publishing Richard Congreve's sermon 'Human Catholicism' in 1876, and in a letter to Congreve mentioned that he had been introduced, on a visit to Cambridge, to two young men who told him 'they were *the* two Positivist undergraduates'. This was in the summer of 1887.[33] He started to go to mass the next year.

Paul plunged himself vigorously into his apprenticeship with King, learning the business of typography, printing and bookbinding, of contracts, commissions, profit sharing and copyright. Where so much was new, the middle-aged man, who was after all accustomed to being an authority not a novice, must have taken special pleasure in matters where his expertise was appreciated. King 'knew no language but his own'; Paul could check translations and prevent embarrassing howlers. When the New York publisher, D. Appleton & Co. (with whom King was deeply involved in the multi-lingual International Scientific Series), sent them *Heredity*, by the controversial French psychologist Théodule Ribot in 1875, they included an assurance that the translation was impeccable. (The publication books reveal that they had paid £250 for it, of which King was committed to contribute half.) The contract had been initiated by Appleton's but King was to publish the book and charge back to the American publisher half the costs of production. Henry King would have had to be content with his colleague's assurance, but Paul 'dipped into the book quite at hazard', and found that the translator had expressed 'à la fête d'une commune voisine' as 'to the feast of a woman in the neighbourhood', rather than 'to the feast of a neighbouring parish'. Paul says he 'occupied the better part of a well-earned holiday' overhauling the translation completely.[34] When in 1876 another book of Ribot's (*English Psychology*, 1873) came up for reprinting, the revised translation was entrusted to Margaret Agnes Paul and she earned £5 for her services.

Margaret published two more novels with her husband's new

firm, *Vanessa* (1875) and *Gentle and Simple* (1878). The earlier books were still in print. The *Publishers' Circular* had reviewed *Thomasina* as 'a plain wholesome story of life without much trouble or heroic combustion . . . very pleasant and placid reading [the anonymous author] . . . writes well, and delineates character without much force, but fairly, and with considerable tone and colour'. (April 1872.) The children were growing up, ranging in age from nine to sixteen in 1874. Louis went to Eton, while Maurice would later attend University College School in London; the daughters' careers are not so well documented, but Paul mentions that they attended a school in France, at Fontainbleau. All this is context for the one place in *Memories* where Paul devotes more than a line or two to his wife. She was concerned, he tells us, when he first visited the unconventional ménage of George Eliot and George Henry Lewes, about 1874.

> At my first visit Mrs Paul was absent from London, and when she came home I asked her to call with me one Sunday afternoon. This she did not wish to do, but had no objection to my going alone. I did not, however, choose to visit at any house without her, and in consequence simply did not go. A few Sundays after Mrs Paul, not wishing to shut me off from what had been so evident a pleasure, made up her mind to accompany me, and when walking home, she said, 'I am convinced that she is a good and pure woman, and I will go whenever you like.'

Taken out of context, this anecdote makes Margaret Agnes Paul seem out of sympathy with her husband's literary interests and his new London circle. But with a fuller knowledge of her upper-class background, her own writing, and remembering that she, too, had friends, family, interests and a reputation to keep up in London, the anecdote comes to life. Victorian ladies in polite society had to be careful about what practices they seemed to condone, and living together out of wedlock was normally out of the question. Margaret had survived her husband's philosophical peregrinations, and probably felt that it was her duty to repress his enthusiasms when they seemed to threaten the family's social position. In any case, she overcame her initial scruples.

Paul's early years in London are marked with a spirit of emotional liberation: discontinuing his tortuous attempts intellectually to reconcile his own unbelief with preaching the Christian gospel must have been both a relief and a source of spiritual energy. In the stimulus of London society, where not only books but plays, concerts and picture-galleries, clubs and dinner parties, and even daily life were novelties, the aesthetic virtues he had formerly found in Anglican ritual and liturgy, and would later seek in Catholic practice, were otherwise supplied. Positivism was not just a much-needed alternative ideology, it was also a setting in which Paul met some interesting people. He thrived on the intimate associations with George Eliot and George Henry Lewes, and with Thomas Hardy.

The closest relationship, outside Paul's family, was with his employer, Henry Samuel King. Paul's 1879 memoir of King, the *Academy* obituary, has been quoted extensively. It reveals his admiration of King's business acumen, King's urbanity and toughness, and his capacious memory, as well as lingering on the literary interests that were closest to Paul's own. There is no direct evidence of hero-worship, but there is room to speculate that for Charles Kegan Paul, King was one of those larger-than-life figures who appear in his biography at vulnerable moments, as Kingsley did: a role model, upon which Paul could shape the outlines of his new life.

IV

The one attribute King possessed, however, and Paul indisputably lacked, was capital, the financial wherewithal to publish the books in which both delighted. Where, then, did the money come from in October 1877 to 'make arrangements with a partner to purchase this business'? Paul's legacy from his mother was long gone; he claims to have saved nothing at Sturminster, and told Ludlow he was in difficulties when pupils were withdrawn. Funds from Margaret's marriage settlement had not, apparently, been accessible to subsidize any earlier ventures. The answer, presumably, is to be found in the partner, Alfred Chenevix Trench. The association between the two men is not, however, easily unravelled.

The most significant thing about Alfred Trench, at least in the minds of Paul and his other contemporaries, seems to have been that he was the son of Richard Chenevix Trench (1807–86), the Archbishop of Dublin. Since the father has become, nowadays, almost as obscure as his son, it is important to emphasize two things about the Archbishop. He was a very well-known person, both in his ecclesiastical aspect and as a popular writer, and he was rich. He presided over the disestablishment of the Irish church initiated by Gladstone's Liberal government in 1869. Trench's poetry and philology had resulted in numerous well-known books in those branches of literature, as well as in divinity and history. In 1877 he was seventy years of age; at that point his works were being published by Macmillan and Co. He had been disabled two years previously in an accident, but did not retire from his high ecclesiastical office until 1884; between 1871 and 1877 he was involved in the controversial project of revising the Anglican prayer book. Archbishop Trench was a very wealthy man, whose name and reputation were prominent.

Almost as prolific as the Colviles, Richard Trench and his wife Frances had eight sons and five daughters. Alfred was the third of four surviving sons, born in 1849 when his father was rector of Itchenstoke, Hampshire. He attended Eton and University College, Oxford and was married in 1873 to Isabella Moore. These facts have been gleaned from school and college records, census and registration materials, a family memoir and the Archbishop's will.[35] Alfred Trench died in 1938, in the south of France, long forgotten by any colleagues who might earlier have memorialized him. He had been living out of England since his firm's collapse in 1889. Even the 'notes' supplied by him to F.A. Mumby for the supplementary chapter on Kegan Paul, Trench in Mumby's *The House of Routledge* (1934) are meagre and uninformative.[36]

Here is the mystery. King announced in October 1877 that his business was now in the hands of 'Messrs Kegan Paul and Company'. It was not until 1881 that title-page imprints, including periodicals published by them, changed to 'Kegan Paul, Trench & Co.'[37] If Trench was a partner from the first (Mumby says he arrived in 1878), why not announce it to the public and, particularly, to the irate Alfred Tennyson who desperately required reassurance about the new firm's *bona fides*? Tennyson and the Archbishop, both Cambridge Apostles, knew each other well. If it was a secret, why did Paul refer casually in letters, even to Tennyson as 'my partner Mr Trench', as early as August 1878? It is reasonable to speculate, in the absence of clear documentation, that the Archbishop's wealth subsidized his son's new venture, and that the Archbishop's political and social position dictated that the family name not be associated publicly with the notoriously heterodox 'Kegan Paul'.[38]

Nor is there any documentation about the personal relationship between Trench and Paul. Twenty-one years younger, Trench might have been one of the young men to whom Paul served as teacher or mentor, but his time at Eton (1863–6) and Oxford (matriculated 1868) coincided with Paul's Dorset years; Paul did know, and probably tutored, Alfred's cousin, Philip Trench.[39] Paul was scrupulous, in writing *Memories*, about suppressing comments on people who were still living.

There is more evidence for Trench's active participation in the publishing business. He was not merely a silent partner. He negotiated the contract for a major project of the firm, the Pulpit Commentary series of 49 books of biblical exegesis beginning in 1880.[40] He travelled to the United States in 1881 and 1883 on the firm's behalf, and in an 1887 letter to Congreve, Paul was pressed for time because 'my partner is in Australia'. The firm's Publication Books show that Trench drew up contracts with authors, negotiated with other publishers, and authorized the clerks to make decisions about printing and binding. Arthur Waugh, a manager with the firm in the 1880s, observed that Trench brought to it 'something of his father's dominant and driving power'.[41]

But Trench's life was never tied to London: at the time of his marriage his father had turned over to him an estate at Ballyroan, in Leinster in Ireland[42] and in 1885 Paul apologized to a correspondent that 'Mr Trench will be away in Ireland'.[43] It was not until the Archbishop died in 1886 that the firm began publishing his works, the copyrights of which had been left to Alfred in his father's will.

Whatever financial contribution the Trench family made to the purchase of the new firm, it seems unlikely that Paul had absolutely nothing to offer. Once again, speculation must take the place of evidence, and once again, the wealth of the Colvile family comes into consideration. Margaret later had funds to dispose of under the will of her brother James, who died in 1880.[44] There is no evidence of what funds she, or her brothers and sisters, may have put up in 1877, but they remain the most likely source of the capital required to set Paul up in business for himself and thus be enabled to continue to support his wife and children appropriately.

To be a successful publisher, however, required not only capital, but a combination of literary and commercial judgement. Although Paul probably exaggerated his own ineptitude in the latter skill, it is important to note his views on the subject.

> It may, I think, be laid down that a literary man is not as a rule a good publisher. He is on the one hand tempted to accept books unlikely to succeed because they fall in with his own literary tastes, and on the other, to reject those which may have a considerable sale at the time, because they are in no true sense literature. I call to mind several books . . . rejected by our firm which, in other hands, proved a great financial success, but happily will never be heard of beyond the decade which saw their production.

Henry King was not so fastidious, though he could better afford to be, having funds at his disposal other than those he made by selling books. Nevertheless, the matter is not easily dismissed. Paul's correspondence, and the firm's records, certainly give evidence of some tough-minded business decisions. Many of the poets under their imprint appeared there not at the company's risk and expense, but at their own.

Paul had written encouragingly to Austin Dobson, a poet he particularly admired, in May 1877: 'it is so easy to criticize, so hard to write'. But the next year he told Dobson that his work 'certainly deserves it [material success] more than some verse I wot of, which pays more – with rare exceptions rougher, ruder and worse work is more appreciated by the stupid public'.[45] In April 1882 Martin Conway, who wanted to publish some lectures, was told that 'although they would make a book with which we should be exceedingly happy to be associated – looking at the matter from the literary point of view – we regret to say that, having regard to the usual sale of works on art, we should be indisposed to take any part of the risk of their production'.[46] The author-sponsored 'commission book' came to dominate the company's list, and this dominance is evidence of Paul's commercial abilities.

Nevertheless, what Paul valued was being a man of letters, not a man of business. As well as publishing poetry and essays in book form, he had the *New Quarterly Magazine* to edit from January 1879 to April 1880. The *New Quarterly Magazine* had been founded by Oswald Crawfurd in 1873 and later edited by Francis Hueffer. By 1879–80 weeklies and monthlies were much more common publication formats than quarterlies, whose format required that all fiction had to be published as complete stories in a single number, not serialized or in parts. The quarterly model had created difficulties for the earlier editors and publishers, and the editorship and publication, and probably the ownership, were transferred to the firm of Kegan Paul late in 1878. Paul enjoyed being an editor, although he wrote to Richard Garnett, 'The great difficulty which I suppose all Editors find is to get *first rate* stories, self contained, that is in one number.' Garnett had just contributed an article on libraries, for the April 1879 number.[47] Paul himself wrote articles about the Oxford Catholic poets and about Cardinal Newman for the magazine. In October 1879 he was able to use the periodical to strengthen the link between his life in Dorset and the new career in London: he wrote a sensitive and appreciative review of the Dorset novelist, then just arrived in London and needing introductions and publicity, Thomas Hardy.

The two men had already encountered each other when King published the one-volume edition of *A Pair of Blue-Eyes* in 1877 (the novel was first published by Tinsley in 1873). Like Paul himself, Hardy was familiar and sympathetic with the lives of agricultural labourers in rural England. Paul praised Hardy's characterization, and even his style, the literary point on which he was most particular. He was able, more so than a critic who had grown up in London, to judge Hardy's familiarity with Dorset customs and dialect. 'A new genius,' he told his readers, 'has arisen in the intellectual sky.' Paul also used the *New Quarterly Magazine* to give Hardy a forum to review a book by William Barnes, the Dorset poet. In the 1870s, Paul developed with the novelist what Hardy's biographer Michael Millgate calls 'a kind of working partnership useful and profitable to both. . . . [Paul] was, after Leslie Stephen, the literary figure who did most to assist Hardy and advance his reputation at this still early period.' The partnership was a family friendship: the Hardys visited the Pauls' drawing room, and young Louis Paul's knowledge of telegraphic instruments was transmitted by his father to fill a gap in Hardy's research for *A Laodician* in 1881.[48]

Charles Kegan Paul was beginning to impress his personal imprint on London's literary society. In the words of Wilfrid Meynell's memoir, 'Kegan Paul in those days was still the hope of authors. He was their fellow clubman; he had excellent taste; he had a pen of his own. They did not reckon with the great natural forces who believed that a golden day had dawned for the writer, when the man of schoolbooks had put them aside, and the parson had come forth from his rectory and knew no other Paternoster but the Square.'

CHAPTER 3

KEGAN PAUL, TRENCH – THE PARTNERSHIP WITH A REPUTATION FOR SERIOUS AND BEAUTIFUL BOOKS, 1877–1888

I

Trading from their premises at 1 Paternoster Square, Kegan Paul, Trench & Co. settled down to the business of publishing. Their title-pages carried the device of two trees, bound together by a scroll bearing the inscription 'Arbor Scientiae; Arbor Vitae' – the tree of knowledge and the tree of life. The *Publishers' Circular* in its annual survey of the British book trade in December 1881, characterized the firm in terms of the International Scientific Series, which offered 'a wide selection of illustrated scientific works, to which additions are constantly being made from the finest writers in Europe', but continued: 'It is, however, as the publishers of the Poet Laureate's works that this firm stands on ground which few can reach, and in the varied editions – the Author's, the Cabinet, the Royal, the Guinea, and the Crown – the purses of all sections of Her Majesty's subjects are considered and consulted.' Enduring poetry, formatted to meet the needs of nation and empire, and innovative science, importing and imparting knowledge from abroad: these two contrasting, almost conflicting, images demonstrate how Charles Kegan Paul and Alfred Chenevix Trench, together, were earning the respect of their peers, a reputation for publishing serious books.

From 1877 to 1888 the firm produced an average of about 125

new titles every year. In addition to this impressive level of production there were numerous reprints, revised editions and reissues in alternative formats. The list was still a general one, as King's had been, but the new firm concentrated on religious subjects and poetry, and on history, biography, essays, *belles-lettres* and science. Some important Victorian novelists appeared briefly under the imprint and then passed on, taking the lustre of their increasing fame with them: Hardy, Meredith, and Robert Louis Stevenson. The contract with Tennyson was renewed in 1878 for a further five years. The negotiations were exacting, as the poet Laureate's dislike of Charles Kegan Paul was countered by his wish that his title-pages give evidence of continuity.[1] King's policy of publishing books in series was continued, and expanded in directions that suited the new managers' tastes and inclinations. And, relatively limited as they were in terms of capital, they continued and greatly expanded their predecessor's policy of publishing on commission, that is, of putting their company name on the title-pages of books whose production costs were sponsored by their authors.

The even tenor of business in Paternoster Square was interrupted on 17 April 1883. The Kegan Paul, Trench warehouses were severely damaged by fire. The following day the story appeared in *The Times*: eight warehouses were involved, 'lofty' buildings of five or six floors each, stocking the books and records of sixteen different firms, were now nearly burnt out; the roofs were gone. The fire had been the occasion of the first use of new ladder trucks by London's fire fighters. The *Publishers' Circular* was more expansive:

> An alarming fire broke out about midnight on April 16 in Paternoster Square, in an immense block of buildings occupied by Messrs Kegan Paul, Trench & Co., and other publishing and printing firms. . . . Some idea of the extent of the fire may be gathered when it is stated that not only smoke, but the flames were distinctly visible from the committee-room windows of the House of Commons, the dome of St Paul's Cathedral being plainly seen. The great difficulty with which the firemen had to contend was that the neighbourhood of Paternoster Square

consists entirely of narrow streets and huge modern buildings filled for the most part with highly inflammable materials.

The Kegan Paul, Trench property destroyed included their whole stock of bound books, but, the *Publishers' Circular* announced, the unbound printed sheets were stored elsewhere. 'Little, if any, delay will therefore arise in meeting the demands of the trade, while the disaster will not in any way interfere with the publication of any of the new books which they have announced for immediate issue. ... The firm have secured temporary premises in White Hart Street, close to the scene of the fire.' They returned to Paternoster Square six months later, in November. Wilfrid Meynell, commenting years later, caustically observed that without the fire some poets would never have seen a second edition of their books. Certainly the detailed Publication Account Books of the firm meticulously note the numbers of copies destroyed by fire.

Many of the company's records were also destroyed: most of the Publication Books and Publication Account Books survived, but very little correspondence. One document lost in the fire would have been of great biographical interest. The opening sentence of Charles Kegan Paul's *Memories* is an account of the fire at his company's premises, followed by the statement that 'In them was burnt a volume in which, for a few years past, I had been writing my reminiscences from time to time, and I have felt some disinclination to work at them again.' That lost manuscript, written at the height of Paul's Positivist years, when he was still a successful publisher, still vigorous and confident, would have been very different from the one he left us.

Coincidentally, on the same day as the fire, there appeared in the *Fortnightly Review* an article by Paul entitled 'The Production and Life of Books'. It had been delivered, initially, as a lecture at the Albert Institute, in Windsor, and it was also one of the pieces Paul thought worthwhile to include in his collection, *Faith and Unfaith, and other Essays* (1891).[2] Although contradicted at some points by Paul's actual business practice as evidenced by the records of his company, and at others by critical colleagues writing in the *Publishers' Circular*, the essay may nevertheless be taken as a statement of his, and the firm's, approach to the making of books. It therefore serves as an introduction to this chapter on the firm's finest decade, the eighteen-eighties.

The essay began with what the *Publishers' Circular* critic regarded as a 'somewhat magniloquent prelude': 'It is intended to trace in the following pages the life of a book, from its first conception in the womb of an author's mind to its grave, that long home, unknown, often long deferred, yet which surely awaits all which is wrought by man, as well as the toiling hand and busy brain which made it.' Paul, holding forth in his journalistic pulpit, now announced his subject:

> the processes connected with the production of books; who can or who cannot write them; the mechanical act of writing them; how they are printed, on what paper, and how bound; how they are sold and distributed; how they are treated by buyers and readers; how and on what principle authors are paid or not paid; finally, what books live for longer or shorter periods, how they die, are buried, and are forgotten, and sometimes reappear, like ghosts, from the realm of the dead.

Paul insisted that 'a true book' requires inspiration, that is 'the author's feeling that he has something to say which will benefit others to hear'. He decried those with nothing to say: 'If a person have fallen into poverty, say a lady left, by the death of father or husband, with limited means, or a gentleman who has failed in business, the lady is recommended to keep a school, the gentleman to take pupils, and both to write a book. The whole outfit is supposed to consist in a few quires of foolscap, a steel pen, and a bottle of ink.' But beyond inspiration, the former Eton master argued, authorship also required a liberal education: ' . . . the turn of a phrase, the allusion to a character, and other indications which show an intellectual reader that he and the author are denizens of the same spiritual land, and have wandered through the same scenes, often make the whole difference between the sensations of delight and weariness'. Also essential were a knowledge of logic and of the rules of metaphor.

Passing quickly over the mechanics of authorship, the standards for a legible manuscript, Paul moved quickly to the question of a book's value. 'Let it be carefully remembered that not every book which has a literary has also a commercial value; and that the one is not necessarily in any degree the measure of the other.' Paul believed that the market, the prevailing public taste, determined the reception of most books: 'if the writer be not a Robertson as a preacher, or a Macaulay as historian, a George Eliot as a novelist, or a Browning as poet; if he be one of the average public who has written a fairly good book, success will depend on whether the book at the moment hits the fancy of the public or supplies a want just then felt: it rarely creates the demand'. He then scouted the notion that publishers were in the habit of overlooking good books: such properties were too rare to be ignored.

Perhaps the most illuminating part of the article is its analysis of the three 'ordinary ways of publishing', which Paul listed as the sale of copyright, the payment by royalty, and publication on commission. The sale of copyright, where 'the publisher takes all the risk, the author receives a lump sum down, and, as far as he is concerned, there is an end of the transaction', Paul regarded as acceptable only for the 'ordinary novel'. Books likely to require revision, such as scientific treatises or schoolbooks, benefited when their author retained a pecuniary interest in their quality. An analysis of his and Henry S. King's contracts with authors shows that King was much more inclined to purchase the copyright than was the Paul–Trench partnership. King also published more 'ordinary novels' than they did, as well as having more capital at his disposal for risky but potentially very profitable investments. Some of the copyrights he acquired from Alexander Strahan, for example, brought income into the firm for years to come. The analysis of types of contracts is summarized in Table 6.

Paul claimed to prefer the payment by royalty, whereby 'the author assigns the book to the publisher, taking, by agreement, so much on each copy sold, either from the first or after a certain reserved number of copies, or on each edition'. The principle, whatever the 'modifications' concerning reserved numbers of copies, was that 'the publisher takes the risk, and the profits are divided in a definite specified manner'. In 1883 the royalty system was just beginning to come into use. Publishers who did not purchase the copyright were likely to agree to share the profits with the author in some agreed-upon proportion, after undertaking the risks of publication. This system frequently led to abuse and to disputes, since the publisher controlled the expenses of production as well as the record of those expenses, and could easily inflate or obscure the real figures, or be accused of doing so. The Society of Authors, founded in 1884, urged its members to seek royalty agreements in preference to the share-profits system, in order to avoid these problems. Of the contracts that Kegan Paul, Trench signed between 1877 and 1889, about 28% could come under Paul's broad definition of 'royalty'. But over half of these (15%) included an important clause to protect the publisher, the reserve clause, whereby no payment was made until a fixed number of copies had been sold; and in many cases a further clause included a 'guarantee': the author promised to pay the cost price of the reserve copies if they were not purchased otherwise. A further 7% were old fashioned share profits arrangements, usually two-thirds to the author and one-third to the publisher. Only about 5% were true royalty arrangements, whether a percentage or a fixed payment of so many pence per copy. In his Paternoster Square office, Paul was not quite so liberal as he made himself appear in the pages of the *Fortnightly Review*.

Paul's comments on the third method of payment, publication on commission, are significant because over half the books on his own list appeared that way. In his definition, 'the writer bears the whole expense, the book belongs to him, the publisher taking a certain commission on the sales'. Paul admitted freely that 'the fact of taking it on commission usually shows that in [the publisher's] judgement the work has but a slender commercial value'. In the next breath he defended the practice, in a way that may have seemed odd to readers familiar with his high standards for work of lasting literary value, but perhaps not to those who knew his democratic political sentiments: 'And if it be the mere whim of the writer, the £100 or £200 spent upon it, some of which is sure to be returned, is of more good to the world, and of more pleasure to the writer, than would be the case did he buy a picture or a gem of the same cost, to be seen by fewer than those whom his book may instruct or amuse.' And he added that 'some books are also published on commission because the author is so confident of his work that he prefers to take for himself the risk and the profit'. Archbishop Trench's works, when they finally came to the firm, appeared on commission.[3]

Having brought his imagined book from conception through birth, Paul added some astute and perceptive comments on the matter of book design and composition, comments that revealed his low opinion of contemporary printers. He laid out the process by which a manuscript went through the printing process,[4] and then passed to the more amusing question of 'the strife as to spelling between author and printer'. With respect to spelling and usage: 'If we left it to the printers we should, unhappily, soon cease to write English, we should write American. We should have "favor" and "honor" for "favour" and "honour"; we should "commence" instead of "begin"; we should have the vulgarity of "did you have?" instead of "Had you?"' And about English printers who insisted upon 'correcting' words in French, setting aside the careful writing of foreign authors, he remarks 'How could a Frenchman possibly know better than a British workman? If this were so, where were the uses of Waterloo?'

Paul was a prophet, as well as a critic, of fine typography and book design: 'There could scarcely be a better thing for the artistic future of books than that which might be done by some master of decorative art, like Mr William Morris, and some great firm of type-founders in conjunction, would they design and produce some new types for our choicer printed books.' Eight years later, Morris would found the Kelmscott Press, the first fine art press in England.[5] Meanwhile Paul decried all mechanical processes, from paper-making to typography to printing. Although he preferred leather, in which he tellingly referred to books being 'really bound', he spared a comment for cloth bindings, 'more or less ornate, fairly inoffensive in the hands of a person of taste, but also frequent vehicles for pretension and vulgarity'. The edges should be left uncut. His book-trade contemporaries would have noticed the irony: books bearing the Kegan Paul imprint routinely appeared in publisher's cloth with the edges cut.

Turning to distribution, he commented disparagingly on booksellers and on the 'monster circulating libraries', like Mudies, that in his opinion 'fostered the growth and development of the second-rate novel'.[6] Bookshops and commercial circulating libraries were the means by which 'our supposed book is launched on its life voyage'. That life would vary according to genre as well as to quality.

Poetry was important to Paul. He had told Austin Dobson, 'it is so easy to criticize, so hard to write'. But as a publisher, he knew that in the case of a volume of poetry 'it is a miracle indeed if it attain success in life. For poetry, refined, subtle, romantic, unconcerned with the most obvious things of life, is ill-suited to make its way in a material world.' The very best of poetry would of course make its way, and so, unfortunately, would the rubbish. But as for the middle ground, where he probably placed his own verse, 'Nor gods, nor men, nor booksellers' shops will have anything to do with middling poets.' As for novels, the vast majority of them were ephemeral, and history was equally transitory. Libraries were like cemeteries, or catacombs, shelving the works of the greatest classical and modern authors, next to '"the ingenious" Mr This, or "the celebrated" Mr That, now forgotten'. And he concluded on a note of optimism, concerning 'the spiritual nature of books, . . . by [which] alone we come to know intimately the mind of the mighty dead or of the living writer . . . We, not Hamnet who died young, not Susanna and Judith, who survived their father, are Shakspere's true children.'

Charles Kegan Paul's 1883 ruminations on 'The Production and Life of Books' have been discussed in detail because his attitudes to literature on the one hand, and to books as physical objects and commercial products on the other, are important evidence of the policy of his firm. To continue the history of that firm, however, a more statistically and less discursively organized narrative is employed, one that is not rigidly chronological. Most of the evidence for the publishing policy of Kegan Paul, Trench in the 1880s is a reconstruction of its list of books offered for sale, based on the database of publishing records described in the Introduction and summarized in Table 4. The remainder of this chapter on the Paul–Trench partnership, therefore, is divided into sections in which titles are counted, analysed and organized by genre, by type of contract and by the gender of the author.

This methodology aspires to be more rigorous than that of the classic house history, in which the author traces the annals of the firm year by year, or decade by decade, highlighting some contracts and suppressing others, citing some particularly amusing or enduring titles and leaving others aside. Such an arbitrary selection is apt to be tedious, and is likely to be incomplete and therefore

Table 4 Genres of books published under the three imprints

Genre (followed by percentage of the trade for 1871)	H.S. KING (1871–7)		C. KEGAN PAUL (1877–81)		KEGAN PAUL, TRENCH (1881–8)		TOTAL	
	No.	%	No.	%	No.	%	No.	%
Theology, Sermons, Biblical (16.0%)	89	13.1	88	20.3	190	19.4	367	17.6
Education, Philosophy, Classics (11.2%)	17	2.5	34	7.9	51	5.2	102	4.9
Juvenile (13.7%)	11	1.6	10	2.3	2	0.2	23	1.1
Novels (7.5%)	112	16.5	21	4.8	51	5.2	184	8.8
Law, Jurisprudence (2.4%)	6	0.9	4	0.9	6	0.6	16	0.8
Political and Social Economy, and Trade and Commerce (2.3%)	44	6.5	28	6.5	90	9.2	162	7.8
Art, Science and Fine Arts (6.8%)	60	8.9	42	9.7	61	6.2	163	7.8
Travel and Geographical Research (6.7%)	52	7.7	27	6.2	53	5.4	132	6.3
History and Biography (7.8%)	55	8.1	34	7.9	92	9.4	181	8.7
Poetry and Drama (7.2%)	100	14.8	69	15.9	181	18.5	350	16.8
Year books and bound volumes of series (6.7%)	1	0.1	0	0.0	0	0.0	1	0.0
Medicine and Surgery (3.8%)	17	2.5	7	1.6	18	1.8	42	2.0
Belles-lettres (4.9%)	21	3.1	22	5.1	61	6.2	104	5.0
Misc., Including pamphlets (not sermons) (3.1%)	92	13.6	47	10.9	122	12.5	261	12.5
Totals	**677**	**100**	**433**	**100**	**978**	**100**	**2,088**	**100**

inaccurate. The approach used here is based upon an examination of the choices made by publishers, with the assumption that such choices are valuable evidence of contemporary cultural practice. Publishers, deciding what to do with a manuscript, mediate between the authors who articulate ideas and the reading public that interprets them. Publishers' judgements are often idiosyncratic and all too often faulty: but they are informed, by a professional sense of the contemporary market-place. Not only did Victorian publishers represent Victorian morality (as the editors of the *Graphic* did when they refused to publish the seduction scenes in *Tess of the D'Urbervilles*), they also mediated such important questions as how science was to be presented in popular form to the reading public, and how schoolchildren were to be introduced, in the shape of cheap reprint translation editions, to the ancient Greek and Roman classics.

To understand a publisher like Kegan Paul, Trench we need to understand their list, by reconstructing that list dynamically, so that it reflects the quotidian decisions they made. The reconstruction takes into account all the books on the list, registering them as they appeared, with details about the subject matter, the kinds of contracts the authors signed, and the kinds of interventions the publisher made in the developing text. Such a reconstruction makes it possible to calculate how many (or rather how few) of the books on such a list comprise the great novels and poetry of Victorian literature, and how many of them were written to express their authors' engagement with the ideas and society of their time. Such a reconstruction may lead its readers to discover hidden treasures and useful sources for a variety of studies. But even in its own right, the dynamic reconstruction of a publisher's list makes a statement about its time.

II

The genres of books published by Charles Kegan Paul and Alfred Chenevix Trench from 1877 to the end of 1888 are considered in order of numerical significance: (1) Theology, sermons, and biblical subjects; (2) poetry and drama; (3) novels; (4) history and biography; (5) science and art; (6) political and social economy (including trade and commerce); (7) travel and geographical research; (8) *belles lettres*; (9) education, philosophy, and classics; (10) medicine and surgery; (11) juvenile; and (12) law and jurisprudence. The categories were defined by the trade journal the *Publishers' Circular* for their annual analysis of national statistics. Table 4 displays the number and percentage of books published in each of these 12 generic categories under each of three publishers' imprints from 1871 to 1888. For purposes of comparison, the aggregate Kegan Paul figures are compared with those for the trade as a whole for 1871.[7] Books in these twelve categories, with the addition of a large number coded as 'miscellaneous', made up the Kegan Paul, Trench list.

THEOLOGY, SERMONS, AND BIBLICAL SUBJECTS

Religious subjects, despite Charles Kegan Paul's own spectacular apostasy, dominated his firm's list as they dominated the overall production of the British book trade. Almost 20% of Kegan Paul, Trench books fell into the category 'theology, sermons, biblical', as compared to 16% for the trade at large and only 13% in Henry S. King's day.

One of the last books to appear under the King imprint, in 1877, was a memoir of Charles Kingsley, who had died in 1875, written by his widow, Frances Kingsley. The same year there was the first series of sermons from the popular George Dawson, whom Kingsley had thought the ablest speaker in Britain.[8] Dawson's sermons were edited by his widow Susan, with assistance from Marie Beauclerc, who had transcribed the discourses and shared in the considerable royalties. And in 1878 appeared three books by Reginald Haweis, the exponent of music and morals. There was a market for the works of Kingsley, Dawson and Haweis, but not for sermons as such. Many sermons and theological essays were published on a commission basis, books like the Rev. Thomas Pinches' three sermons on Samuel Wilberforce, subtitled *Faith, Service, Recompense*, or the Rev. Charles Shakspeare's nine sermons entitled *St Paul at Athens: Spiritual Christianity in Relation to Some Aspects of Modern Thought* (both 1878). Pinches paid over £100 to publish his book on commission; Shakspeare agreed to wait for 550 copies to be sold at 4s 6d before he was to begin collecting a royalty. Paul's new humanist interest can be identified with Richard Congreve's *Religion of Humanity, the annual address delivered at the Positivist School . . . on the Festival of Humanity, Jan. 1st, 1878*, but his cautious business interest is registered in the commission agreement for the title.

Another book in the genre of sermons was *England's Sin. Honour Sold. Truth Betrayed. Plain Words Delivered at Finchley on Good Friday, 1884* by the Rev. Cecil B. Carlon, M.A. For a 5 guinea fee and a further guinea for advertising, plus printing costs, Carlon had a fourteen-page pulpit to express himself: 'Oh for one burst of honest wrath and indignation against the prevailing curse; against the underground life of the day; against the subtle, creeping, dastardly sins of modern society, so little denounced, so little thought of, while the grosser, more patent sins of the poor are exaggerated and declaimed against!' And the same year Kegan Paul, Trench began publishing *Thirty Thousand Thoughts, being extracts covering a comprehensive circle of religious and allied topics*, in six volumes on commission for J.S. Exell and others. Completed in 1888, it failed to sell in the open trade, but two years later a bookseller reported that his largest purchase in the way of a publisher's remainder was this very work; he changed the title to *Treasury of Religious Thought*, and got rid of 1,300 sets in less than two years.[9] Exell was an Anglican clergyman living in Colchester, who was editor of the *Homiletic Quarterly*. He was one of the general editors of the Kegan Paul, Trench series *The Pulpit Commentary*, a much more commercially viable project designed as a useful handbook for preachers tackling their own weekly duty, rather than for the purpose of preserving particularly memorable sermons.

When Archbishop's Trench's works finally came to the firm at his death in 1886, the association of the name of the firm and the name of the distinguished author intensified their reputation for religious books. Trench's *Notes on the Parables of Our Lord*, first published in 1841 by John W. Parker, had gone through fourteen editions with citations in the notes printed only in Greek and Latin. Now Alfred Trench and his partner decided that with a view to making the book more accessible, these should be translated into English. Alfred Pollard, later keeper of the Department of Printed Books at the British Museum, was in 1886 a young and struggling junior member of that department. One evening, Paul asked the Reading Room superintendent to recommend 'some one who could translate the Greek and Latin quotations in Archbishop Trench's treatises on the Parables and Miracles'. Pollard undertook the task and in the process of preparing the fifteenth edition, he and Paul became close friends.[10]

POETRY AND DRAMA

After religion came poetry. Here was literature where Charles Kegan Paul could act as editor and mentor to young poets, and also present their work to the public. But in his role as publisher, Paul knew that he could make money on mediocre verse by the likes of Emily Jane Pfeiffer, and was apt to lose on Andrew Lang, Austin Dobson or Wilfrid Scawen Blunt.[11] Poetry, with drama, accounted for nearly 17% of Kegan Paul, Trench contracts, and only 7.2% of the output of the trade at large. Their reputation as Tennyson's publisher, as well as Paul's personal standing in the literary community, may have attracted some poets to their imprint.

Andrew Lang has been described as 'a literary landmark for forty years', a generalist who could write as a novelist, classical scholar, folklorist and journalist, as well as a poet.[12] Three of his books were published by Kegan Paul, Trench, the most important being *XXXII Ballades in Blue China* (1880; second edition in 1881). This was published on commission, but the firm's staff were admonished that the costs be kept low, and a minimal 2 guinea fee was charged to Lang. The firm purchased the copyright of *Rhymes à la mode* in 1884, for £25, and in 1886 paid the same amount for *In the Wrong Paradise*; but in this case there was a promise of further payments after the sale of each 1,000 copies. Paul seems to have enjoyed and admired Lang's verse, but been exasperated by the waste of his poetic and scholarly talents in writing very light verse. In *Memories* he regretted 'that the brilliancy of [Lang's] fugitive work has interfered with the production of some exhaustive treatise on one of the many subjects in which he is a master', and in conversation he was more sarcastic: 'Ah! There is Andrew Lang – there was a time when he had something to say. Alas! now he has to say something.'[13]

Austin Dobson is remembered as a writer of light verse incorporating French forms, what Paul called *vers de société*. King had published his first collection, *Vignettes in Rhyme* in 1873, sharing the profits with the poet. There was a second edition the following year. When Paul appeared on the scene he began to correspond with Dobson, and later commissioned him to edit works in the Parchment Library series. Wilfrid Blunt was not only a poet, but also a diplomat, a traveller and student of Arab culture. His poetry included such diverse themes as love lyrics and adaptations from the Arabic. His first volume had appeared in 1875, but he switched to Kegan Paul, Trench in 1881. His *Love Sonnets of Proteus* was published on commission, and for *The Future of Islam* there was a royalty arrangement: 1,000 copies were printed, and after 500 had been sold, Blunt would receive 1s 6d on each copy sold at 6s. Similar arrangements were made in 1889 for the sonnet sequence *In Vinculis*. Their friendship continued until Paul died.

Lang, Dobson and Blunt, along with Archbishop Trench, Aubrey de Vere and Sir Henry Taylor whose work King and Kegan Paul, Trench also published, have become part of literary history. Although not often reprinted in modern editions or taught in the curricula of university departments of English, their books are important parts of collections both public and private. Poetry of this kind, the books that Paul in his essay claimed would live forever in the hearts and minds of readers, formed a distinct minority on the company's list.

Much more typical was the execrable *Dolores: A Theme with Variations* (1880). Published anonymously, this three-part poem appeared under the imprint of C. Kegan Paul & Co., in a neat blue cloth binding decorated with an unobtrusive black band. The publisher's records show the author to have been Miss E. Bond, who paid £65 to see her work in print. This seems to have been her only published poem: no other works by a woman called Bond have been found in the catalogue of the British Library. The poem concerns the 'gentle, girlish' Dolores, who is the object of the affections of her cousin Nigel. She, however, does not return his love.

> ... Thus, in the flame of her imagination,
> Dolores hero, Rex, first took his station.

To summarize brutally, Rex murders Nigel in a jealous rage, goes mad, and dies. In Part II the middle-aged Dolores, still single, rescues a shipwrecked sailor, Victor, nurses him and falls in love. But Victor deserts her for another woman. Finally, in Part III, Dolores discovers the virtues of charity and of caring for children; at her death she affirms faith in God. Her downfall was her extraordinary philanthropy:

> Dolores lingered, hour by hour,
>   while help and sympathy were needed:
> She gave them with inspired power,
>   And let the time go by, unheeded:

Charles Kegan Paul's chagrin at having this sort of verse appear under his imprint may be imagined. But just as he predicted, *Dolores* was catalogued and shelved in the collections of Britain's copyright libraries, and survives to demonstrate the immense eclecticism of his list.

NOVELS

As with poetry, so with novels: ephemeral tales outweighed the works which were to enter the canon of Victorian literature. Paul regarded himself as an authority on the genre, rating George Eliot as the greatest of living English novelists. He judged Walter Pater, Thomas Hardy and, surprisingly, Hesba Stretton to be stylists who 'show the perfection to which, in this age, our language can be wrought'.[14] He and King published two of Hardy's works in one-volume editions, subsequent to their first appearances in three volumes. But Hesba Stretton returned to the Religious Tract Society in about 1880, and none of Pater's works appear in the firm's list. While novels accounted for 7.5% of the book trade in general, they were only 5% of the output of Kegan Paul, Trench. Not only was this below the trade average, it was a significant decline from Henry S. King's 16.5%. Paul complained in his memoir of King that some books, hastily selected in the years before his own influence was brought to bear, 'were difficult to eliminate when better material flowed in'.

Paul's contemporaries were struck more by the novels, and

novelists, he attracted and then lost, than by those few he continued to publish. Thomas Hardy in these years regarded Smith, Elder as his publishers and Paul never had the opportunity to do more than produce one-volume editions of earlier novels.[15] Robert Louis Stevenson was a much more dramatic example. In *Memories*, Paul merely remarked that Stevenson, at the time of their association, had not 'attained the fame which he was afterwards to enjoy'. But Wilfrid Meynell, writing the *Academy* memoir, was convinced that the novelist had been so impressed with Paul's paradoxical personality that he had used it 'as the germ of Jekyll and Hyde', his most famous characterization. 'Other versions of that conception have been given,' he insisted, 'but I adhere to mine. Jekyll and Hyde, Kegan and Paul – the very names have a sort of aural association.' When Trench made his contribution to Mumby's *House of Routledge* he obligingly recalled 'the worst bit of business that I ever did in my life', the fiasco of losing the author who was to become familiar to everyone as 'R.L.S.'

Paul and Trench had paid Stevenson £20 for *An Inland Voyage* in 1878, promising a further royalty of one shilling per copy after a reserve of 1,000 copies had been sold. This was Stevenson's first book-length work, the description of a canoe tour in Belgium and France. When there was a delay in preparing the frontispiece, Stevenson wrote to the artist, Walter Crane, conveying a vivid impression of Paul's sense of urgency as well as his own.

> It appears that there is a tide in the affairs of publishers which has the narrowest moment of flood conceivable: a week here, a week there, and a book is made or lost, and now, as I write to you, is the very nick of time, the publisher's high noon. I should deceive you if I were to pretend I had no more than a generous interest in this appeal. For, should the public prove gullible to a proper degree, and one thousand copies net, counting thirteen to the dozen, disappear in its capacious circulating libraries, I should begin to perceive a royalty which visibly affects me as I write.[16]

Only 485 copies, however, were sold in the first year, although there was a fresh agreement in 1880 for a cheap edition. The firm refused in 1879 to bring out the 'Latter-Day Arabian Nights' (eventually published as *New Arabian Nights* (1882) by Chatto and Windus), 'on account of their preposterous character'. But they did publish *Travels With a Donkey in the Cevennes* (1879), with a lump sum payment of £30 and the promise of royalties if 700 were sold. Trench at one point told the author it was the only book of the firm's that was selling at all. Stevenson's *The Amateur Emigrant* was set in type for publication in April 1880 but withdrawn by the author in August because of doubts about its quality and because his need of money was now less urgent. The following year there was a collection of essays, *Virginibus Puerisque* (1881), which they accepted for a single payment, with no promise of further remuneration. Stevenson told his mother 'I only got £20 for Virg. Puer. I could take Paul by the beard and knock his head against the wall.' Interestingly it was Paul, not Alfred Chenevix Trench, with whom Stevenson remembered dealing. The book that Paul and Trench declined was *Familiar Studies of Men and Books* (1882). Chatto & Windus acquired it, along with the first refusal on new works, for £100, paying an additional £100, approximately, to Kegan Paul, Trench for the rights to the earlier books. When this at length was arranged, in 1884, the ledgers were still showing a loss of £180 on all three early titles.[17]

In the hindsight of the nineties, when Trench and Meynell and even Paul himself knew Stevenson to be a popular as well as talented novelist, their policy looked short-sighted. But how were they to have known that the travel writer and literary critic for whom they had done the best they could (not everyone, as we have seen, received lump-sum payments in advance of publication), was to transform himself into an adventure and mystery novelist of the first rank, and make a hit with *Treasure Island* and *The Strange Case of Dr. Jekyll and Mr. Hyde*?

George Meredith was different, like Stevenson a serious novelist, but unlike Stevenson admired primarily by a narrowly discriminating audience, and only late in his career by the broader reading public. Charles Kegan Paul expressed some ambivalence about Meredith's innovative style. 'To understand George Meredith,' he remarked in *Memories*, 'it is perhaps necessary to belong to a somewhat esoteric circle who can enter into a literature which will probably increase as time brings a wider education.' But later he labelled Meredith 'among the first of living writers, whose novel, *The Ordeal of Richard Feverel*, I put on the highest level of English literature'. Although Meredith's books were chiefly published by Chapman & Hall, for whom he served as publisher's reader for many years, he brought out two novels with Kegan Paul and Company. In 1878 they published the second English edition of *The Ordeal of Richard Feverel*, a cheap edition at 6s 0d with a royalty of 1s 6d paid after 750 were sold. In 1879 they published *The Egoist* in three volumes, with a one-volume cheap edition in 1880. Paul paid £450 for the copyright, then infuriated Meredith by selling (for £110) the serial rights: 'The diplomatic Kegan has delt me a stroke,' he told a friend, 'Without a word to me, he sold the right of issue of the *Egoist* to the *Glasgow Herald*, and allowed them to be guilty of a perversion of my title. I wrote to him in my incredulous astonishment.'[18]

With both Stevenson and Meredith we see Paul struggling to balance his literary taste against the knowledge of the realities of commercial publishing he had learned from Henry S. King. Privately he identified with the authors and their interests, but it was his public and commercial aspect that they related to, his way of treating their cherished texts as mere commodities, and his own property at that. Good books did not always sell; the books that sold were not always good; and funds had to be secured, even if it required making deals with the *Glasgow Herald*, or printing pictures of Tennyson's home. But Paul suppresses these more sordid arrangements in *Memories* and in his essay on publishing, implying that he limited himself to the good books, to his financial discomfiture: 'For good or evil our firm always preferred to be literary and scholarly.' On the contrary. They were perfectly willing to publish mediocre novels on a commission basis, but not to profit from publishing mediocrity.

HISTORY AND BIOGRAPHY

The craft of history was changing, in the late nineteenth century, as professional historians, many of them working out of universities, began to extract material from the archival records created by governments, organizations and private individuals. The literary form used so effectively by Macaulay and Carlyle now gave way to a more empirical, research-based scholarship. This 'transformation of Victorian historiography' has been described in terms of 'an immense change in the concept of the historical enterprise, in many ways illustrative of the changing contours of Victorian intellectual life'.[19]

This new way of studying history was often epitomized by Leopold von Ranke's motto, 'wie es eigentlich gewesen'— the study of what actually happened. Ranke's *Universal History: the Oldest Historical Group of Nations and the Greeks* was published in translation in England in 1884, by Kegan Paul, Trench. The translator was Sir George Prothero, who received a payment and a royalty; Ranke also received a 5% royalty, and the firm recovered part of their outlay from Harper Brothers in New York, for the right to reprint in the United States.

Although Kegan Paul, Trench were never identified as major publishers of history in the way that the university presses were, they did nevertheless bring out some important works. Another 'modern' historian published by the firm was Samuel Gardiner, who with J.B. Mullinger wrote a two-part *Introduction to the Study of English History*. Royalties in this case were paid on a per-edition basis, rather than per copy, and the American publisher this time was Henry Holt.

In addition to these major works, there were numerous books, ranging from scholarly to banal, on the histories of Rome, of Ireland, of Japan, of Holland. With biography, history accounted for 9% of the Kegan Paul, Trench firm's new titles, which was a little above the trade average of 7.8%.

Biography, too, was one of the principal literary forms of the Victorians: soon after an illustrious person's death, the two- or three-volume life and letters could be expected to appear. It was also a genre where there was great scope for the commission author: the life and letters of a beloved husband or wife, or an admired teacher, seemed to many to be a suitable memorial, a way of ensuring that the person whose life was written would never be forgotten. Two- and three-volume tomes were the common format, and in the text all scandal and controversy was veiled in a seemly obscurity. As St John Adcock remarked: 'In the Victorian age biographies without tears were produced, and all great men were described as paragons. . . . If we so fear the truth that we prefer to shut our eyes to it, and desire biographies without tears, we should be honest enough to call them by another name, and change the first letter of the word and spell it with an "L."'"[20] Maria Trench's memoir of her uncle, the Archbishop, is just one of several works she produced in this genre.

Autobiography, too, permitted people of the record-keeping classes to shape the narrative of their own life. Paul's *Memories* fits easily into a genre with which he was familiar: he introduced his text with the observation that 'since I have taken interest in the narratives of several men I have known, and am inclined to think that the careful memories of the somewhat varied life I have lived may prove in the same manner entertaining to others'.

But the 'somewhat varied life' of a publisher was one thing: the daily record of a national hero, written at the very moment when facing a martyr's death with Christian fortitude, was quite another, 'the most remarkable book published by Mr Trench and myself'. This was *The Journals of Major-Gen. C.G. Gordon, C.B., at Kartoum*, published in 1885. The cult of General George Gordon in the 1880s was a notable example of popular imperialist pride, and whatever religious musings he wrote in his last hours ought to have constituted a best-seller. Gladstone's Liberal government, which delayed too long in sending off a relief expedition to Khartoum, suffered political damage because it was held responsible for Gordon's martyrdom, by patriots from the Queen down. But Paul tells us that the book was delayed in its turn, by problems with translation from the Arabic and with editing, and thus came out after the first flush of enthusiasm was past, a fickleness of public opinion that was reflected in disappointing sales. However the rescue mission, the fall of Khartoum, the hero's death and retrieval of his journals, the contract, the entire publishing process and the first edition all took place within 1885. In that year, Paul and Trench outbid other publishers for the journals, which were in the hands of Gordon's brother, offering 5,000 guineas, £5,250, to top the £5,000 offered by Longmans. The complexities of translation and printing raised the expenses to £7,000. They were able to spread out the risk, however, by selling off the American, foreign and colonial rights, and the right to a serialized version in newspapers. A facsimile edition (*General Gordon's Last Journal*, 1885) and a biography (Henry William Gordon, *Events in the Life of Maj. Gen. Charles Gordon*, 1886) were further spin-offs from the project. As for the timing, perhaps Victorian public opinion was more fickle than we have believed. Much more likely, however, is the conjecture that Paul's deprecatory account in *Memories* was designed to support his self-portrait as unbusinesslike gentleman publisher.

SCIENCE AND ART

The juxtaposition of the history of science with the history of the book is just beginning to be recognized as a promising approach to scholarship in both fields. Adrian Johns, in an article in the journal *Publishing History*, speaks of 'the simultaneous arrival over the last generation of both a new history of the book and a new history of science', and suggests

> that a *rapprochement* might be highly beneficial to both camps. For the historian of science, attention to the history of the book adds a valuable perspective to those detailed considerations of the construction and maintenance of natural knowledge now increasingly prevalent in the field. On the other hand, the history of science offers a way of showing how the culture of books affects apparently the most fundamental and objective aspects of knowledge in our society.[21]

The way in which Charles Kegan Paul and his colleagues, working as publishers, approached the scientific developments in their society provides some useful evidence of contemporary attitudes.

In the mixed category of science and art, books in the International Scientific Series accounted for 98 of the total of 163 titles, and accounted for the Kegan Paul firm's reputation as a major scientific publisher. A review in November 1880, for example, described the series as 'fast placing in the hands of English students all the most important works of foreign authors on scientific subjects'. By 1882 it was the series that seemed to guarantee the quality of the title, so that in the case of Sir John Lubbock's *Ants, Bees, and Wasps* (1882), 'the fact that the publishers include this treatise by the popular banker, senator, and defender of ancient monuments in their "International Scientific Series" is a sufficient testimony of its value from a scientific point of view'.[22]

Occasionally a book commissioned for the series turned out to be longer or more expensive to produce than the one-volume, five-shilling format of the series permitted, and the book then spilled over into the firm's general list. This happened with W.B. Carpenter's *Principles of Mental Physiology* published by King in 1874. Science and art together comprised 7.8% of Kegan Paul, Trench's list, a shade more than the 7.2% share of the trade as a whole.

Many books with 'science' in the title are more properly counted among works on religious subjects. Examples of these are *Genesis in Advance of Present Science* (Henry Smith-Warleigh, 1883) and *The Science and Art of Religion* (1888, Samuel Mackinney), both published on commission. The latter part of the nineteenth century was the time when the military metaphor of a 'war' between religion on the one hand, and science on the other, was coined. Coincidentally, H.S. King published the two most influential books concerning this theme: Draper's *History of the Conflict Between Religion and Science* was enormously popular in the International Scientific Series from its first publication in 1875; and Andrew White's 1876 *The Warfare of Science and Theology* also remained in print during the Kegan Paul, Trench years.

Of the relatively few books on artistic subjects published by the firm, an important one was Emilia Pattison's *Renaissance of Art in France* (1879). Pattison, later Lady Dilke, was one of the few women scholars who wrote with authority about the history of European art. She had to contribute £150 towards the production of her two-volume work. And in 1886 Bernard Bosanquet produced a translation of *The Introduction to Hegel's Philosophy of Fine Art*, which was published on a commission basis. It was for the subtleties of book design, rather than for printing elaborate engravings or lithographs, that Charles Kegan Paul was remembered. Although the firm printed a number of illustrated books, on scientific as well as artistic subjects, and books for children, they were never among the leading publishers of Victorian book illustration.

POLITICAL AND SOCIAL ECONOMY (INCLUDING TRADE AND COMMERCE)

A substantial 7.8% of the company's list comprised books on political and social economy, which outweighed slightly the trade average of 6.8%. As usual, many of the books were the effusions of private individuals wishing to express in print their views on subjects from free trade in land, to home rule in Ireland, to proportional representation in voting. An exception was Kegan Paul, Trench's publication in 1881 of *Progress and Poverty*, by Henry George. This had been first published in New York, by Appleton, and the firm initially purchased copies already printed. George's book, subtitled 'An Inquiry into the Causes of Industrial Depressions and of Increase of Want with Increase of Wealth', was very influential in Britain in the eighties. Members of the Fabian society used it to help explain disturbing economic changes that were affecting society. George Bernard Shaw and Alfred Russel Wallace were only two of the many who were persuaded by the book. The firm published a popular edition at sixpence in 1882, and also continued to publish editions at 1s, 1s 6d and 2s 6d, in almost as many formats as Tennyson's poems. They seem to have acted as George's agents in the British empire, collecting a payment in 1888 for the copyright in Australia.

TRAVEL AND GEOGRAPHICAL RESEARCH

Travel literature, closely connected with reports on geographical research, grew enormously in the Victorian period, as men and women reported on their adventures and discoveries abroad. With its tradition of service to the colonial community in India, Henry S. King & Co. published numerous accounts of this kind, and the Kegan Paul firm continued the practice, at 6% of the whole list almost exactly on a par with the trade in general. And as we shall see, when the imprint later expanded to take in all the titles published by Nicholas Trübner, the firm's reputation for travel and geographical expertise would expand even further.

In the 1880s it was the travels of Sir Richard and Lady Isabel Burton that dominated the list. Richard Burton was already well known in 1878, when Kegan Paul & Co. published his *Gold Mines of Midian* (paying him an advance of £100 to be followed by a share in the profits); he had been the first Englishman to enter Mecca in 1853, the beginning of a dramatic and well-documented career of travel, exploration and writing. He returned to the subject in 1879 with *Land of Midian, Revisited*. Lady Burton had already used H.S. King to publish, in 1875, her book *The Inner Life of Syria, Palestine, and the Holy Land. From My Private Journal*. Because she could satisfy readers' curiosity by reporting on her experience of the harem and other eastern mysteries restricted to women, Isabel Burton's book was a great success. First published in two volumes, a one-volume cheap edition (still 10s 6d), with photographs and coloured plates appeared in 1879. Her payments amounted to £100 for each edition, plus royalties. Paul recounts Lady Burton's wish that the firm publish her guidebook in an edition 'interleaved with the historical parts of the Bible, the Prophets and Gospels, because, she said, every one must take her book as a travelling companion, and it was by no means certain that they would take the Bible also'. Readers were left, however, to do their own cross-referencing.

BELLES-LETTRES

As with science, the class of literature labelled *belles-lettres* was largely contained in an important series (discussed below), the Parchment Library initiated in 1880.

Essays on literary subjects often appeared as commissioned works. One title that ought not to be lost to posterity is *The Sweet Silvery Sayings of Shakespeare on the Softer Sex*, published in 1877 and proclaimed on the title-page to be 'compiled by an old soldier'. He is revealed in the publication records to be Col. G. D'Arcy, who commissioned Henry S. King to publish his book. Kegan Paul Trench's titles in *belles lettres* comprised 6% of their list, as compared with just under 5% of the trade as a whole.

EDUCATION, PHILOSOPHY AND CLASSICS

The Kegan Paul firm never entered the increasingly profitable and competitive market for textbooks, but it did publish a number of books on the theory of education. These are counted in book trade statistics along with philosophy and classics, and amount to 5% of the firm's list, as compared with 11.2% in the trade overall. Beginning in 1881, the Education Library, edited by Sir Philip

Magnus, contained five of these books, but the publishers were disappointed in the public response to the series. At a more practical level was Charlotte Mason's 1886 book, *Home Education: a Course of Lectures to Ladies*. She was founder of the Parents Educational National Union. Acquired initially on a royalty agreement reserving the first 2,000 copies, this turned out to be a successful publication, and eventually it spawned a series, the Home Education Series.

Philosophy and, particularly, classics appealed to Charles Kegan Paul's personal notion of the intellectual equipment of an educated person. Editions of Camoens, of Horace, of Aeschylus and of Virgil flowed steadily from the Kegan Paul press, most of them commissioned by their editor-translators.

MEDICINE AND SURGERY

Medical books were specialized texts whose professional authors customarily took their work to specialized publishers. Only 2% of the King and Kegan Paul, Trench, list was directed to this market. One distinguished medical author was Henry Maudsley, the psychiatrist whose book *The Physiology and Pathology of Mind* (1867) has been described as 'a landmark in the development of British psychiatric thought'. That book had been published by Macmillan. Maudsley was one of the earliest contributors to the International Scientific Series, 'the logical person to invite to write a book on medical jurisprudence'. *Responsibility in mental disease* appeared as volume 8 in 1874. Over the next twelve years he entrusted two more books to Kegan Paul, Trench, both on commission-publishing arrangements: *Body and Will* (1883) and *Natural Causes and Supernatural Seemings* (1886).[23]

JUVENILE

The children's book, by the 1880s, was also becoming a genre in which certain publishers specialized. As a result, general firms like Kegan Paul, Trench found it difficult to compete. Sarah Smith, the prolific and popular 'Hesba Stretton' who had written *Jessica's First Prayer*, returned to the Religious Tract Society. Her original publisher was now prepared to pay what her books were worth.

Similarly Jean Ingelow, whose novels King had acquired from Strahan, did not add further books to the Kegan Paul, Trench list, although they kept *Off the Skelligs* (1872) in print, and included it in their reprint fiction series, the Colonial Library, in 1888. But at just over 1%, the firm's list of juvenile works did not have much of an impact on the large, and growing, market in the general book trade.

LAW AND JURISPRUDENCE

The smallest category of books published by Kegan Paul, Trench was books on law and jurisprudence. A mere ten titles fell into this grouping. One very successful one, though, was Sir George Sherston Baker's edition, in 1878, of *International Law* by the American jurist Henry Wager Halleck. The first publication had been in San Francisco in 1861. The contract called for the book to be known as 'Sherston Baker's "Halleck"', but advertistments referred to 'Halleck's International Law'. Initially the agreement was with H.S. King and Co. in 1876, but when the book came out in 1878 the imprint was C. Kegan Paul & Co. Baker improved on Halleck's original work by adding notes and bringing the classic text up to date. After a reserve sale of 300 copies at 38s 0d per two-volume copy, Baker was paid a royalty of 15s 0d per copy, as usual reckoning 25 copies as 24. This arrangement survived a new edition in 1893 and another in 1908. When a representative of the reorganized firm travelled to North America in 1899, he sold 250 copies to the Boston publisher Little, Brown, thus returning Halleck to his home country in the form determined by Baker.

MISCELLANEOUS

Finally, books labelled 'miscellaneous, including pamphlets not sermons', accounted for 12.5% of the Kegan Paul, Trench list, as opposed to only 3.1% of titles in general. The wide variety of idiosyncratic titles and subject matter gathered under this heading is discussed below in the section on the practice of publishing by commission.

Analysed generically, the list of books published by C. Kegan Paul & Co. and by Kegan Paul, Trench & Co. from the autumn of

Table 5 Series published by C. Kegan Paul & Co. and by Kegan Paul, Trench & Co., 1877–88.

International Scientific Series (initiated by King: 98 titles, 1872–1911)

Parchment Library (40 titles, 1880–94)

Pulpit Commentary (49 titles, 1881–97)

Education Library (5 titles, 1881–8)

Military Handbooks for Officers and Non-Commissioned Officers (7 titles, 1883–8; revived with a further 10 titles, 1897–1910)

1877 to the end of 1888 throws some new light on the history of Victorian publishing. The well-known stories of how badly Charlotte Brontë was treated by her publishers, how well George Eliot by hers, and how Charles Dickens revolutionized his, are by no means typical. They are the publishing histories of books that not only registered with readers in their own times, but survived those times to become the subject of scholarly examination in the twentieth century. The history of a general publishing firm of the middle rank, like Kegan Paul, Trench and its predecessor and successor, presents a much fuller, and more nuanced, picture of that part of Victorian culture that was concerned with authorship, printing and publishing, and ultimately with reading, using and enjoying books.

III

Charles Kegan Paul did not mention the series as a publishing form in his essay on 'The Production and Life of Books'. The tone of that article implied that a book is always an individual text: written and published, read and catalogued as an autonomous unit, and destined to stand or fall on its own literary or scholarly merit. Victorian publishing, however, did not work that way, and the reputation of Paul's imprint as a publisher was made largely on the prestige of series extending over years, rather than for single texts like the Gordon journals or Dobson's first volume of poetry.

INTERNATIONAL SCIENTIFIC SERIES

The credit for founding the London edition of the International Scientific Series was due to King, but it was Paul who carried it on for a quarter century. Nevertheless in *Memories* Paul subtly disparaged the series, partly by emphasizing faulty translations, and also by mentioning that some authors 'gave merely old magazine articles', rather than writing original works that would meet the series' dual standard of scholarship and accessibility. And when someone like T.H. Huxley 'gave new and admirable original work, . . . in these cases the cost of illustration was far greater than could reasonably have been expended for the price at which these volumes were sold'. Moreover, he criticized King for arranging with Youmans and Appleton 'extremely liberal terms, too liberal indeed to make the "Series" a great financial success'. If this were so, Paul would have had to explain why the International Scientific Series, standing at twenty-two volumes when he took over in 1877, expanded to sixty-five by the time he lost absolute control of the firm at the end of 1888, and survived even under the new management to a ninety-eighth volume appearing in 1911. The memoirist of 1899, now a pious Catholic, preferred to distance himself from the coruscating success of a set of books whose aggregate reputation was for challenging religious belief with secularism.[24]

For an accurate and contemporary view of Paul's work on the International Scientific Series during the 1880s we can turn to his correspondence with one author whose book, as it happened, he failed to attract. Francis Galton was a well-known scientist of wide interests, best known for his interest in heredity, and his development of eugenic theories of inheritance. He had written *Hereditary Genius: An Inquiry into its Laws and Consequences*, published in 1869. In November 1877, immediately after taking over from King, Paul reminded Galton that he had promised the series founder, Edward Livingston Youmans, that he would contribute a book on 'Psychometry, or the measurement of Mental Actions in Time and Quantity'. Statistics, and especially psychological statistics, was a subject of great interest to educated people in the late 1870s, and this book would have been very significant. Paul explained the financial terms for such a book, and added that he would like to advertise it with other titles forthcoming in the series. When would the manuscript be ready? Would there be illustrations? Galton replied that these questions were premature, the book was not yet written and in fact research was still in progress. But he was interested enough to note that Youmans had told him the American royalty was 10%, not 7.5 as Paul had mentioned. Responding the following day, Paul insisted he hadn't intended to press, merely to formulate the firm's understanding of the conversation between Galton and Youmans. He understood not only that the book was unwritten but that it would be 'published in Scientific Memoirs and in popular Magazines before reaching our hands'. And Youmans had been correct about the rate of American royalties. But nearly a year later, Galton wrote that he couldn't see his way to writing a good book for the series. Still not prepared to give up, Paul asked Galton to suggest a subject, other than Psychometry, on which he would write for the series.[25] Written nearly twenty years earlier than *Memories*, these were the business letters of a committed editor–publisher, fully engaged in promoting the success of a series of books on the latest scientific subjects, by prominent scientific authors.

PARCHMENT LIBRARY

The elderly Charles Kegan Paul was happier to remember his part in the Parchment Library. Here, Paul himself had been the moving spirit, combining the roles of Henry King, Edward Youmans, and the three-person editorial committee of the International Scientific Series. 'The intention of this series,' he remembered, 'was to present in thoroughly good paper and print some of the most distinguished English classics, and we certainly set the fashion of really beautiful books. No doubt many have now surpassed them, but at the time these reprints were a distinct advance.' And Paul's claim to primacy is corroborated by J.M. Dent, who wrote in 1938 of his Temple Library, begun in the early nineties, that 'The idea of the format of the series I began with was very little of my own, but was reminiscent of a series published by Kegan Paul called "The Parchment Library". I was, however, not conscious of this; probably the real suggestion came from the printers, The Chiswick Press, ... who I believe printed some volumes of The Parchment Library.'[26]

In the 1880s, book collecting evoked almost as much passionate interest as scepticism, agnosticism and science, and some of the same people were interested in both. Paul was on the fringe of a circle that included Thomas J. Wise, Clement Shorter and others who, having among themselves acquired most of the available stock of modern first editions, began to take an interest in publishing beautiful new books that were destined to become collectors' items.[27] Book lovers who could not afford to collect manuscripts or first editions were attracted by the idea of owning well-printed, uniformly-bound copies of the English and European classics.

Four titles appeared in the first year, 1880. The series began with editions of two particularly popular poems by Tennyson, as Paul struggled to make the most of his expensive contract to publish the poet laureate, then in the second year of its second five-year term. *In Memoriam* and *The Princess* both appeared in the small and compact Parchment Library format that became familiar. Each edition was about sixteen by ten centimetres in size, printed on good paper with the wide margins and untrimmed edges that Paul preferred. The titles were printed on the title-pages in red capitals, followed by names of authors and editors in black and then by the 'Arbor Scientiae; Arbor Vitae' mark. The imprint, all in capital letters, was the place name London, in red ink, the publisher's name, in black, and then the date in red roman numerals. On the outside cover the title was printed in red capitals, in the upper left hand corner, balanced by the Kegan Paul device in the lower right. The binding was limp 'parchment antique' and the selling price was 6s 0d; copies could also be had in vellum at 7s 6d, For some titles a large paper version (20 × 12.5 cm), in a limited, numbered edition of fifty copies was also offered, at 12s 0d bound in parchment and 15s 0d in vellum. The printer of the first volumes was the Chiswick Press, under the direction of Charles Whittingham, and the binder was Burn and Company.

Alfred Trench wrote to D. Appleton and Co., the co-publishers of the International Scientific Series, and found they were willing to publish this new series in New York. In this case, however, editorial control remained in London. Appleton's agreed to pay for half the cost of composition, and for the stereotyping of one set of plates. No royalty would be paid to the English publisher on the sales.[28] Royalties were not to figure largely in the expense of the Parchment Library in any case. When, as happened with the third book, a title was edited by a scholar, there was a flat fee of £10 or 10 guineas, occasionally more, and the book was thereafter treated as the company's own property. Richard Garnett, a good friend of Charles Kegan Paul and a rising literary star, edited *Poems Selected from Percy Bysshe Shelley*. The remaining book in 1880 was an edition of a text that was particularly important to Charles Kegan Paul, *Of the Imitation of Christ*, by Thomas à Kempis.

Oddly enough, Paul had made his personal discovery of the Christian, and particularly Catholic, devotional classic after reading August Comte on the subject of Positivism. Later on, daily reading of the mystical meditation on the progress of a soul to Christian perfection, and eventually to union with God, did much to shape his conversion to Roman Catholicism. George Eliot had used Maggie Tulliver's encounter with the book to great effect in *The Mill on the Floss*. A few days before her death, Paul sent her a copy of the new edition, and her husband John Cross let him know that the book had been laid on her coffin. He discussed the text of the translation with Cardinals Manning and Newman. Paul was not, however, the editor or translator: the book is attributed to Frederick Apthorp Paley.

The year 1881 saw three further volumes, *English Odes* edited by Edmund Gosse, and Edgar Allen Poe's poems, edited, with an introductory essay, by Andrew Lang. Edward Dowden, a distinguished Shakespeare scholar and another friend of Paul's edited *Shakespere's Sonnets*. Each editor received £10 for his contribution. In 1883 there were seven more titles, and the series, as a series, began to attract serious attention: in the *St James*, in a February 1882 article on 'Bibliography and Bibliomania', Charles Kains-Jackson, referred to the editions of *In Memoriam* and *The Imitation of Christ*, which, 'in size, printing, and style leave *nothing* to desire, and are, at the same time, within the reach of a moderate purse. Classical works, they represent their publishers' judgment and taste.' The *Publishers' Circular*, in December 1884, called the Parchment Library 'a series of books which, whether as single volumes or in the set, will always be certain to please a cultured taste. The style in which they are produced makes them beautiful to the eye, and a very wise discrimination has marked the choice of the volumes honoured with a place on the list.'

One of the titles of 1883 was the beginning of a twelve-volume set, nothing less than an edition of Shakespeare's plays. These were prepared by Edward Dowden. As each successive volume appeared, the *Publishers' Circular* became more enthusiastic: on 15 June 1883, for the third volume, they remarked, 'If "good wine needs no bush", the "Parchment Library" certainly need no praise, although in typography, paper, and "get-up" – or should we say "absence of get-up" – it is worthy of the warmest praise.' And with the eleventh, on 15 September, 'Another volume of the dainty Parchment Library with its choice binding by Burn, and the imprint of the unrivalled Chiswick Press. If there is such a thing as gilding refining gold without offending against the laws of good taste it is when Shakspeare is thus presented.'

Some titles did better than others. Paul's friend Oscar Browning, the Cambridge historian whose contribution to the Education Library was selling poorly, offered to make an edition of Dante's *Divine Comedy*. But Paul replied

> Touching the Dante: we have had already several offers from competent persons to edit the Divine Comedy . . . but we have as yet been deterred for two reasons. 1. It is too long to go into a single volume in at all a pretty form of a page, in that series. 2. The foreign books in that series do not take in at all the same proportion as the others. Frank [Cornish]'s Horace has had a very limited sale, and the French Lyrics also are far behind most of the series. I wish it were not so for we should particularly have liked to bring out a good Dante.[29]

Frank Cornish was yet another Eton and Oxford friend of Paul's whose edition of *Q[uinti] Horatii Flacci opera* must have meant a great deal to both of them. In 1882 George Saintsbury had edited a volume of *French Lyrics*.

Much more successful, and even more of a consuming interest for Charles Kegan Paul personally, was his own edition, published in 1883, of *Living English Poets*. The preface is unsigned, but its tone is distinctly Paulian, and a letter to Algernon Swinburne confirms his involvement. The Publication Book records an unattributed payment of £20 for 'literary services'. The scholarly principle of selection was novel, in that an anthology of the work of writers still living was presented in order of their dates of birth: 'no casual or desultory assemblage of beautiful poems, but one which presents in chronological order examples of the highest attainment, and none but the highest, of the principal Poets of our own age'. The rule about living poets was adhered to rigorously: some poems of Dante Gabriel Rossetti had to be dropped at the last moment. Writing to Swinburne, Paul stressed that

> the Editors, persons who can be trusted will sedulously exclude all who are not Poets in the narrowest sense. The number of lines selected will be more from the greater, less from the lesser Poets, though there will not always be a strict numerical proportion. Thus it comes that we venture to ask your leave to incorporate a somewhat large number of your poems. . . . We shall have a large number of Mr Tennyson's Poems, including I think Rizpah, and Mr Matthew Arnold has given his cordial assent to our plan; and his permission to include all for which we asked.

All eight of the requested poems and selections appeared in the finished volume. Now that Robert Buchanan's works were safely off the company's list, and the unfortunate King imprint obliterated, Swinburne was willing to comply.

Austin Dobson was among the younger poets included in the anthology, but not Frederick Locker. The preface had explained that 'The present age has been particularly rich in facetious and fantastic verse, but the Editors of the present selection have only ventured to avail themselves of it sparingly, and where an underlying seriousness of purpose and a close attention to form seemed to give it more than an ephemeral value.' He wrote to Dobson, 'The sentence in the preface about *vers de société* was meant to soothe Locker. I shall be sorry if he be hurt, but is he a *Poet*? If we once brought in feeling one would have wished to include many. As I read the volume I think of no one whom I would include, & see two, at least, whom I would our Edition had kept out.'[30]

The partners took advantage of the closing months of their contract with Tennyson to publish a two-volume edition of his *Poems* in the Parchment Library in 1883. Austin Dobson edited Goldsmith's *The Vicar of Wakefield*, and Oswald Crawfurd an anthology of *English Comic Dramatists*, both in 1883. The series continued through the 1880s, with John Gay, John Milton and John Keats, the book of Psalms, a collection of *English Sacred Lyrics* and even *The Gospel According to Matthew, Mark and Luke*. In 1885 appeared Paul's own translation of *The Thoughts of Blaise Pascal*, translated from the text of Auguste Molinier. The standard fee to editors and translators was in this case varied, to a share-profits agreement. George Saintsbury edited *Specimens of English Prose Style from Malory to Macaulay* in 1885, and Chaucer's *Canterbury Tales* were presented the next year by yet another of Paul's friends, Alfred Pollard. Pollard would have liked to include Browning's play *Strafford* in the series, but Paul told him that, although Browning was an intimate friend of his, the firm of Smith, Elder nevertheless held the rights. And George Smith 'would not like any one else to poach on his preserves'.[31] The thirty-fourth title, and the last to appear under the Kegan Paul, Trench imprint was in 1888, *Selections from Wordsworth*, by William Knight and other members of the Wordsworth Society. But even under the new management of the limited company, Paul continued to manage the fortunes of the Parchment Library. The last title was in 1894, Jane Maria Strachey's *Poets on Poets*. 'In the dainty "Parchment Library" so charming a book finds a fitting home', commented *The Bookman* in January 1895.

With the Parchment Library, Paul came as close as he ever did to reconciling, in his publishing work, the diverse aspects of his personality: his aesthetic sensitivity was gratified by the beautiful 'get-up' of the volumes; his intellectual interests were served by organizing good scholarly editions of important works; and his business instincts also flourished: if Dante would not sell, then no edition of *The Divine Comedy* could be included. The series also created the opportunity for him to help the young poets and scholars who were his best London friends.

PULPIT COMMENTARY

Despite the austere charms of the Parchment Library, their bibliophilic and scholarly quality does not encompass the full range of the Kegan Paul, Trench imprint. A second series was initiated in 1880, one with a very different mandate, focus and market. The Positivist ex-parson and the Archbishop's son were now promoting The Pulpit Commentary.

In contrast to the 'dainty' parchment and vellum of the literary series, and the aggressively modern black-stamped red cloth of the International Scientific Series, both in small formats, the Pulpit Commentary ran, eventually, to forty-nine magisterial volumes. These were so massive that when a representative of the firm tried to sell the series in Australia, in 1899, he found that the district clergymen in Melbourne had 'such small houses that the introduction of 49 substantial volumes would be a serious inconvenience to their comfort'.[32] Each volume ran to about 24 × 15 cm, and five to six hundred pages, cloth-bound in blue with marbelled edges and endpapers. The studies of English clergymen, for whom the series was originally contemplated, could accommodate it easily, however. Paul may have remembered Sunday mornings in Sturminster Marshall when a well-organized commentary organized according to the books of the Bible, and broken down into references for each chapter and each verse, would have been invaluable.

The Pulpit Commentary had been initiated by the Rev. J.S. Exell, the author of *Thirty Thousand Thoughts*. His specialty was preaching. Four volumes of his 'new commentary of the Bible' had already been published, and two more were finished to the point of being committed to stereotype plates, when he signed an initial agreement with C. Kegan Paul & Co., as it then was, on 17 February 1881. The existing books would be assigned to the company, and the £2,000 he had already spent would be repaid by 1888. Kegan Paul would continue to publish the Commentary, paying Exell £100 for editing each volume, plus a royalty of one shilling per copy sold up to 2,500, and then 1s 6d for copies over that number. Profits for sales in America would be divided equally between the editor and the publishers. An assistant editor, the Reverend Canon H.D.M. Spence, would receive a ten guinea fee for each volume (and a further 10 guineas after 2,500 copies were sold), and the various contributors would also be paid. The net price per volume was 12s 6d.

Each volume had a general title-page giving the names and positions of Exell and Spence, and the names of the authors of the introductions. This series title-page was dated. The individual volume title-page started with the series title and editors' names again, then the 'title', which was simply the name of the Bible book or books under consideration. Authors of the introductions, of exposition and homiletics and of homilies were then named. After a lengthy general introduction and an introduction to the book being discussed, each Bible book was divided into sections, by chapter and verse. Each section had a two-column Exposition, a brief introduction on the character of the text. Genesis, for example, was characterized as not history, not science or myth, but revelation. Then followed detailed exposition of the text, one phrase at a time, then homiletics (applications), and finally homilies by various authors, that is, the texts of sermons. For each Bible book there was a bibliography.

The books appeared between 1881 and 1897, Old Testament books followed by New Testament books, although not in strict canonical order. The Pulpit Commentary involved Kegan Paul, Trench in printing the text of the Bible, and specifically of the Revised Version of the New Testament, which was completed in 1881. They therefore had to sign a licensing agreement with the Vice-Chancellors of Oxford and Cambridge Universities, since the Universities were 'proprietors of the Copyright in the Book entitled "The New Testament of Our Lord and Saviour Jesus Christ translated out of the Greek being the Version set forth A.D. 1611 compared with the most ancient authorities and revised A.D. 1881" herein after called the Revised Version.' This involved a token payment of one guinea per volume.

By the time the final volumes on Psalms and Daniel appeared in 1897, Exell had been with the firm for seventeen years and had seen two changes in management. In February 1886 Trench had persuaded him that it was 'rather onerous' for the publishers to pay double when a single book of scripture ran into two volumes of commentary, and a fee of £150 for two-volume books was arrived at. At the same time Exell agreed to forego royalties, receiving instead a payment of £1,200. And, as we shall see, in 1896 the limited company then using the Kegan Paul imprint made an agreement to furnish plates to Funk and Wagnall's in New York, in exchange for royalties on copies printed in the United States.

Paul says nothing about the Pulpit Commentary in *Memories*, and the only record of the firm's initial dealings with Exell is the contract itself, and some acrimonious correspondence in 1893–4 when Exell felt he was being deprived of royalties due to him. The series was a very significant investment, and also a source of profit. But those profits were slow to reach the firm during the 1880s, when the Pulpit Commentary was appearing volume by volume. Unlike the International Scientific Series or the Parchment Library, it was a finite series, limited in terms of content by the books of the Bible, and controlled editorially by Exell's scholarly decisions. This meant much less involvement in the textual history of the series for Charles Kegan Paul and Alfred Chenevix Trench. But it was very much a part of the commercial history of their publishing business.[33]

EDUCATION LIBRARY

If the Pulpit Commentary looked back to the traditional scholarship of scriptural exegesis, the Education Library looked forward, towards the professionalization of pedagogy. In 1880, when primary, secondary and university education, as well as technical training, were the subject of Royal Commissions, reforms and debate, the series must have looked like a viable proposition. The collection amounted to only five volumes, however, appearing between 1881 and 1888, and although some individual titles are significant in the history of education, the series made no mark as a series. In fact, as Paul wrote to contributor Oscar Browning in June 1883, 'the Education Library has proved a very unfortunate failure'. But because Browning kept tenaciously in touch with his publishers about the progress of his contribution, and Browning's college preserved his voluminous papers, the series' history may now be reconstructed.[34]

The Education Library, like the Pulpit Commentary, had an editor who was named, cited and paid for his part in the process.

The publishers may have learned from problems they experienced in the management of the International Scientific Series, where a three-member committee supervised the editorship without title-page attribution, and without any clear understanding of their duties and responsibilities. This time the editor was Philip Magnus, a pioneer in the field of technical education. Magnus directed the City and Guilds of London Institute, and was principal of the Finsbury Technical Institute, the first college for technological studies in England.[35] The series included Magnus's book *Industrial Education* (1888), but its scope was much broader, the theory, history and practice of education in all its aspects.

Magnus 'having procured a number of gentlemen to contribute separate works to the Series', as the agreement put it, was to receive £60 for the first edition of 2,000 copies of each volume and pay his contributor out of that sum; the issue of further printings from the stereotype plates would generate additional payments. The price per volume was lower than for the International Scientific Series, since no illustrations were involved: 3s 6d. But to publish at this price Kegan Paul insisted on limiting the texts to 208 printed pages, using the International Scientific Series as a model for size and design. As usual an American publisher was offered and accepted the series. This time it was Harper and Brothers. There was still no international copyright agreement in place, and as they told Browning years later, their payments bought them no more than 'a few days' priority in the publication; and in consideration of that priority by the use of advance sheets, we paid Twenty pounds'.[36]

Browning's contribution, *An Introduction to the History of Educational Theories*, 1881, launched the series. Browning was a fellow of King's College, Cambridge. He and Paul were old friends, with a correspondence dating back to 1860 when they had worked together at Eton. Browning had been forced to leave Eton in 1875 as a result of a scandal involving accusations of sexual misconduct, and Paul had written to him kindly, assuring Browning that his reputation was unstained, at least in the London circle he frequented, and recommending a Knightsbridge bookseller to handle the removal of Browning's collection of 7,000 books.[37] By 1881 he had settled into his Cambridge post, developing a reputation as historian as well as educational reformer, but finding his career blocked by what biographer Ian Anstruther calls 'a deeply held suspicion' that 'he was not serious'.[38]

Magnus, presumably, solicited Browning's contribution, but Paul involved himself in the production of the book, correcting the manuscript and corresponding with Browning about details. 'Surely,' he chided his friend, 'you cannot say [on p. 45 line 23] that the curriculum of the Middle Ages included the mathematics of Newton, and the science of Herbert Spencer. In the first place it is only misleading to use these modern names, and in the next Herbert Spencer is not a man pre-eminently of Science.'[39] And once the book was out, Browning initiated a correspondence with both Paul and Magnus, and later with Paul's successors and with the American and Canadian publishers, in which he insisted on further and larger payments for his book.

The remaining books in the series were much less trouble, if no more successful. Simon Laurie, another distinguished educationalist (or, the contributors asked each other, should it be educationist?), based in the University of Edinburgh, wrote a biographical study. *John Amos Comenius, Bishop of the Moravians: His Life and Educational Works* came out in 1881. By June of 1883 the initial 2,000 copies were sold, but Laurie found Kegan Paul, Trench and Co. reluctant to put a reprint in hand. He told Browning, 'The reprinting of Comenius is transferred to the hands of Mr Magnus who is naturally much annoyed by the action of Kegan Paul. Until he has done his best therefore I shall take no further action.' Magnus's best, however, did not move the London publishers, and the book eventually went to the Pitt Press of Cambridge University Press. Laurie had anticipated the possibility:

> The book, however, is so honest and exhaustive a statement of all that Comenius did & is the result of so much tedious labour on my part that I cannot allow it to go out of print. I need scarcely say that I would prefer to see it emanate from the Pitt Press rather than from any Publishing House and . . . I do not think the Pitt Press would lose by it although I am well aware that the sale of such books is slow.

Browning had apparently shared with Laurie his view that Kegan Paul, Trench were 'unsatisfactory publishers'. Laurie agreed:

'Kegan Paul seem to take a purely money view of everything.' Philip Magnus, as series editor, seems to have been caught between his irascible authors and his disappointed publishers. In October 1881, as soon as *Educational Theories* had appeared (just barely in time for the start of the University term, which was important for marketing) he forwarded to Browning £45 of the £60 honorarium for this title, and later an additional £5.

Only three more books appeared in the series, and a further six that had been advertised never materialized.[40] In print were *Old Greek Education* (1881) by J.P. Mahaffy, *School Management* by Joseph Landon (1883) and finally Magnus's own *Industrial Education* (1888). Looking at the titles that appeared, and those that didn't, it is easy with hindsight to see that the series was too eclectic, and too theoretical, to appeal to teachers themselves, and that the market among educational generalists was a small one. Simon Laurie remarked in an 1883 letter to Browning, 'It is uphill work trying to persuade educationalists that they should study Education.' In some ways, too, the series was ahead of its time. As Browning's correspondence with the firm extended into the 1890s and past the turn of the century, the management began to tell him that his book, still in print, occasionally reprinted, had become 'a classic'. In 1909, B.W. Willett told Browning how gratifying it was to know the book was being used in Servia [*sic*], although 'it certainly seems unfortunate that it should be most appreciated in the countries where the rights cannot be or have not been protected'.

MILITARY HANDBOOKS FOR OFFICERS AND NON-COMMISSIONED OFFICERS

Five years after Willett's letter to Browning, the assassination, in Serbia, of Archduke Ferdinand heralded the beginning of the First World War and the end of Britain's nineteenth-century military amateurism. In 1883, however, when Kegan Paul, Trench initiated a series of handbooks for army officers, interest in military subjects was limited to a specialized audience. The series editor was Charles Booth Brackenbury (1831–90), a specialist in artillery training, a lieutenant-colonel in the Royal Army, and a veteran of the Crimea. He had been military correspondent for *The Times* during the Franco-Prussian war. Although Brackenbury's editorship began in 1883, with a payment of £120 in connection with C. Pratt Sisson's *Field Artillery*, two books published earlier were incorporated into the series, *Military Sketching and Reconnaissance* (Hutchison and MacGregor, 1878) and *The Elements of Modern Tactics* (Wilkinson J. Shaw, 1879). Following Sisson's book there were volumes on military administration and military law, and in 1884 a contribution from Alfred Trench's brother, Frederick Chenevix Trench, *Cavalry in Modern War* (1884). After a seventh volume, Brackenbury's own *Field Works* (1888) the series appeared to have terminated. The firm changed hands the following year, and Brackenbury died in 1890. However, as we shall see, the series was revised in 1897, with a new editor and a further ten titles. Some volumes in this first segment of series are remarkable for their endurance. The second was reprinted a dozen times, the third eight times, and the fifth, C. Pratt Sisson's *Military Law*, eighteen times; the last reissue occurred in 1910 just before the merger of Kegan Paul with Routledge.

Charles Kegan Paul and Alfred Chenevix Trench were highly skilled at publishing and marketing books in the series form. Some of their best-known titles appeared within the shelter of a series format. Their relations with series editors brought them into contact with leaders in scientific, religious and military circles: Huxley, Tyndall and Spencer of the International Scientific Series; Exell of the Pulpit Commentary; Magnus of the Education Library; and Brackenbury of the Military Handbooks. Each of these was a series of new books, specially commissioned, where the conditions of authorship were shaped by the commercial and literary exigencies of the series format. This places them in contradistinction to those series of reprint fiction so popular with their contemporary publishers.[41] The reprints of classics in The Parchment Library were in a separate class from the profitable but competitive reprint market, in which Kegan Paul, Trench only dabbled, with their Colonial Library.

The Colonial Library was the firm's series of reprint fiction. The binding was distinctive, a crisp red cloth with the title, author's name and an ornament (a wine goblet, or sometimes a bunch of oak leaves and acorns) picked out in gold. At the tops and bottoms of the covers was a border, a wide band with a floral pattern and

Table 6 Types of contracts issued under the three imprints

	H.S. KING 1871–7		C. KEGAN PAUL 1877-81		KEGAN PAUL, TRENCH 1881-1888		TOTALS	%
	NO.	%	NO.	%	NO.	%		
Commission	202	29.8	218	50.3	562	57.5	982	47.0
Sale of Copyright	184	27.2	52	12.0	109	11.1	345	16.5
Reserved Royalty	68	10.0	80	18.5	163	16.7	311	14.9
Share Profits	108	16.0	22	5.1	10	1.0	140	6.7
Royalty	32	4.7	25	5.8	54	5.5	111	5.3
Series	23	3.4	20	4.6	40	4.1	83	4.0
unidentified	35	5.2	5	1.2	37	3.8	77	3.7
not published	25	3.7	11	2.5	3	0.3	39	1.9
Totals	677	100	433	100	978	100	2,088	100

two black rules. The series was treated as a series in the Publication Books and Publication Account Books. The odd thing is that it does not seem to have been marketed as a series, but simply to have emerged in a uniform format. There are no lists or advertisements, even in copies of the books themselves. The 'series' started with a reissue of George MacDonald's novel *Malcolm* in 1887; it included many other books by MacDonald, other works previously published by the firm, by Jean Ingelow and 'Maxwell Grey', as well as several novels whose first appearance had been with other publishers. It is impossible to be more precise, because the Colonial Library (sometimes referred to as the Indian and Colonial Library) is a bibliographical morass: even the series binding is not always identical from one book to the next. It amounted to about forty volumes, from 1887 until about 1896. Nor is it possible to give a definitive explanation of why the Colonial Library was not marketed as a series. Perhaps Paul and Trench capitulated, in the late eighties, to a form of publishing they had previously eschewed, but which they identified as a source of rich profits to their contemporaries. Their reluctance to advertise may have had to do with contractual arrangements between them and the original publishers of some of the Colonial Library novels, but no documents have survived to confirm this speculation.[42] In any case, their preference was clearly for publishing, in series format, serious original non-fiction works of high quality.

IV

Books in series were, as the *Publishers' Circular* once put it, 'sustained literary ventures'. Individual titles, transitory literary ventures, were riskier, if more exciting and interesting projects. The excitement and interest were shaped by the literary taste of the publishing partners, and their perception of the public taste, while the degree of risk they undertook was determined by the kinds of contracts they signed. As Charles Kegan Paul had explained in his essay 'The Production and Life of Books', contracts could be divided into purchase of copyright agreements, royalty arrangements including shared profits, and commission publishing.

PURCHASE OF COPYRIGHT

Only 12% of Kegan Paul, Trench books were what the company's records described as 'own' books, where for one reason or another the company owned the copyright and could print as often as they wished, in whatever form they wished, without any further recompense to the author after the initial payment of a lump sum. Nevertheless this 12% comprised 161 titles, and these included some of the best-known books associated with the firm.

Paul approved of outright copyright purchase for 'ordinary novels', and the records demonstrate that he used it; to the limited extent that such books were published by his and Trench's firm. George Meredith's *The Egoist* was published that way, and so were the George Macdonald novels that Paul continued to publish after King's retirement. Books for children, by juvenile authors Nancy Meugens (known as N.R. D'Anvers) and Isabel Reaney, normally became the company's own property. The 'Last Journals of General Gordon', as Paul referred to his grand gesture in 1885, represented at 5,000 guineas the largest amount spent by the firm on a copyright. In fact historical and biographical works were, in general, more likely than other non-fiction subjects to be purchased by the publishers.

Another trend can be discerned: books written or edited by people associated with the firm often went on the records as 'own' titles, rather than under royalty or share arrangements. Margaret Agnes Paul sold her copyrights to her husband's firm, for sums of £75 and £50. Harriet Eleanor Hamilton King, whose poetry continued to be published by Kegan Paul after her husband's death, usually sold them the entire copyright, making it possible for them to reprint individual poems in collections like the *Living English Poets*. Paul's *Biographical Sketches* (1883) was the property of the firm, although most of his other books were a matter of shared profits.

In some cases it was the publisher who conceived of and planned a book, and then selected someone to write or edit it. Arthur Pollard, whose ill-paid work at the British Museum was supplemented by editorial work supplied by Paul, produced *Victorian Hymns: English sacred songs of fifty years* in 1887, anonymously, for a fee of ten guineas. The book gave Paul the opportunity to write to Mr Gladstone, the Prime Minister: 'After H.M. the Queen, who has graciously accepted the Dedication of Victorian Hymns, there is no one to whom we feel more pleasure in offering a copy than to yourself, whose interest in the literature of which this is a specimen is so well known.'[43]

One more group of books for which the publishers owned the copyright, at least in Britain, was those purchased already printed from the United States. In most cases the books were obtained in printed sheets and bound in London, usually with cancel title-pages bearing the imprint of the firm. Paul and Trench regularly arranged for American publishers to bring out their books. There was a brisk trade in both directions. Until the 1891 copyright legislation in the United States put an end to literary piracy, publishers on both sides of the ocean who preferred to give their transatlantic colleagues, as well as their authors, at least token recompense for sales in the other country commonly made this sort of arrangement. After 1891, the American legislation that protected the literary property of foreign authors was dependent on their books being printed in the United States, a stipulation that put an end to the trade in printed sheets.

Alfred Chenevix Trench's visit to New England in 1883 resulted in several agreements for his firm to be the English publishers of books published and printed in the United States. Houghton, Mifflin of Boston and New York had just published George DeLong's *The Voyage of the Jeannette: the Ship and Ice Journals*, edited by Emma DeLong, in 1883; it came out in England the same year, under the Kegan Paul, Trench imprint. More memorable was Trench's acquisition from the same company of *The Complete Works of Nathaniel Hawthorne* in twelve volumes to be sold for 7s 6d each, also in 1883. The Hawthorne bibliography describes this as the 'Kegan Paul Edition', that is the English issue of the Riverside Edition of Hawthorne's works, using American sheets with cancel titles (printed by Houghton, Mifflin) in Kegan Paul binding. Only 250 copies were involved, at a price the American publishers regarded as very low, 62½ cents per copy.[44] Another Houghton, Mifflin book published by Kegan Paul in 1884 was 262 copies of *James Fenimore Cooper* by T.R. Lounsbury. And in 1886 the relationship was still in place. Five cases of the sheets of Theodore Roosevelt's *Hunting Trips of a Ranchman: Sketches of Sport on the Northern Cattle Plains* were received from Houghton, Mifflin and published in London.

SHARED PROFIT AND ROYALTY CONTRACTS, INCLUDING RESERVE AND CONTRIBUTION AGREEMENTS

Although Henry S. King had purchased numerous copyrights, he also agreed to share profits with many of his authors. This was how he acquired the right to publish the one-volume six-shilling edition of Hardy's *A Pair of Blue Eyes* in 1877; it was the standard arrangement for translations, for books in the classical languages, and for Stopford Brooke's sermons and essays. But when the C. Kegan Paul and then Kegan Paul, Trench imprints succeeded King's, the proportion of share-profit contracts declined, from 16% to 5% of the total, while royalty agreements remained nearly the same, at about 5%.

It was unusual for a royalty to be paid from the beginning, since the company wished to recover the cost of typesetting (and stereotype if that was done), of printing an initial run of several hundred to several thousand copies in sheets, and binding enough copies for review and for the expected initial demand. When Susan Dawson brought the second volume of George Dawson's *Sermons on Daily Life and Duty* and his *Sermons on Disputed Points and Special Occasions* to the firm in 1878, they published both at six shillings. After a reserve of 500 copies of each title had been disposed of, Mrs Dawson began to collect a royalty of two shillings per copy, or one-third of the selling price. But she had to wait until the initial 'reserve' was sold. In many cases, that number was never reached.

Dawson's sermons sold steadily to a loyal but limited, and declining, public. A book like Richard Burton's *Gold Mines of Midian* (1878) would make a more dramatic one-time impact, and it evoked a more generous, but still cautious agreement. Kegan Paul paid Burton £100, and then promised a two-thirds share in the profits after a reserve of 750 copies had been sold. The following year, *Land of Midian, Revisited* earned Burton £150, but this sum was counted as an advance on his two-thirds share of the profits, which would begin to accrue after the reserved 650 copies were gone.

Neither Susan Dawson nor Richard and Isabel Burton, however, expected to have to contribute to the publication of their own books. They were, or in Dawson's case they represented, established authors, part of whose living was made by writing books. In other cases, profits were to be shared, or royalties paid, not merely after a reserve number of copies were sold, but only if the author guaranteed the sale of that number. Charles Kegan Paul took his annual holiday with Edmund Gosse, and he admired Gosse's poetry. But *New Poems*, in 1879, came out in an edition of 500 copies, of which Gosse had to guarantee the sale of 250 within twelve months. In 1882 the University College London professor of law, Sheldon Amos, offered the firm his *History and Principles of the Civil Law of Rome; an Aid to the Study of Scientific and Comparative Jurisprudence*. Kegan Paul published the book in 1883, 750 copies at a selling price of 16s. Of these, Amos guaranteed the sale of 400 at 10s 6d, up to a maximum of £50; however if the 400 were sold he would collect a 5s royalty. Corrections to the proofs, above a certain minimum would, as usual, be charged to the author. Amos had to pay over £16 for excess corrections, and, in 1884, the price of ninety-five unbound copies. One last example is H.M. Hyndman, the first spokesperson in England for Marxian socialism. The publication of Hyndman's 1885 book *The Historical Basis of Socialism in England* is one of the landmarks in the history of the Social Democratic Federation and eventually of the Labour Party. But its political and textual significance was not reflected in its commercial history. One thousand copies were published, to be sold at 6 shillings; Hyndman guaranteed that if fewer than 650 were sold in eighteen months he would pay for the balance at the rate of 3s 4d unbound. He later purchased 182 copies. Arrangements of this kind did not account for the firm's entire stock of such books: small numbers of bound and unbound copies were kept in the warehouse for years, and gradually brought in monies to supplement the author's original contribution.

When authors guaranteed Kegan Paul against loss on their books, they did not have to pay until after the loss was a reality. At the time when Amos and Hyndman made their arrangements with the publishers, they must have hoped, perhaps even expected, that they would soon be collecting from the firm, not paying out. Another class of authors was required to contribute to the cost of publishing their books as a condition of acceptance. The philosopher F.H. Bradley made this kind of a deal with King in 1876, and again with Kegan Paul, Trench in 1883. *Ethical Studies* cost him £45, for which he received six free copies and the promise of royalties after the sale of 200; *The Principles of Logic* required a contribution of £100. Bradley was a serious, mainstream scholar, although never a fashionable one. His books remained in print for many years, and eventually recouped their costs; second editions of both eventually appeared, from the Clarendon Press at Oxford, in 1927 and 1922 respectively. One more writer whose reputation took a long time to develop was Walter Bagehot, who died in 1877. In 1883 his widow Eliza Bagehot offered the firm his *Essays on Parliamentary Reform*. She contributed £50 for an edition of 1,000 copies, on which she would receive royalties after 230 were sold.

When authors contributed to the cost of producing their books, or had to make good their guarantee to purchase a reserve number of copies, they, not the publishers, were taking the risk. Their books appeared at their own expense, which meant that the power of the publishing decision was reversed. Instead of saying that Kegan Paul decided to publish Amos or Bradley, we have to say that these authors decided that the Kegan Paul imprint was right for their books. This important class of titles added to the lustre of the publisher's list, and in some cases to their profits. Significantly, the publisher's reputation for serious books may well have been a factor in an author's determination to pay for the privilege of appearing under the imprint.

COMMISSION BOOKS

No such ambiguity was involved in commission publishing. In those cases, Paul had written, 'the writer bears the whole expense, the book belongs to him, the publisher taking a certain commission on the sales'. Apart from serving authors like Archbishop Trench, who preferred to control the production of their own very profitable works, commission publishing created a wide field for Victorian obsessions, idiosyncrasies and eccentricities to flourish in print.

Hundreds of commission books fill the Kegan Paul list. More than half the books the firm published were sponsored directly by their authors in this way. The difficulty is that the vast majority of them are altogether obscure: nothing is known about Miss E. Bond, the author of *Dolores*. Nothing is known about Edward Gough, a congregational minister of Barrowford, near Nelson in Lancashire, either, except that two letters from him to the firm are among the surviving documents. Edward Gough commissioned Kegan Paul to publish his projected multi-volume work, *The Bible True from the Beginning: Designed as a commentary on all those portions of Scripture that are most questioned and assailed.* Gough presumably expected his book to be consulted as frequently as the Pulpit Commentary, but unlike Exell he had to agree to pay a 5 guinea fee for each volume, in addition to printing and binding costs and a percentage commission on sales. Gough began the great work, and in May 1888 *The Bookman* reviewed Volume VI: 'There is something irresistibly pathetic in the spectacle of a learned man issuing a work in eight large volumes to illustrate a theory which will certainly not find acceptance by any mind but the author's.' Despite this discouragement, Gough had brought out eight volumes by 1903 and had four more ready. He wrote to Kegan Paul, Trench, Trübner as the firm then was, that he had now 'come to an age when I cannot expect to do more expository work. I must rather turn my attention to getting through the press what I have written.' He continued, observing that 'Thus far the work has not met with much favour from the press or the public. Reviewers put down to my account difficulties which I believe to be owing to the fulness of Scripture. None of them have given any attention to the question whether there is or is not a gradal system in Scripture, as the gnostic Christians alleged . . . Even if my means would allow me to go straight on with the publication . . . which they will not, it is probable that the new volumes would just meet with the same treatment as the old ones.' Gough's proposed solution was to commission his publishers to bring out yet another book, which he estimated would be about 320 pages, entitled *With Singing unto Zion, and Miscellaneous Poems*, as a form of advertisement to *Bible True* ('it may help to beat down prejudice'), as well as to raise money for the remaining four volumes. The preface to the poems would reiterate his theory, and challenge the National Federation of Free Church Councils to establish a committee to test the question, using the Book of Joshua for the test. Nine volumes of *Bible True* appeared, and so did the *Poems*. For Gough, commission publishing through Kegan Paul, Trench was a worthwhile expense, essential to the self-evident importance of circulating his views in the world.

Edward Gough, like Charles Kegan Paul, was in deadly earnest about theology and about the rituals appropriate for use in English churches. 'The Prig' took a lighter view of these questions. Thomas Longueville began writing under the pseudonym 'the Prig', in 1885, with a commission agreement for Kegan Paul, Trench to publish *The Life of a Prig. By One*. The estimate for 750 copies was £20 for composition, printing and publishing, 7d per copy for binding an initial 250, a further £20 for advertising and a two guinea fee. Other 'Prig' books, all published on commission, followed. In 1886 there was an 'expurgated, expounded and exposed' version of *The Venerable Bede*, better known as 'The Prig's Bede', and in 1887 *How to Make a Saint: or the process of canonization in the Church of England.* By 1888 Longueville was ready to commission a combined edition, *The Prigment*, which included all the books already published plus *The Churchgress*, a satirical account of the Church Congress of 1887.

Commission publishing, whether it carried Gough's high seriousness, 'the Prig's' arch humour, or philosophy, politics or poetry, gave the Victorians a vehicle for self-expression. Or for self concealment. One final example is found in another of the few letters from commission authors found in the Kegan Paul archives: Claude Reignier Conder (1848–1910). Conder does not, however, rank among the unknown. He had other reasons for publishing on commission.

Conder published three books with the firm: In 1881 there was *Rabbi Jeshua: An Eastern Story*; it was described by the *Academy* as 'A very clever attempt at a rationalistic life of Christ.' *Bible Folk Lore* (1884), subtitled 'A Study in Comparative Mythology', was 'an attempt to apply the principle of evolution to the history of Hebrew and Christian belief'. Conder – or rather the anonymous 'Author of "Rabbi Jeshua"' as the title-page identified him – concluded that the books 'bound in the English Bible . . . [were] but part of the great library of Sacred Books of the East'. And his *Paul of Tarsus*, published by George Redway in 1889 and brought into the amalgamated firm, was another biography, this time of St Paul, that took nothing for granted. It incorporated the same sceptical, rationalistic and radical thinking, an attempt to come to terms with biblical criticism and with new findings about the holy land in the fields of history, literature and archaeology. 'Mankind has recognized [Paul's] proper place in history', the author observed. 'Buddha and Jesus have been made gods; Paul has never been more than a saint.' Claude Reignier Conder became a colonel in the royal engineers, well known for his work in the exploration of Palestine and deciphering of its ancient languages, and author of several popular books based on his experience. But Conder's identified publications include none of the three works published by Kegan Paul. Instead these works are attributed to the political economist James E.T. Rogers, presumably because Rogers published an anonymous book, in 1872, entitled *Paul of Tarsus*.[45]

In 1884, when Conder was thirty-five years old and in the midst of a very successful career, his contract commissioning Kegan Paul, Trench to publish his second anonymous book, *Bible Folk Lore*, specified that 'the author's name will not be divulged without his consent'. Conder's experience with publishing ('I have some experience in the matter from 12 years of literary work') shows up in his confident handling of the details of typeface and advertising. Five years later, Conder told George Redway that he was the author of *Paul of Tarsus*, the incomplete manuscript of which had been sent to London by a colleague, and continued.

> You will no doubt regard this information as Confidential. Not being in the Church there is of course no real bar to my acknowledging the authorship of this or other works at any time when I see fit and considering the sums I receive for work defined by my name, I do not think the sale would be thereby damaged. My reason is a purely private one. I have relations and kind friends who would be much pained by thinking I held such views. My published works bear of course no reference to religion but they contain I think not a word which clashes with my views which are well known to those who agree with me and in whom I have confidence. Your letter shews that in event of agreement you expect such confidence.

Conder's letter reveals a Victorian man of science, holding advanced views that he wished to share with sympathetic others, while at the same time wishing to protect his family from the distress of anxiety about his immortal soul. Anonymous publication was the answer. He asked whether Redway had 'suspected the real author as several people claimed R. Jeshua'. A month later a contract was hammered out for *Paul of Tarsus*. Conder told Redway that 'Mr K. Paul has kept my secret faithfully.' He also referred to reviews of *Rabbi Jeshua*. 'I do not mean that the reviews are favourable because the writers evidently hated the book but they shew it attracted attention and now I think the public mind is a little more open.' One review was by Conder's own father, Francis Roubiliac Conder, 'who never suspected the authorship'. The senior Conder had collaborated with the junior in 1879 on a *Handbook to the Bible*, and it may be significant that he died in 1889, the same year that Conder began to think about

Table 7 Gender of the author in the publication books. Total number of titles and percentage of total output are entered in parentheses for each genre

A) BY TYPE OF CONTRACT

	MEN	WOMEN	UNIDENTIFIED
Commission (982, 47.0%)	82.8%	13.1%	4.1%
Sale of Copyright (345, 16.5%)	77.4%	19.1%	3.5%
Reserved Royalty (311, 14.9%)	75.6%	21.9%	2.6%
Share Profits (140, 6.7%)	75.7%	22.1%	2.1%
Royalty (111, 5.3%)	69.4%	28.8%	1.8%
Series (83, 4.0%)	98.8%	1.2%	0.0%
unidentified (77, 3.7%)	59.7%	26.0%	14.3%
not published (39, 1.9%)	89.7%	0.0%	10.3%
Totals (2,088)	**79.5%**	**16.6%**	**3.8%**

B) BY GENRE OF TITLE

	MEN	WOMEN	UNIDENTIFIED
Theology, Sermons, Biblical (367, 17.6%)	91.8%	6.5%	1.6%
Education, Philosophy, Classics (102, 4.9%)	88.2%	8.8%	2.9%
Juvenile (23, 1.1%)	17.4%	82.6%	0.0%
Novels (184, 8.8%)	45.1%	53.8%	1.1%
Law, Jurisprudence (16, 0.8%)	93.8%	0.0%	6.3%
Political and Social Economy, and Trade and Commerce (162, 7.8%)	90.7%	4.3%	4.9%
Art, Science and Fine Arts (163, 7.8%)	95.2%	4.3%	0.6%
Travel and Geographical Research (132, 6.3%)	82.6%	10.6%	6.8%
History and Biography (181, 8.7%)	76.8%	21.0%	2.2%
Poetry and Drama (350, 16.8%)	73.4%	22.0%	4.6%
Year book and bound volumes of series (1, 0%)	100%	0.0%	0.0%

Table 7 – cont.

	MEN	WOMEN	UNIDENTIFIED
Medicine and Surgery (42, 2.0%)	85.7%	9.5%	4.8%
Belles-lettres (104, 5.0%)	81.7%	12.5%	5.8%
Misc., Including pamphlets (not sermons) (261, 12.5%)	77.8%	13.8%	8.4%
Totals	**79.5%**	**16.6%**	**3.8%**

publishing the half-finished *Paul of Tarsus*. Here we have a classic Victorian double life: the public Conder was a pious and filial professional soldier, who published his scholarly and popular books with John Murray and A.P. Watt as well as through the Palestine Exploration Fund. But the private Conder was a different sort of public figure, the mysterious 'author of the *Rabbi Jeshua*'.

Now that the secret is revealed, over one hundred years later, there is no particular interest in who wrote *Rabbi Jeshua*, or in Conder or his alter-ego James Rogers, to whom librarians have attributed the books. But there is an abiding interest in the psychology of the Victorians, in the relationship of sons and daughters with their parents, in the tensions created within families by doubt and unbelief. We are also interested in the way that reputations, both professional and personal, were created, in the ways they could be damaged or destroyed by scandal, and in the ways they could be protected by such conventions as the customary cloak of anonymity. The evidence of Claude Conder's letters casts a little light on all these matters, and at the same time it illuminates thoroughly the central importance of commission publishing in the literary and business interests of the Kegan Paul managers.

V

The question of sorting the firm's authors by gender is quickly dealt with. Table 7 shows that more than 80% were men, and fewer than 20% women.[46] When the gender of the authors is examined in relation to the genre of their books, it appears that women were a majority only in writing for children and in fiction, and the proportion of women's books within a genre exceeded their overall share only in history, poetry, *belles lettres* and miscellaneous pamphlets. Only in royalty and series contract agreements did their share of the number differ significantly from the norm. Royalty agreements were frequently used for novels, while women were excluded almost totally from the networks that formed around the editors of scientific and other series. Although women wrote a number of biographies and memoirs, and a few books in the category of *belles lettres*, only one woman was asked to edit a book in the Parchment Library.

The two publishing practices that stand out from this analysis of almost twenty years and over two thousand books are the predominance of books published on commission and the importance of the edited, non-fiction series. Both characterize the ways in which Paul and Trench, and King before them, differed from the typical practices of the trade, publishing fewer novels, juvenile books and yearbooks, and many more works of science, of theology, and of poetry and literature. These findings should be useful for the critical and bibliographical study of individual authors and series, alerting scholars to the cultural and economic context in which particular books appeared. As for publishing historians seeking to place the firm in the context of the Victorian book trade, the predominance of commission publishing is conspicuously important, ranking equally with Paul's literary preferences, and King's romance with poetry.

Commission publishing, and other methods by which the author took the risk, made sense for Kegan Paul, Trench because their firm was operating with limited capital. They could not afford to finance all the books they would have liked to publish, in the elegant form that Paul, at least, admired. Nor could most of their colleagues in Paternoster Square, other publishers who were their competitors in the London book trade. And those who could afford large lump-sum payments for copyrights, such as Chatto & Windus, attracted the popular authors, such as Robert Louis Stevenson. But Paul's experience, his basis for comparing business practices, was not with other ordinary publishers but with his exceptional predecessor, Henry S. King. He may not have realized, or it may have taken him a long time to learn, that he was never going to have the kind of money that had been available to fund King's ambitious programme of publishing.

CHAPTER 4
KEGAN PAUL, TRENCH, TRÜBNER & CO. LTD.: A FINANCIAL CRISIS AND A REVOLUTION IN MANAGEMENT, 1889–1911

I

Charles Kegan Paul, reflecting in *Memories* on the financial limitations of his quarter-century career in the book trade, observed 'that publishing is not by any means the ready road to wealth that many people think it is, and that it is very inexpedient for any one without a large capital and considerable literary skill to enter such a business. Supposing, however, any one to have the capital and the literary skill,' he continued, 'I can imagine no more interesting work.' Paul certainly regarded himself as having plenty of literary skill: what was missing was the 'large capital'. Henry S. King had swashbuckled through the seventies, investing his mercantile wealth in copyrights; now, on the eve of the 1890s, Paul became involved with another larger-than-life entrepreneur of publishing, Horatio William Bottomley. Paul first met Bottomley in 1888 or 1889 when the promoter called upon him with an invitation to become a member of the board of directors of a small printing company, Macrae, Curtice and Co. Ltd.[1] Macrae, Curtice had recently secured the lucrative and prestigious contract for publishing the parliamentary debates, replacing Messrs Hansard; Bottomley was its managing director. Paul joined this board, and remained a director until the business was merged into the

Table 8 Chronology of proprietorship and management of Kegan Paul, Trench, Trübner & Co. Ltd. 1889–1911

Kegan Paul, Trench, Trübner & Co. Ltd.: the result of the 1889 merger of

- Trübner & Co. (owned and managed by Nicholas Trübner from 1851 until his death in 1884 and subsequently owned by his heirs and managed by Frederick Düffing)

- Kegan Paul, Trench & Co. (owned and managed by Charles Kegan Paul and Alfred Chenevix Trench, since 1877)

- Redway & Co. (owned by George Redway and Alfred Sinnett; managed by Redway since ca 1882)

Directors: Coleridge J. Kennard; W. Crookes; C. Kegan Paul; A. Chenevix Trench; F. Düffing; A.P. Sinnett; Horatio Bottomley. Share Capital £100,000; Debenture Capital £50,000.

Management:
1889–95: Charles Kegan Paul and George Redway, with participation by Alfred Sinnett located 1891–1903 at Paternoster House, Charing Cross Road.

1895–1905: Spencer Blackett (with Arthur Waugh until 1902; Charles Kegan Paul involved until his October 1895 disability)
   located 1903 at Dryden House, 43 Gerrard Street, Soho.
Chairman of the Board of Directors: John Hubert Schmitz.

1906: H. Wingfield.

1907: Basil W. Willett.

1911: Laurie Magnus and William Swan Sonnenschein.
   Management and control in the hands of George Routledge & Sons.

Hansard Union, whereupon he became a director of that ill-fated enterprise.

While Horatio Bottomley was using Paul's name to enhance the respectability of his main scheme, for amalgamating printing establishments in a 'Hansard Union', he was also involving the publisher in a separate arrangement, one that involved the amalgamation of publishing houses. On 14 November 1889, Kegan Paul, Trench & Company was sold to the newly created firm of

Kegan Paul, Trench, Trübner & Company Limited. Initially both Charles Kegan Paul and Alfred Chenevix Trench were members of the board of directors. A prospectus announced that shares in the new limited company were being traded on the Stock Exchange.[2] But Alfred Trench almost immediately retired, in ill health, to Italy, and his partner became 'literary manager', as well as a shareholder and member of the board. The new firm capitalized upon the respected names of Kegan Paul and Trench, but the partners' list was only one of three combined under the new form of management. The prestigious international publisher and bookseller Trübner, specialist in Indian and Asian literatures, was much larger; and although George Redway's name did not appear on the new imprint, his sparse and idiosyncratic list was slated to be merged with the other two, and he would share with Paul the management of the limited firm. The name of Horatio Bottomley appeared only as a member of the board of directors, but to insiders in the London book world in 1889, it would have been clear that the promoter of the Hansard Publishing Union had achieved another dazzling success.[3] Charles Kegan Paul must have looked back on twelve years of financial stringency, and perhaps forward to a vision of the kind of financial underpinning that would finally be able support his literary ambitions.

Before sketching the histories of the two businesses now associated with that of Charles Kegan Paul and Alfred Chenevix Trench, and that of the Hansard Union, it is worthwhile to note some of the conditions in the publishing trade that surrounded the merger. Change was under way, and both authors and publishers were combative and wary. Authors had formed the Society of Authors in 1883, to protect themselves against unscrupulous publishers; many of them used agents for the same reason. The three-volume novel format, which had been agreed upon by novelists, publishers and the commercial circulating libraries, came to an end, by mutual arrangement, in 1894. The government of the United States finally legislated protection of the copyrights of foreign authors, in the Chace Act of 1891, but only when the book was manufactured by an American business. A Net Book Agreement, concluded in 1899, ended half a century of price war among booksellers, as publishers agreed to give fixed discounts that would enable all booksellers to sell their products for a uniform 'net' price.[4] The nineteenth-century transition of the publishing industry, from a business in which a small number of books were sold to libraries at high prices, to one in which large quantities of cheap books flooded a mass market-place, was complete. Arthur Waugh had a trenchant comment to make on the transformation he observed, of 'the traffic in books from a business select, scholarly, and, if not aristocratic, at least oligarchical in essence, into a vast democratic machine, working, wheel within wheel, with the spread of education, and the dissemination of literary culture among the masses'.[5] N.N. Feltes, in *Literary Capital and the Late Victorian Novel*, offers a provocative reading of this period, in which he 'begins to theorize publishing as a decentered totality in transition', a machine not so much democratic as capitalist.[6] Much had changed since the time when Henry S. King and George Smith, and contemporaries like Nicholas Trübner had entered the mid-Victorian book scene.

Nicholas Trübner, known for years in the London book trade as the 'prince of oriental publishers', had died in 1884 and Marie Trübner now sold her substantial inheritance to the new limited company. Nicholas Trübner was born in 1817, in Heidelberg, where he studied languages and began his working life as apprentice to the university bookseller.[7] He later worked for a bookseller in Frankfurt. Like Henry S. King, Trübner continued his broader education while learning to deal in books. Trübner's employer did business with Longman's, and William Longman engaged Trübner to move to London in 1843 as his foreign corresponding clerk. In 1851 he and a partner started the firm of Delf and Trübner at 12 Paternoster Row,[8] subsequently moving to larger premises in Ludgate Hill. The firm, later known simply as Trübner and Company, established a reputation for handling oriental literature, works in philology and philosophy, and also for expertise in American literature. Nicholas Trübner wrote and published a *Bibliographical Guide to American Literature* (1855) and travelled several times to the United States. In 1872 he compiled *A Catalogue of the Dictionaries and Grammars of the Principal Languages and Dialects of the World*.

Besides philology and oriental literature, Trübner published four of the novels of Charles Reade, on commission, between 1858 and 1861, and *The Breitmann Ballads* (1871) of the American writer Charles Godfrey Leland. Trübner, however, seldom competed with his fellow-publishers of London for novels or *belles-lettres*. In the words of one of them, William Heinemann,

> Nicholas Trübner was the friend and adviser of all who were engaged in the study of Oriental literature. His firm during this period has been the intermediary between Europe and the East. His agents are scattered all over the globe, and they send from the remotest parts the literary productions of every people of the world to London. Here they are catalogued and carefully described, and *Trübner's Record* makes them widely known among librarians and scholars.

Trübner's American and Oriental Literary Record (1865–91) was a 'register of important works', widely used by scholars of the eastern languages.[9] In 1878 he launched Trübner's Oriental Series, edited by the distinguished linguist, E. Reinhold Rost. The first book was E.W. West's edition of *Essays on the Sacred Language, Writings and Religion of the Parsis* by Martin Haug (1878), and the sixth was John Dowson's *Classical Dictionary of Hindu Mythology and Religion, Geography, History and Literature* (1879). The series was encouraged and supported by the India Office Library, where Reinhold Rost worked from 1869 to 1893. Another series was the English and Foreign Philosophical Library (1877–99), which included *Enigmas of Life* by William R. Greg. Through Greg, who was Controller of the government Stationery Office, Trübner acquired lucrative contracts, becoming the supplier of reference books and periodicals to government offices. Trübner combined his oriental interests with the contemporary popular market when he published Edwin Arnold's *The Light of Asia* in 1879. This rendering of the Life of Buddha in blank verse was very popular and was frequently reprinted as well as translated into several languages.

Samuel Butler is perhaps the best-known to a modern scholarly audience of Trübner's authors. After his *Erewhon* (1872) was rejected by Chapman & Hall, Butler sent it to Trübner and Co. They began by returning the manuscript unread, saying 'they supposed it was something to do with the Contagious Diseases Act'. Presumably they were thinking of Josephine Butler, who was outraging contemporary London with her feminist campaign against the legislation for controlling venereal disease. When that mistake was rectified they agreed to publish it on a commission basis, anonymously. When Butler offered *Life and Habit* (1877) to Trübner, they initially agreed to share the costs of production, but the publisher, according to the author 'insulted me so grossly that I offered to pay for the whole myself and take it away at once'. Butler departed briefly to David Bogue, then returned to an apologetic Trübner, where he stayed until his move to Longmans at the time of the amalgamation with Kegan Paul, Trench and with Redway.[10]

Trübner and Company was still a going concern in 1889, five years after the founder's death: massive, substantial and respected. Ownership had initially been divided among Trübner's widow and his two senior managers, Edwards and Düffing. When Edwards died soon after, his share became the property of Edward Hanson. Both Hanson and Marie Trübner seem to have been anxious to extract their capital and dissociate themselves from the business, since their names appear no further in the records. Frederick Düffing, however, remained involved with the management of the new firm for a few months, until, on the advice of his friend Alfred Sinnett, he linked the affairs of Trübner with those of George Redway.[11]

George Redway was only thirty years old in 1889, a partner with Sinnett in the small publishing house in Covent Garden that bore his name. He was the son of a footman, Charles Redway; his brother William Redway later became known to book collectors of the 1920s as the bookseller and publisher of works on chess, Frank Hollings. Charles Redway may have been in service in the household of a bibliophile and learned enough to install himself and two sons in the world of 'bookmen'.[12] In any case the three men started a small publishing business in London's York Street about 1882. George Redway recalled his career in an article for *The Bookman* in December 1931, 'Some Reminiscences of Publishing Fifty Years Ago'. As a young man he had worked with Rivingtons and later with Henry Vizetelly and he had also been a journalist. Rivington ('At the sign of the Bible and Crown') was a conservative publisher specializing in religious works and textbooks, while Vizetelly was on the *avant garde* of the London book trade. Here

Redway felt more at home. Vizetelly published Zola and other French naturalist writers in English translation; this was a strongly political act in 1888, for which Vizetelly was fined and later imprisoned for obscene libel.[13] By that time, Redway was established in York Street, specializing in esoteric books, such as Hargrave Jennings's *Phallicism: Celestial and Terrestrial, Heathen and Christian*, Arthur Machen's *The Anatomy of Tobacco* (both 1884) and Rosa Baughan's *The Handbook of Palmistry* (3rd edition, revised, 1885). It was during this period that Redway acquired the copyright of Swinburne's poem *A Word for the Navy* and published a limited edition.[14] He became London agent for the *Theosophist* in 1884, and was so much associated with the fashionable spiritualist movement that a contemporary described his own encounter with theosophy in terms of 'going in for a course of Redway'.[15]

The colleague who 'introduced the theosophical element' was Alfred Percy Sinnett, who joined the little firm as a partner at the death of Charles Redway. And it was Sinnett who forged the connections among Redway, Bottomley, the Trübner estate, and the Kegan Paul, Trench partners. Sinnett had begun his career as a journalist, reporting on Indian and Asian affairs for various London papers, and had served as editor of the colonial journal *The Pioneer of India*.[16] According to Redway's interview with *The Publishers' Circular*, Sinnett was an old friend of Frederick Düffing. When the latter became overwhelmed by the work of managing the huge Trübner concern after the deaths of his two partners, he was ready to consider the idea, proposed by Sinnett, of a merger with George Redway and Company. Redway was a young, ambitious and energetic manager, Düffing an elderly and experienced one. And Redway had some knowledge of international publishing because of his connection with theosophy. Sinnett, their mutual friend, reasoned that an amalgamation would be fruitful. Then, as Redway said in an interview, Bottomley 'appeared on the scene, was interested in the scheme, but found it altogether too small a matter to meet his ideas'. With the addition of the Kegan Paul, Trench business, of course, 'the affair, from being initially of a more modest scope, gradually assumed its present magnitude'.[17]

That magnitude can be seen in an early copy of the stock prospectus, which appeared 18 November 1889, announcing the amalgamation, the firm's directors, its bankers, brokers, solicitors, and auditors, its temporary offices and its official secretary.[18] The share capital amounted to £100,000, divided into shares worth £10 each; the debenture capital was £50,000, consisting of 500 mortgage debenture bonds. The merger of three existing businesses was expected to effect 'great economy in management expense, together with many other advantages which will arise from the combination'. Although no detailed breakdown of financial apportionment has survived, the intangible contribution of each vendor was articulated. Kegan Paul, Trench were 'well known as one of the leading firms of London publishers', with a 'highly successful and lucrative business which embraces a large and varied list of publications'. Trübner's global reputation and government connections were glowingly described, while Redway's business 'although of more recent origin has been thoroughly successful'. And Redway was going to be co-operating in the management of the new company. Of the £150,000 capital, the vendors received £130,000 in debentures and shares, which left £20,000 as working capital.

These large sums and well-publicized financial arrangements were presumably as unfamiliar to Redway and Sinnett as they were to Paul and Trench: but they were familiar to speculators in the Hansard Publishing Union, popularly remembered as the 'Hansard bubble'. The Hansard Union was only the first episode in Horatio Bottomley's long and remarkable public life. The impact of this extraordinary financial promoter on the genteel and tradition-bound London book world has never fully been examined. Bottomley (1860–1933) combined the careers of journalist and financier, having begun as a printer in 1884 with the *Hackney Hansard*, a suburban weekly, which soon expanded to other local 'Hansards'. In 1888 he was Managing Director of Macrae, Curtice and Co. Ltd. and managed to acquire an extraordinarily lucrative contract, the right to publish the *Hansard Parliamentary Debates*. With the new income, Bottomley purchased several other printing and publishing firms, and by April 1889 they were working under the umbrella of the Hansard Publishing Union in Great Queen Street. In Bottomley's own words,

> the Union aimed at being a combination of every department of the printing and publishing trades. The object was to give

newspaper printers and others the opportunity of securing the benefit of a co-operative organization dealing with every detail of newspaper and book production, from the growing of the wood from which the pulp for making paper is obtained to the distribution and sale of the finished periodical or book – with the intermediate supply of every technical requisite, commercial, literary and artistic.

Begun with a capital of £500,000, the Union failed in just over two years, and Bottomley was bankrupt and in court, defending himself, successfully, against charges of conspiracy to defraud. In the meantime, however, there had been a time when the company 'was employing about a third of the members of the London Society of Compositors; was paying several thousands of pounds per week in wages; had a thousand printing machines at work night and day; and produced every week over two hundred . . . newspapers and other publications'.[19] And during those same exhilarating months Bottomley set out to replicate the 'union' model of combining printing firms in his vision for the amalgamation of three publishing firms in Kegan Paul, Trench, Trübner & Company Limited.

Some of the impact of Bottomley's personality may be sensed in the evidence given by Charles Kegan Paul to a subsequent public inquiry into the demise of the Union, of which he was a board member. He testified that 'he heard of the formation of the union not very long after Macrae, Curtice and Co. was formed. Mr Bottomley told him, in reference to the starting of the union, that a number of firms might be easily amalgamated and would make one very good business.' The notion of vast profits to be made by exploiting the commercial possibilities of publishing was appealing, and Bottomley was persuasive. But details, such as the value of each individual business, were never made clear. Paul was asked by the prosecutor 'You were dealing with over half a million of the company's money; cannot you say what the committee did to ascertain the value of the businesses?' Paul replied 'that he could not state exactly, but he ascertained that they were worth what was about to be paid for them, and they showed a good profit'. He had naively relied for this opinion largely on a report from the general manager 'to the effect that every department was full of work'. Paul had to admit that he did not even know who was promoting the financial deal, and was unaware that Bottomley was personally involved in purchasing printing businesses and reselling them to the Hansard Union. In fact the expression 'did not know' recurs throughout Paul's testimony. At a second bankruptcy hearing in January of 1893, Paul testified that 'We thoroughly and entirely agreed with every word said by Mr Bottomley . . . I had implicit confidence in [his] character and integrity. . . . I bought some [more shares] a few days before the collapse, so great was my confidence in the company.'[20]

By May of 1891, barely two years after its founding, the Union was bankrupt. Bottomley blamed this debacle on the Debenture Corporation, which had initially underwritten an issue of debentures and now expressed its misgivings by appointing a Receiver and initiating 'the inevitable Winding-up'. A debenture is the sealed bond with which a company acknowledges the sum on which interest is due at a fixed rate, until the principal is repaid. Such interest normally constitutes a prior charge on assets. Because the debentures could not be supported, a receiver was appointed to administer the property and the Hansard Union had to be 'wound up', or liquidated, its liabilities ascertained and its assets apportioned fairly. A committee of investigation gave its opinion that 'it is more desirable that the Union should be wound up by an official liquidation than by voluntary action'. The report, printed in *The Publishers' Circular* on 30 May, stated that £200,000 would have to be raised if liquidation were to be stayed. This was not possible, and the bankruptcy hearing went ahead in November. Then Bottomley was charged with conspiracy to defraud. He defended himself in court, was acquitted, and later launched himself on a career of finance, stock promotion, and sensational journalism.

Although Paul's new firm remained independent of the Hansard Union and therefore weathered the débâcle, it must have been a great blow to his pride, as well as to his personal finances. He had been a member of the Union board, and the board of his new company shared members with the Union. Members of the initial Kegan Paul, Trench, Trübner & Co. Ltd. board were Paul, Trench and Bottomley; Coleridge Kennard (banker); Sir William Crookes (chemist); Alfred P. Sinnett (journalist in India and theosophist;

already involved with Redway's firm); and Frederick Düffing (of Trübner's). Members added later were George Redway, William Lindsay (of the *Windsor Herald*) and General Sir Richard Strachey. The Hansard Union's directors were Paul, Kennard, and Sinnett, with Sir Henry Isaacs (Lord Mayor of London) and Sir Roper Lethbridge (former Press Commissioner to the Government of India). Bottomley was managing director.

Bottomley had undoubtedly traded on the prestige of the Kegan Paul name. In *Bottomley's Book* he named Paul first among the directorate as 'one of the most eminent London publishers, and a gentleman of the very highest reputation'. He had also taken advantage of Paul's trust. In testimony on the matter, Paul told a public inquiry that 'so far as figures were concerned I left that to the accountants, and all legal questions I left to the solicitor to the Union'.[21] He did not know what Bottomley was up to. Paul must also have succumbed to acquisitiveness, to the wish to have much more capital available for the purchase of copyrights and for investing in the increasingly expensive manuscripts of his chosen authors. Now, however, he was poorer not richer. And instead of making his own publishing decisions with only Alfred Trench to consult, he was dealing with Trübner's and Redway's books, their lists, their authors and editors, their customers, their reputations, and their managers.

II

Charles Kegan Paul shared management of the new limited company with George Redway from early in 1889 until beginning of 1895. His own list, carefully selected and lovingly promoted, was now dwarfed by the massive Trübner catalogue. Trench had left England for Italy, Düffing for Heidelberg: it was George Redway who remained in London, in the office, inescapably involved in Paul's life. The two men were so different in their intellectual and cultural interests that it is difficult to imagine a very deep sympathy between them, and little evidence survives to characterize their relationship. Paul's *Memories* suppresses Redway altogether; the younger man's brief memoir claims that he enjoyed a 'close and cordial' relationship with his new colleague; at their daily lunch together Paul would 'pour out his stores of information about the men of his time . . . at sixty-five he was as entertaining as men can be who have followed many vocations'. Redway was about the age of Paul's eldest son, Louis, and of his protégé Arthur Pollard. His account of the relationship, however, does not have the tone of Paul's affectionate friendships with other young men such as Pollard or C.R. Ashbee. And Paul was preoccupied at the time with his final and wrenching decision to embrace the Roman Catholic religion. There is not enough evidence to be certain about the relationship, but enough to speculate that it was at best remote.

It was not only the two publishers who had to come to terms with the new arrangements. Authors had, over the years, become accustomed to dealing with Paul or Trench, with Redway or Sinnett, or with one of the Trübner managers. Each writer expected his or her book, or books, to continue appearing under the imprints under which they were first published. In the context of a merger of lists, misunderstandings and distress were unavoidable. A particularly eloquent example of this problem was Marie Sinclair, Countess of Caithness and Duchesse de Pomar. Widow, successively, of General le Comte de Medina Pomar, and of James Sinclair, the fourteenth earl of Caithness, she lived in Nice and was an ardent theosophist and prolific writer. So was her son, on whose behalf, as well as her own, she wrote. Although her initial contact, via theosophy, was with Redway, two coincidences made her feel a personal interest in the new amalgamated firm. Nicholas Trübner, years earlier, had been her first publisher and a personal friend, and Paul had once been her son's tutor. Now, however, in February 1890, she was aggrieved, telling George Redway:

> . . . allow me to say that the last letter I received on the subject of my books, *was not from you*, but from the new firm of Kegan Paul &c &c – & also to tell you that I felt very much hurt by it which is the reason I sent no reply at the time. . . . [furthermore,] in consequence of beginning to feel a personal interest in the new publishing company of which you formed a part I was absolutely induced to invest the sum of £500 in it – when immediately after doing so – I received a short note signed with the business stamp of the firm – saying they could only agree to take *The Mystery of the Ages*, as the latest of my publica-

tions, & advising me to sell off all the rest by Public Auction!

In the first place The Mystery of the Ages is not the latest – for "*The Midnight Visit to Holyrood*" was published at least a year or two later and is not known at all in the literary world, though all my friends who have seen it call it a little gem . . . Of course sooner than sell this book off by Public Auction I will have it sent over to Paris & give *every* copy away to friends as occasion offers. Allow me to ask whether your own Library in York Street still continues under your direction – & whether you have seen the books the new firm so much despises.[22]

Both Paul and Redway had more to think of in 1890 than one outraged writer of recondite 'little gems', published on commission. The magnitude of their new enterprise was overwhelming, and in that context £500 meant little. But the sense of personal betrayal expressed by Lady Caithness must have been experienced by many authors sensitive to the fate of their beloved books.

Redway and Paul had now to deal not only with authors, but with shareholders. At the March 1890 general meeting, where Horatio Bottomley presided, the directors announced that they had decided to build their own premises. This 'would be better for the purpose of the business itself, as well as from a financial standpoint'. The chosen site was in Charing Cross Road, and the new building was expected to save a large sum in rentals. Nothing was said about what the building would cost. Bottomley also explained that no dividend was to be declared for 1889; the directors would wait until the end of the first half of 1890. One of the stockholders, identified in *The Times* as Mr Schmitz, and elsewhere as J.E. Smids, was almost certainly John Hubert Schmitz, a prominent German sponge merchant working in London. He asked several pointed questions. Why had the directors 'departed from what was stated in the prospectus, and . . . decided to build premises of their own?' And was it not unfair to ask the shareholders to wait six months for information about what profits had been made in the past year? Bottomley replied that the Trübner offices had been discovered to require extensive and expensive structural alterations. And to declare a dividend and divide profits would have required the company to 'go through the difficult process of stock taking'. Schmitz was unimpressed: he moved a resolution that a dividend be declared, but the meeting did not support him.[23] The company was prepared to go to the trouble and expense of building new premises, but not of taking stock. One shareholder, at least, was able to see through the dazzle of Bottomley's grandiose plans.

It was in October 1891 that the company duly moved out of Redway's 'library in York Street', Kegan Paul, Trench's offices in Paternoster Square, and the old Trübner headquarters in Ludgate Hill, to its own new building. Named Paternoster House, it stood in Charing Cross Road at the corner of Cecil Court. The operations of the three founding firms were now consolidated.[24] The *Publishers' Circular* celebrated the occasion by publishing the lengthy interview which has already been cited. Redway guided their reporter on a tour of the 'new and more commodious premises'. The publisher and the reporter worked their way down through five storeys. 'At the top of the house' was the general export department, from which shipments were sent to international customers, mostly large libraries and public institutions. On the same floor was the department 'devoted to the Continental trade, that is, to the exportation of English books to Continental booksellers'. One floor down was kept the stock of bound books, arranged alphabetically, and below that was the Oriental book department, which, Redway proudly observed, had been 'always a feature of the Trübner business, but now much more largely developed'.

The first floor housed the 'counting house' and the private offices of the managers. The ground floor was devoted to the import department. 'Here . . . you will find Mr Child, who for the past 45 years has been connected with the importation of American literature.' With the addition of a department for importing books from the European continent, the new firm was in a position to supply its customers with books from around the world. The basement housed the packing department and other domestic offices, and the premises was served throughout by electricity and 'fitted up with every modern convenience, and excellently arranged for the business that has to be transacted in them'. Redway told the reporter: 'You see, we are cosmopolitan booksellers as well as publishers.'

As Redway explained, the management was now in the hands of

Charles Kegan Paul and himself. The reporter inquired about changes in the constitution of the company since its formation nearly two years earlier. On the board of directors, Bottomley had been replaced by Reginald Lake, a publisher with the firm of Gilbert and Rivington's; the banker Coleridge Kennard had died. On the management side, Trench had 'broken down in health', and Mr Düffing, who had operated Trübner's in 1889, was now back in Heidelberg. Alfred Sinnett, however, had been 'allotted a share of the work' of management. Redway finished up his interview by holding forth on how little appreciated are publishers by their clients, the authors: 'the publisher's business is a difficult one, and taxes heavily not merely his knowledge of commerce and literature, but his courage and temper'.

The *Publishers' Circular* interview occurred in the fall of 1891; by the next summer, rumours were circulating in London about the fragile nature of the new company's business. One author, Louise Chandler Moulton, told her American publisher 'since I sent you the offer of Kegan Paul I have heard from *three* different sources that the firm can't be depended upon – & is supposed to be near bankruptcy'.[25] More sinister was the *Stock Exchange Year Book* report, that while no report had been received, 'it appears from a newspaper paragraph (in January, 1893) that the last accounts showed a debit [of £313] to profit and loss'.

The problem seems to have been one of over-capitalization, and the ambitious building scheme must have constituted a further strain. As Redway reflected forty years later, he, Sinnett, Paul and the others had 'failed to see . . . that in spite of auditors' certificates, a share capital of £150,000 was far too great for dividend earning purposes. Within their proper limits all the businesses were sound . . . but my £10 shares were sold for two shillings and sixpence, and £100 debentures for £40 apiece.' Their confidence 'in the integrity and astuteness of Mr Horatio Bottomley' had been misplaced. The initial 'interim dividend' promised by Bottomley had been declared, at the rate of 7 per cent, at the eighteen-month anniversary, 30 June 1890. It turned out to be the last dividend the shareholders ever saw. There was at that time a reserve fund of £2,000, with a balance of £359 carried forward to the next year. Henceforth accounts were to be submitted in January. But in January of 1892 no report appeared, and the *Stock*

Exchange Year Book could only report that the newspapers had mentioned a debit. The same thing happened a year later. However in January of 1894 an Annual Report appeared, covering the firm's affairs up to the previous June.

The delay in the completion of accounts for 1892–3 was explained by 'the prolonged and serious illness of the business manager'. It is not clear to whom this refers. The report continued, 'though not showing a large profit, the business is now fully paying its way'. This was, however, 'not due to any fortunate literary speculation, but to careful management and persistent retrenchment in expenditure'. Investors were reminded of the contemporary commercial depression, because of which sales had decreased by about 9%. Purchases of stock, and production of new books, had not decreased, and as a result the value of the stock as a whole had increased slightly. The directors had arranged to have a valuation made of the firm's stock, a valuation to be made by the staff under the direction of the business manager, with the results to be checked by the board of directors and investigated by auditors. Meanwhile, in an attempt to reduce the general expenses of management, the directors were drawing half-fees. Moreover, it was announced, 'Mr Paul and Mr Redway also have again relinquished a part of their remuneration, and the Board has thought it fair under the circumstances to allow them the privilege of taking a pupil.' The initial £150,000 value had now increased to £165,777, of which the stock was valued at £49,462, the goodwill at just under that amount, and the new premises at £9,800. The bottom line was a debt of £313. It was based on some rather over-optimistic accounting.

The firm staggered through 1894 without making a report, but in 1895 it faltered badly, and publicly. By June, people in the book trade could read in their copies of *The Publishers' Circular* that Spencer C. Blackett had been appointed to replace George Redway as manager of Kegan Paul, Trench, Trübner & Co.

The annual report told a fuller story. The new manager was reporting to a new board of directors, their predecessors having been discredited. The new chairman of the board was John Hubert Schmitz, the nay-sayer of five years earlier. Alfred Sinnett had departed, and he had commenced legal action against the board, 'nominally on behalf of the Debenture holders'. George

Redway had disappeared with him. 'All will recollect,' the report stated, 'the circumstances under which the Board was elected at the last Meeting, and with a view of maintaining continuity in the business and of obtaining full information of its affairs, the Directors then elected, requested Messrs Lake and Lindsay to resume their seats on the board.' This had been done. The new board excluded Paul and Redway, as well as Sinnett and General Sir Richard Strachey. It included some new members, and it was now chaired by Schmitz, whose interest was presumably more financial than literary. Part of the problem was with the valuation of the stock. A new independent valuer, Arthur J. Rayment, had drastically reduced the balance-sheet valuation of the stock to £44,437. But in the face of Sinnett's debenture action, 'and of the undoubtedly heavy losses ... during the past years', the directors decided to issue the remaining debentures, which meant their value was extinguished. Most importantly, the decision was made to write off the loss accrued by the firm's reduction of capital, 'in order that the shares may become dividend paying'. Each share of £10 was converted to one of £1, so that the capital was now a mere £10,000.

George Redway, discredited together with Alfred Sinnett, was back to independent publishing, where he remained until about 1899 and the Boer War, when his full-time military career began. Oddly, he was to be associated with the firm again in 1901, as a contributor to the revived series of Military Handbooks. And Charles Kegan Paul survived the débâcle of 1895 to play literary manager to a new business manager, Spencer Collinson Blackett.

What can be said about the books published between 1889 and 1895, under the joint management of George Redway and Charles Kegan Paul, with the influence in the background of Horatio Bottomley? Were there more popular best-sellers than before, or fewer? Was the atmosphere conducive to the courting of serious writers, or to the establishment of distinguished new series? Only tentative answers to these questions may be suggested, because the detailed database of authors, titles, genres and contracts prepared for the years since 1871, which was the basis for the analysis in chapter three, has not been extended past 1889. The incorporation of two disparate lists would have made comparison impossible.[26]

4 PAUL, TRENCH, TRÜBNER & CO.

Kegan Paul, Trench, Trübner & Co. Ltd continued many of the policies of the old company. Austin Dobson, whose poetry Charles Kegan Paul so much admired, now entered into correspondence with the firm about an illustrated edition of his poem *The Ballad of Beau Brocade*. In July of 1892, he wrote to confirm the arrangements made in a meeting with both Paul and Redway. The drawings were to be entrusted to Hugh Thompson. He asked, politely and very firmly, for a ten per cent royalty. In November, he told Thompson, 'I have written to them [Messrs Kegan Paul] that I propose to run up tomorrow and have asked them to see me. They have written such extremely nice letters that I hate the idea of bargaining with them at all but I must. One cannot have the money slipped generously into one's pocket without any trouble to oneself.' Thompson shared Dobson's scruples, observing that Paul and Redway had sent him

> a very nice letter, the only sting to my self-consciousness lying in the phrase about 'driving bargains' which makes my ears

Table 9 Series published by Kegan Paul, Trench, Trübner & Co. Ltd., 1888–1911

International Scientific Series (initiated by King: 98 titles, 1872–1911)

Parchment Library (initiated by Paul: 40 titles, 1880–94)

Pulpit Commentary (initiated by Paul: 49 titles, 1881–97)

Modern Science Series (6 titles, 1891–3)

Military Handbooks for Officers and Non-Commissioned Officers (initiated by Paul: 7 titles, 1883–8; revived with a further 10 titles, 1897–1910)

Pamphlet Library (3 titles, 1897–8)

Out of Door Library (4 titles, 1897–8)

Wolseley Military Series (9 titles, 1897–1902)

Westminster Biographies (6 titles, 1899–1901)

burn. . . . I hope, dear Dobson, that you don't think I have been too grasping. I have certainly grasped as much as I could get, but it is now time the poor unknown author and artist should turn and board the enemy's craft. I wish in my case that it had been some other firm against which I had a grudge. Messrs K.P. have been so nice and agreeable that I have been ashamed to try my bold buccaneering measures first on them.

Back in the 1870s, when Paul had written to praise Dobson's verse, there had been no relationship of enmity between author and publisher. Twenty years later, their private relationship had changed with the larger world of publishing and the book trade. Grasping, and 'bold buccaneering measures' were expected on both sides.

The International Scientific Series continued to produce two or three new titles a year as well as reissues of the older books. Sir John Lubbock had been engaged to edit a new venture, the Modern Science Series, in 1891, and Redway mentioned in his *Publishers' Circular* interview that it was meant to replace the older series. The Modern Science Series, however, amounted to six titles by 1893 and then ceased; the International Scientific Series generated the same number of books in that time, and moreover went on to include a further twenty-one before 1911. Similarly the Pulpit Commentary volumes continued to appear until it finally finished in 1897. Six more volumes in the Parchment Library came out between 1889 and 1894, with both Paul and Pollard lavishing careful attention on them. The Military Handbooks were allowed to lapse, but the Colonial Library, the reprint fiction series, continued to flourish.

Paul's friendship with Arthur Pollard had already produced several publishing projects that served the interests of both men. It was George Redway, however, who 'casually suggested' Pollard's editing a series of six Books About Books, starting in 1892. An agreement between editor and firm laid out the contract: Kegan Paul, Trench, Trübner & Co. Ltd. would pay Pollard £5 per volume for his services as editor, and purchase from each author the copyright of his or her book for £40. An additional royalty began after the sale of a fixed number of copies. Their timing was impeccable; the Books About Books were published just at the moment when a number of antiquarians and bibliophiles in London began to be serious about collections and bibliography. The series comprised the following volumes: E. Gordon Duff, *Early Printed Books*; Charles J. and Mary Elton, *Great Book Collectors*; W.J. Hardy, *Book Plates*; Herbert P. Horne, *Book Bindings*; Falconer Madan, *Books in Manuscript*; and Alfred William Pollard's own, *Early Illustrated Books*. Pollard remembered that 'The series started at the height of a craze for large paper copies, and the sale before publication of 150 sets of these secured its financial success.' And the editor's reputation was further enhanced: 'The success of "Books About Books" encouraged the publishers to accept my proposal for a bibliographical quarterly.' This was the distinguished journal *Bibliographica*.[27]

Another new venture was the Home Education Series, edited by Charlotte Maria Shaw Mason from 1886 to 1905. A preface to the series of five books noted that it was 'so called from the title of the first volume, and not as dealing, wholly or principally, with "Home" as opposed to "School" education'. Mason was interested in 'the study of the laws of education as they bear on the bodily development, the moral training, the intellectual life and the religious upbringing of children',[28] and this approach seems to have been more popular than the theoretical studies included in Philip Magnus's Education Library in the early eighties. A German publisher, G. Braunsche Hofbuchdruckerei und Verlag, negotiated in 1905 for the rights to produce a German edition.

An Eminent Actors Series, edited by William Archer, began in 1890 with Archer's own biography of Charles Macready. Although the *St James's Gazette* noted that 'No "series" of eminent men has made a more excellent beginning', only three titles appeared. Robert Lowe wrote the life of Thomas Betterton, and Edward Abbott Parry the life of Charles Macklin (both 1891). A few years later the Westminster and Beacon biographies were to return to the idea of a series of 'lives', this time not limited only to actors.

A new scientific series that failed to supersede the existing one: domestic pedagogy: a stagnant series of biographies. Only the Books About Books stands out as a really successful innovation of the Redway–Paul years, perhaps because it represented a subject that was of genuine interest to both managers. The other series give the feeling of grasping at straws, of projecting books that might impress the board of directors, if not the reading public. After Redway's difference of opinion with the board, when he had re-established himself as an independent publisher in Hart Street, Bloomsbury, he published in 1897 William Hazlitt's *Confessions of a Collector*. Redway wrote a rather tactless but also very revealing letter to the author. 'If I had more time,' he told Hazlitt, 'I would try and concoct a sort of trading account to shew how much more profitable it is to deal in rare examples of early English literature . . . than to purchase the right of reproduction of modern authors.'[29] Publishing, in the way that Henry S. King, Charles Kegan Paul, and Alfred Chenevix Trench had understood it, was never Redway's concern.

III

Spencer Blackett's sojourn with the firm lasted ten years, from 1895 to 1905, twice as long as that of George Redway, and no more productive.

Blackett had been born into the book trade, but educated as a soldier. A memoir concerning another young London publisher of the 1890s, William Heinemann, places Blackett in his social context. There was a gambling, music hall-going, man-about-town side to Heinemann's life about which 'an extremely racy book might have been written', and the man who could have written it best was Spencer Blackett.[30] A more detailed narrative, that of Arthur Waugh, takes up the tale.[31] Waugh first met Blackett in the autumn of 1895, when the latter had just taken over the management of the restructured firm and was on the lookout for a literary manager. Up to that time, Waugh remembered, Blackett 'had followed the career of a rolling-stone. Alas, he followed it to the end, but always with a right good heart!'

> Blackett was a man of smart appearance and fascinating address, and he got the post at once. He had the business experience which comes from having been disillusioned once or twice; and he was blessed with overflowing energy, especially for a new interest so long as it were new. But he would never have claimed to know much about literature, and he was now looking round for someone to act as reader to the firm, and to help him

generally as literary adviser. He and I met at Heinemann's and, after a few encounters, he suggested that he should put my name before his Board.

Waugh was to play Charles Kegan Paul to Spencer Blackett's Henry S. King. Paul, however, was still coming into the office every day. His opinion of Blackett's antics, while not documented, is not difficult to imagine. His passing comment in *Memories* ' . . . every such business [publishing] ought to be an autocracy . . . ' may be relevant to a tentative reconstruction of his relations with the two younger men with whom he was saddled in the 1890s. The senior publisher was now sixty-seven years old, his junior partner thirty-seven.

Blackett was the third son of publisher Henry Blackett. The senior Blackett had been a partner of Henry Colburn until 1853, when his firm became known as Hurst and Blackett. He died in 1870, when Spencer was eleven. Three years later, Spencer Blackett entered school at Charterhouse, and about 1876 went to the Royal Military College at Sandhurst. At the age of twenty-one he was commissioned as a second lieutenant in the 21st Hussars, serving in Dublin under Earl Spencer. He left the army in 1882, aged 23.[32] The Heinemann memoir links this change to 'family reverses', noting that Blackett 'remained a Cavalry man in thought and outlook to the end', still a member of the Cavalry Club and still wearing 'his handsome Hussar uniform'. Waugh, however, juxtaposes the event with Blackett's marriage, when 'he sent in his papers, and came up to London to follow the family tradition of publishing'. Not, however, in the family firm, now in the hands of his brothers. Instead he purchased the business of John Maxwell, and began to 'make a fairly good thing out of sensational novels and shilling shockers'.

In fact, the records suggest that Blackett did not take over from Maxwell until 1887, five years after he left the army. Besides 'shilling shockers' like *Whose Wife shall She Be? The Story of a Painter's Life* by James Stanley Little, and numerous luridly-titled works by F.W. Robinson, Blackett's 1887 catalogue included the novels of Mary Elizabeth Braddon, 'the Queen of Circulating Libraries', and author of *Lady Audley's Secret*. There was also a series of British Standard Handbooks, thirty-nine 'illustrated practical handbooks of sports and pastimes'. From 1889, Blackett worked with a partner, Percy Hallam. The firm of Blackett and Hallam was sold in July 1891 to Griffith and Farran. Some indication of what Spencer Blackett was doing during the years not documented in this account may be gained from Arthur Waugh: he 'attempted several rather disastrous enterprises in lines of business with which he was insufficiently acquainted'. Harriet Jane Blackett and their 'high-spirited family of boys and girls' must have been delighted by the promise of security represented by the appointment to Kegan Paul, Trench, Trübner & Co. Ltd.

Arthur Waugh, too, was happy to join his friend, although he regretted having to 'ally himself . . . with the army of black-coated, top-hatted workers who left home immediately after breakfast, attaché-case in hand, and returned towards evening, tired out and probably rather irritable'. But this dismal prospect was mitigated by working with Blackett 'whose sense of humour fell in exactly with my own, and who seemed to regard the day's work as a huge joke, to be made the most of both in and out of office hours'. Waugh had begun his career as a freelance writer loosely connected with Heinemann; he went on from Kegan Paul's in 1902 to serve for thirty-five years as managing director of Chapman & Hall.

Waugh described the firm, at the time he and Blackett entered it, as 'labouring under heavy weather'. Paul, in his opinion 'was a man of fine literary appreciation, but far too fastidious and pedantic in taste to make a successful publisher'. The Charing Cross Road offices were 'bright, sunny rooms, with good accommodation for staff and stock. Nor was the stock of a kind to be regarded lightly.' Waugh alluded to the association with Tennyson, the collaboration with Pollard, and the 'soundest scientific literature of the day' absorbed by the International Scientific Series. But when the capital had been reduced in 1895, 'a little knot of stockholders got themselves elected upon the Board, apparently believing that, because they had succeeded in other lines of trade, they could soon pull a publishing business together'.

Schmitz, the City sponge-merchant who can probably be credited with saving the firm in 1895, was described condescendingly by Waugh as 'a benign old gentleman with an all-embracing smile, [who] bore an uncompromisingly German name, and spoke with a fierce German accent'. Neither he nor any of the other members of the new board knew anything about the book business, a situation Waugh deplored. He became convinced 'that a publishing board of business men, who know nothing about books, is doomed to beat the air, and leave the threshing-floor bare of grain'. It is not clear how familiar Waugh was with the firm's disastrous recent experience, when a combination of book-world people and financiers had been in charge.

The glaring personal incompatibility between the Blackett–Waugh team of playboys and Charles Kegan Paul is obvious and need not be belaboured. Their encounter did not last long, but it must have been terribly difficult on both sides. In October of the first year of the new regime, 1895, Charles Kegan Paul was badly injured in a traffic accident, crossing Hammersmith Road. The board accepted his resignation soon after, but he remained in touch with the firm, and seems to have been consulted quite frequently. They also published two of his translations in 1896 and 1898, and both *Memories* and his poetry in 1899. He suffered from chronic pain for the rest of his life, and this condition must have exacerbated the irascibility with which he expressed himself to his new colleagues. As Arthur Waugh put it, 'his fastidious repulsion from anything cheaply popular grew upon him so keenly with the use of practice, that the "opinions" of his old age consisted almost exclusively of a parade of "terrible examples." . . . Criticism of this kind reduced Blackett to a profound depression.'

Waugh continued, characterizing Blackett's own approach to these matters by putting him into the place of a publisher's reader making a 'commercial estimate', which should take a line something like this.

> 'I am paid by my employers,' such a reader would say, 'to find them books that will be profitable investments. The public taste is low, but that is no fault of mine. This book is vulgar and trivial, but it will sell. Who are we that we should despise a commercial bargain?' (286)

Two readers, two editors, could hardly have been less compatible. But as two publishers, they also embody in their attitudes the difference between an independent entrepreneur on the one hand, and a manager responsible to shareholders on the other.[33]

Stock Exchange reports for the first year under Blackett's management showed a modest posting, £6,770, to the profit account in the company's ledgers, but a closer look would have demonstrated this to be misleading. The auditors' certificate observed that in the valuation some copyrights had been 'written up' since the previous year, while of those newly acquired, some had been valued above the amount of cost, in anticipation of future profits. 'If it were not for such anticipation no profit would be shown on the Profit and Loss Account.' Despite these warning signs, Spencer Blackett's standing and position of trust with the company's directors was confirmed by his election to join their number on 17 February 1897. The same month he embarked on his first business trip to the United States, a journey of some three months.

The figures thereafter were written in red, but the decline was not immediately apparent either to the management or the board of directors. The report for the year ending 30 June 1897, submitted January 1898, explained that the reason why the company exhibited a loss, of £3,577, had to do with 'the difficulties attending upon the valuation of a publishing business'. Despite the auditor's warning, the previous three years valuations, made by Rayment, were now declared too low. Spencer Blackett assessed the copyrights and stock at £8,000 more than did the independent auditor. Moreover, the period in question had 'not been favourable to the sale of high-class literature'. At the annual meeting on 21 January 1898, Schmitz had 'expressed regret' at the unsatisfactory character of the report and accounts. He was told that Rayment's valuations 'had in some cases been cut down to an extravagant extent ... a good many publications which had an actual value had been returned as quite valueless, while in other cases less than the mere cost of the binding had been allowed'. The directors had checked Blackett's figures and gave the opinion that they were not extravagant in the opposite direction. Schmitz may have felt that a sponge in his warehouse which failed, for whatever reason, to find a buyer was not worth very much, and wondered how books could be regarded differently. He remained, however, as chairman of the board, and seems to have been convinced by Blackett's rationalizations and promises for a glowing future.

Less than a year later, the board of directors announced to its shareholders in December 1898 that, despite a debit of over £2,000, they were 'encouraged by the result of Mr Blackett's journey to America in the spring of 1897'. Therefore, 'your Board decided that the trade of the Company in the Colonies might derive benefit from a visit by him to the principal cities in Australasia'. The following year, they reported on his success. 'With the view of again developing the Company's Agency Business, Mr Blackett visited Australasia and the United States . . . and received many promises of support. The progress of the revolution in the publishing trade is watched carefully, and no risks of serious loss are incurred.' Since Blackett's 'Australia Report' has been preserved in the archives of the firm, it is possible to identify just how inaccurate and misleading was the information provided to the stockholders.[34]

Inaccurate because Blackett's journey included Canada, as well as Ceylon, New Zealand, Australia and the United States. Misleading because he documented clearly his near-complete 'failure to sell books'. Blackett was away from 6 October 1898 until 3 April 1899, spending a total of £357 4s 0d on fares. He seems to have been acting on behalf of firms other than Kegan Paul, Trench, Trübner & Co. Ltd. He mentions providing services for his old friend William Heinemann, now an independent publisher. This is not the place for a full exposition of Blackett's journey, which is in fact important evidence for the conditions of the international book trade at the turn of the century. Some details, however, may be noted.

At Colombo, a dry goods entrepreneur about to go into the book business assured him of doing business in the future. In Perth, Western Australia, the public library ordered a few titles, but the major bookseller already had an agent in London. The New South Wales Free Library at Sydney graciously accepted a gift of books from the backlist, but there is no evidence that they followed this up with any orders for new titles. In Brisbane, Blackett's mission was regarded as unfair competition by the local booksellers, and the Labour Party members of the provincial House of Representatives supported their protest. Similar experiences pursued him throughout Australia and New Zealand: large libraries in large towns had dwindled, and new towns were already doing business with local booksellers: 'the advantage we once held of being able to advocate our business by being a London House no longer holds good'. And the Pulpit Commentary was too expensive, and too voluminous, for the modest bookshelves of antipodean clergymen.

In March, Blackett sailed for San Francisco. 'At the Public Library I found our name is well known, and they spoke in very complimentary terms of the catalogues we issue from time to time.' However, 'I fear we do not get the full benefit of our enterprise as they pick up the books through other channels.' One local businessman with a subscription business accepted a copy of the one-volume Shakespeare, 'to canvas amongst dry goods houses'. This was a pattern of selling books, widely used in North America, with which Blackett, not to mention his board, was unfamiliar. He travelled via Portland to Vancouver, where he found that the Public Library bought 'very few new books'. The neighbouring town of New Westminster had been destroyed by fire the previous autumn, but the Municipal Council there hoped to rebuild and restock their library, and left Blackett with the impression that his firm would secure the agency. Victoria and Winnipeg were disappointing, and Blackett, without explaining why he bypassed Toronto, travelled on to Montreal. He 'regained the custom' of the Fraser Institute, but had to admit that McGill University's librarians were perfectly satisfied with their existing arrangements.

Blackett's return to the United States was only a little more successful than the Canadian débâcle. Herbert Putnam had just been appointed Librarian to the Library of Congress: 'I think for many reasons there will be no alterations because Mr Putnam's appointment is mainly to break through the jobbery that has always existed in this library, and although I think for personal reasons he would wish to place the agency with us I gather that he will not make any radical changes where satisfaction has been given to avoid any suspicion of favouritism or benefits.' More tangible was a meeting with a new Boston firm, Small, Maynard & Co. The arrangements for the Beacon/Westminster series of biographies are described in detail below. In New York Blackett took the opportunity to visit Funk and Wagnall 'who seem to be doing their utmost for the Pulpit Commentary', and to sell them 500 sets of the twelve-volume Shakespeare in the Parchment Library. Blackett summarized the results of his tour in the following terms.

> In Australia the difficulties of Bookselling is [*sic*] the fact that Booksellers pure and simple do not exist except in a very few cases. They rely entirely for their livelihood on the sale of Stationery and Fancy Goods. Orders for back stock is [*sic*] a thing of the past, except in educational books where they have the supplying of schools and colleges. In most of the Colonies I find the Board of Education have adopted a series of their own, so that even this branch is limited. Owing to the failure of Messrs Petherick & Moore in Sydney many thousand pounds of stock are still on the market, and our own books in the few popular lines that we [have,] have been so slaughtered in price that it is difficult to secure orders at current rates. Every steamer brings out a large supply of new books which they find it difficult to get rid of. The sale generally means either a great success at the moment and they have not enough to supply, or else the books never catch on and they are unable on any terms to get rid of the stock.
> Unfortunately throughout the whole of Australia, New Zealand and British Columbia there is a wave of unrest caused by the gold speculation. In this way I found my journey considerably hampered by having to make repeated calls before I could see the principals, and then I was invariably asked to call again. Any one representing books only has not the same chance as those travellers who carry Stationery and Fancy Goods, and those who look for their living as travellers can sort up their lines to greater advantage and can afford to give away part of their commission on their books to secure a good general order. Whereas I was limited by Heinemann and others not to break into our 10% commission. I offer this explanation to the Board as some explanation is necessary to account for my failure to sell books. On the other hand I believe that the two agencies of the Perth and Brisbane Free Libraries will bring us a commission within a reasonable time sufficient to cover the whole of my

expenses. The Libraries for whom we act expressed their surprise that no one had called before on behalf of the firm, and they seemed to be exceedingly pleased at my visit. I can assure the Board with every confidence that the Libraries we now act for we shall continue to hold in spite of the great competition and the number of applications which reach them by every mail offering to do the work 10% cheaper than we do. I think it well to call the Board's attention to this as it is a question in my mind whether we should not lower our terms before we are compelled to do so, which I think is bound to come sooner or later. The whole system of Library Agencies has changed within the last few years owing to the facilities offered by the Steamship Coys. It means that the work must be more rapidly carried out. Feeling sure that this will materially affect us I have settled terms with the American Express Co. to the satisfaction of the Boston Libraries to collect weekly shipments up to 100 lbs or £20 in value, which will save a Consular Certificate, and deliver direct to the Libraries saving brokers fees the other end. I expect to hear very shortly that this system has been generally adopted.

This document has been quoted at length because of its astonishing *naïveté*. Blackett's predecessors on the Trübner side of the concern would have been intimately familiar, as a result of years of experience, with the kind of trade information he so painfully learned on his travels. Alfred Trench, travelling on behalf of the firm in the 1880s had merely visited New York and Boston publishers with whom he and Paul were already doing business: he had not dashed around a foreign country assuming that any Londoner would be welcome, and trying to impose upon its booksellers and librarians an alien system of distribution. And Henry S. King, back in the 1870s, had applied to the international book trade his already formidable general knowledge of shipping, markets and distribution networks.

The annual report for 1900 again showed a loss, of £5,247. This time it was attributed to the general depression in the publishing trade caused by the Boer War, and by events in the United States, notably the presidential election in that country. The results of Blackett's world tour were still deemed to be 'satisfactory'. This was the last year in which a formal report was filed with the Stock Exchange. Henceforth the debit figures appeared only in the *Stock Exchange Yearbooks*: 1901, £5,903; 1902, £5,519; 1903, £5,161; 1904, £4,703; 1905, £4,634.

In July of 1903, the firm made yet another move. Their new premises was the house at 43 Gerrard Street, Soho, that had belonged, in the seventeenth century, to John Dryden. Renamed Dryden House, it was much smaller than Paternoster House, the Charing Cross Road building they had opened with such fanfare a dozen years earlier. Blackett wrote an open letter to the Editor of the *Publishers' Circular* which was published under the heading 'What Moving a Publisher's Stock Means'. The job of moving 100 tons of quire stock had taken three months of overtime labour on the part of the regular staff: 'when they left they looked more like a lot of sweeps than anything else'. Bookshelves had to be emptied, dismantled, removed and rebuilt, and refilled. In the absence of other evidence, it appears that the move was an attempt to reduce the firm's indebtedness by selling the building and renting the new premises. A new series, the Dryden House Memoirs, was announced. But before the books began to appear, Blackett's career with Kegan Paul, Trench, Trübner & Co. Ltd. had come to an end. By 1905, after ten years, his ability to convince the board that he could manage a publishing business had finally run out.

IV

The books published during Blackett's administration of Kegan Paul, Trench, Trübner & Co. Ltd. were not particularly distinguished. In 1897, he and Waugh initiated three new series. The Pamphlet Library, which Waugh edited, comprised *Political Pamphlets*, selected, arranged and introduced by Pollard and published in 1897, *Literary Pamphlets: Chiefly Relating to Poetry from Sidney to Byron* (Ernest Rhys, in two volumes, 1897) and *Religious Pamphlets* (the Rev. Percy Dearmer, in 1898). Waugh explained in a preface to his volume that

> The object of *The Pamphlet Library* is to set before readers who are interested in the literary and constitutional history of our

country the text of those pamphlets or tractates which, besides possessing the only saving qualities of distinction and style, have also exercised a striking influence upon the current of events.

A promised fourth volume, of 'pamphlets of dramatic significance', seems not to have appeared.

The Out of Door Library was less ambitious: its four volumes, in 1897–8 were merely reissues of books published in New York by Scribners: *Angling, Athletic Sports, Mountain Climbing* and *Big Game Shooting*. Each set of American-printed sheets was bound in blue cloth, and the covers were embossed with sketches of fishing rods, of golf clubs, of climbing equipment, and of trophy horns. This reissue arrangement was perhaps made during Blackett's first American journey. It scarcely constitutes a series in the usual sense of the word.

But the Wolseley Military Series was more substantial: by 1902 there would be nine volumes. It was literary and historical where the old Military Handbooks were practical. Edited by Captain Walter H. James, the series demonstrates the assumptions of English military writers in the years before the Boer war, when British experience was limited to 'Queen Victoria's little wars', mostly in colonial locations. The series was named for Garnet Wolseley, a hero of the Ashanti war in West Africa and later of the 1882 Egyptian war; from 1895 to 1904 he was commander in chief of the British army.[35] Spencer Blackett's own military experience, and the contacts he had made as a solider, may have influenced the shape of the series. The object of the Wolseley series was a dual one: to provide English translations of the best of foreign military books, and to add original works on neglected 'portions of our military history'. The first title, in 1897, was *With the Royal Headquarters in 1870–71*, by the Franco-Prussian war general J. von Verdy du Vernois. The third, G.J. Younghusband's *Indian Frontier Warfare* (1898) was an original work, and so was the fifth, T.S. Baldock's *Cromwell as a Soldier* (1899). In the latter case, James's editorial preface explains that Englishmen normally see Cromwell 'from a political point of view', not as a soldier. A Prussian author, von Hoenig, 'has written a life of the great Englishman. It is not, however, in all respects accurate, and, although its translation was suggested to me for the Wolseley

Series, I preferred to put forth an original work written by one of Cromwell's own countrymen.' The series ended in 1902 with another translation, Yorck von Wartenburg's *Napoleon as a General.* By that time, after the dramatic impact of the experience of the Boer War on the consciousness of both soldiers and civilians in Britain, James's preface was profoundly outdated. His rationale for publishing translations had been that strategy and tactics had been treated much more widely by foreign authors, who enjoyed direct military experience, than by English writers. His remark that 'England has been engaged in no great war since the beginning of the century', was referred to a footnote: 'This was written in 1897.' There was no further mention of the Boer War. But about the same time, the old series of practical Military Handbooks was revived.

In 1899, Blackett's expensive round-the-world junket paid off for the firm in a small way, in the shape of a series that offered readers an experience of 'short but crisp biography'. It was a co-publishing arrangement with Small, Maynard & Co. of Boston. Blackett had reported to the Board:

> One line I decided to take up which is issued by a new firm who promise to do good business, viz., a biography of prominent Americans. It occurs to me that now is a very opportune moment to put such a scheme upon the market as so much has taken place during the last few months to bring the two nations closer together. It is proposed to start a similar series of prominent men in England which will be taken up by the same firm in America, and from inquiries I made of the sale of this class of book on the spot I find that some editions dealing more exhaustively with the subject are selling very well, so that I hope a short but crisp biography may receive a popular sale.

The Beacon (American) and Westminster (English) biographies together comprise an attractive series, brief, well-designed, and each illustrated with an elegant portrait.

The Boston series, edited by M.A. DeWolfe Howe, aimed 'to furnish brief, readable, and authentic accounts of the lives of those Americans whose personalities have impressed themselves most deeply on the character and history of their country'. Their brevity was designed at pocket size, to meet the needs of 'the average busy man and woman' for whom lengthy, 'more formal lives', were unsuitable.[36] The subjects of over twenty volumes range from Phillips Brooks and Aaron Burr to Daniel Webster and Walt Whitman. Herbert Small and his colleagues had only just incorporated Small, Maynard & Company when he signed a contract with Blackett in April 1899. The American company agreed to sell to their English partners 250 cloth- and 50 leather-bound copies each of the first ten volumes of the Beacon series, at 29 cents and 50 cents respectively. Blackett would supply a brass die with which the Americans could impress his company's device on the leather bindings. Future biographies were to be sold to Kegan Paul on similar terms.

By autumn, the agreement in the opposite direction was settled. Blackett proposed that the American issue of The Westminster Biographies be published in Boston from English plates, furnished at no charge by Kegan Paul; the modest fees paid to authors, up to £25 except in special cases, would be shared. Small concurred; he believed 'that there is every chance that your biographies will sell as well here as The Beacon Biographies, if not, in many cases, better'. He assured Blackett that extra funds would be forthcoming if the English publisher could 'secure from time to time some distinguished name to add to your list of authors'. In terms of subjects, he was looking for an emphasis on 'men of letters', and was particularly delighted to hear that Blackett would be putting out a Browning biography. 'That ought to have a really very large sale in this country.' For his part, Small intended to publish The Westminster Biographies in a format uniform with the Beacon series.

This format consisted of cloth bindings, blue in Boston and green in London, stamped with a decorative border and the respective publisher's device, either Westminster Abbey or the summit of Beacon Hill. The size was about 15 by 10 centimetres.

The biography of Robert Browning that Blackett promised to Herbert Small was written not by a literary scholar commissioned for the purpose, but by his assistant Arthur Waugh. Only five more contributions to the Westminster Biographies appeared, all in 1900–1: *George Eliot* (Clara Thomson); *Daniel Defoe* (Wilfred Whitten); *John Wesley* (Frank Banfield); *Adam Duncan* (H.W.

Wilson); and *John Henry Cardinal Newman* (A.R. Waller and G.H.S. Burrow).[37]

The Beacon Biographies can be characterized as a substantial series, managed by an independent editor, lasting for several years, and launching the reputation of their ambitious publisher. The Westminster Biographies were less impressive. Waugh, once again, had to submit his scholarly talents to the needs of the firm, rather than attract outside writers. It is not surprising that in January of 1902 he departed from 'this uneventful, unambitious routine', to accept 'a very attractive offer' and become managing director of Chapman & Hall. Spencer Blackett survived on his own for a further three years.

V

The final six or seven years of the Kegan Paul firm can be dealt with briefly. By this time, they were no longer in the front rank of London publishers, and when Paul died in July 1902, the *Times* obituary remarked that 'As publishers, his firm used to be more active than it is now.' People began to compare them with a new company, The Bodley Head, owned by John Lane, initially in partnership with Charles Elkin Mathews. Or rather, to compare the Bodley Head to what they had been. Lane's concept of a literary publishing house with a strong vision and a clear sense of its position in the market-place seems to have reminded people of the Kegan Paul of a few years earlier. Roden Noel, for example, told Mathews that he wanted to begin publishing his books with The Bodley Head. Kegan Paul, he explained, 'have now become a limited company. . . . I confess I would like some human being to "publish" me, rather than a limited company! Especially someone with an interest in Literature as such and not *merely* as so much marketable and common retail "stuff".' Another Bodley Head author spoke of the undesirability of publishing verse with 'none of the qualities of poetry save that fatal fluidity which flows like a great river thro' the doors of Kegan Paul'.[38]

It is not clear when Blackett left the firm, or under what circumstances. The *Stock Exchange Year Book* for 1905 lists him as Managing Director, at the new office of Dryden House. But in 1906 the position was filled by H. Wingfield. For Blackett's later history we have only the evidence that he died intestate, leaving an estate of £20, at the age of 61, on 20 September 1920, at Brookwood Railway Station, in Hampshire. And Arthur Waugh's remark on Blackett having 'followed the career of a rolling stone . . . to the end'.

Wingfield's appointment apparently lasted only a year or so, after which he moved to the board of directors; in 1907 Basil W. Willett was Manager and Secretary, and this situation persisted until 1911. In that year he moved on to The Bodley Head, 'There being no direction' at Kegan Paul, Trench, Trübner & Company.[39] The 1912 yearbook listed as Managers Laurie Magnus and William Swan Sonnenschein, who were also managing directors of George Routledge and Sons, Ltd., and noted that 'In September 1911, the management and control of the company for 99 years was taken over by George Routledge & Sons Ltd.' The debit balance at that point was £5,611. In 1914 the directors were Magnus and Sonnenschein with Cecil Franklin, and henceforth the affairs of Kegan Paul, Trench, Trübner were handled by the management of the Routledge firm.[40] Routledge continued to operate it as a separate company, however, until 1947, and even then, after the Second World War, they perpetuated the powerfully evocative name in their new imprint: Routledge and Kegan Paul. The year of transition, 1911, was the fortieth anniversary of the foundation of H.S. King & Co., in Cornhill.

The evidence for the end of Kegan Paul, Trench, Trübner & Co. Ltd. as an independent firm is neither literary nor financial; the evidence is the fact of the 1911 takeover. It might be argued that the firm that began in 1871 with Henry S. King's publication of Stopford Brooke's *Freedom in the Church of England* had really come to an end in 1889, when Paul lost control of his own company. But he remained involved until 1895, alive until 1902, and associated, in the minds of many readers, with the firm for another decade. An echo of the past, and a sense of the continuity which these publishing houses exhibit, may be discerned in a letter to the firm dated July 1910, from Stopford Brooke, now very elderly. Willett had asked if Brooke would accept a 10% royalty on all his books, superseding all earlier agreements. 'I am much obliged by your letter,' he wrote. 'It has cleared my path. It will amuse me if that dead book should suffer a resurrection.'[41] As we shall see, Charles Kegan Paul's dead name also suffered a resurrection, continuing to sell books for Routledge's until 1947 under the Kegan Paul, Trench, Trubner imprint (the umlaut was silently dropped in 1916), and from that date until 1988 as Routledge and Kegan Paul. Since then, when the publishing conglomerate Associated Book Publishers acquired the company and then sold Routledge, a partially owned subsidiary of Associated Book Publishers has been operated by Peter Hopkins: Kegan Paul International. They publish the kind of books on Africa, Asia, the Middle East and the Pacific that were part of Henry S. King's stock-in-trade, that constituted Trübner's specialty, and that fell within the catholic span of the intellectual interests of Charles Kegan Paul.

The final chapter of this book will not trace that history in detail. Despite the continuity embodied in the name of the imprint, book-publishing decisions after 1911 were made by people unconnected with the old firm. The last new book in the International Scientific Series appeared that year. The personal influence of Henry S. King, and of Charles Kegan Paul and the successors with whom they worked, had come to an end. What did continue was the Kegan Paul name, the name which the Rev. Mr Paul had arrogated to himself when he transformed himself into a publisher. It is therefore worthwhile to return to Paul's personality, to his life, and to his autobiographical memoir.

CHAPTER 5

THE KEGAN PAUL LEGACY: THE MAKING, CONSOLIDATION AND SURVIVAL OF A REPUTATION FOR SERIOUS BOOKS

Charles Kegan Paul wrote a poem in 1890, soon after his installation as joint manager with George Redway of the reconstituted Kegan Paul, Trench, Trübner & Company. The title was 'The End of Wandering', and in the preface to his collected poems, *Ont the Way Side*, Paul states explicitly that it refers to his submission to the Roman Catholic Church.[1]

> Except in thee I find no resting-place;
> Except in thee I find no help from sin:
> Beauteous thou art without, beauteous within,
> Mistress of virtue, channel of all grace.
> Through clouds for many years I saw thy face,
> And heard thy gentle voice that strove to win
> Thine erring son, but sounded faint and thin,
> As his who calls from topmost cliff to base.
> I turned, self-willed, to walk in pathways drear,
> Now dark, now led by gleams, and yet the while
> I climbed unknowing; all at once is clear,
> My Mother meets me with her gentle smile:
> 'I watched thee long, my son, I bade thee come.
> Here is thy rest, and here thine only home.'

The contrast between Paul's tortured sensibility and the impetuous vulgarity of Spencer Blackett, or the rather unsavoury preoccupations of George Redway, who had made his name as the publisher of books on theosophy, palmistry, phallicism and tobacco, could hardly be exaggerated. And yet the transformation of the imprint was not a mere change of personality in the manager's office. In the forty years of existence of the King and Kegan Paul house, the book trade had also transformed, with heavy capitalization and corporate direction beginning to take the place of personal attention driven by a literary sensibility. Nor was Paul the helpless victim of circumstance. His ingenuous fascination with Bottomley was obviously an important factor in his difficulties in the late eighties. And although he managed for a long time to keep his impecuniosity out of the record, it is likely that balance sheets for Paul's years in control of the firm would look little better than the Stock Exchange Reports of the nineties. Money was the main reason why he and Trench lost Tennyson, Meredith and Stevenson. It was probably also the main reason why they lost the firm. But Paul and Trench would have invested any money they had in poets and novelists. Bottomley, Sinnett, Redway and Blackett put it into buildings, and into publishing projects that were novel without being innovative.

I

The dominant experience of Charles Kegan Paul's life after the firm became a limited company was his conversion to Roman Catholicism. Some commentators have explained the religious decision in terms of the business and personal disappointments of being associated with the Hansard Union débâcle,[2] and no doubt that humiliating experience did affect him. But he first began to attend Mass in 1888, the year before the trouble began, and as we have seen, the desire for spiritual and aesthetic satisfaction pervaded his whole life. As early as his 1882 essay, 'Faith and Unfaith', he had observed that 'All that lies between the Catholic Church and extreme free-thought is whirling and surging, but gradually settling into two streams, one recurrent, the other dashing rapidly to some unknown cataract, whose roar is heard by almost all, however smoothly glides their barque.' At that time he admitted to feeling 'the difficulty of accepting either hypothesis, but mainly the impossibility of accepting the Catholic solution'.[3] Six years later the impossible had become inevitable.

In *Memories*, Paul strove to explain himself and his need for an explicit creed. Even the experience of Positivism, he found, 'gives order and regularity to life, inculcates simplicity of manners, aims at a certain amount of discipline, and . . . [makes] of humanity the ideal woman, the great mother and mistress of all'. He said, 'I doubt if I should have known the Faith but for Positivism, which gave me a rule and discipline of which I had been unaware.' However, 'Positivism is a fair-weather creed, when men are strong, happy, untempted, or ignorant that they are tempted . . . ; but it has no message for the sorry and the sinful, no restoration for the erring, no succour in the hour of death.' One of the strongest influences in Paul's move to embrace the Catholic church was his reading of, and admiration for, John Henry Newman, and before him of Blaise Pascal.

> Since Pascal none has put so plainly as [Newman] the dread alternative, all or nothing, faith or unfaith, God or the denial of God. I had not denied Him, but had left Him on one side, and now, as it were, God took His revenge. This is no place to explain in detail how in sorrow and desolation of spirit God left His servant alone for awhile to clutch in vain for some help in temptation, for some solution of doubt, and find none, if it were not God and the old creeds. It were to lay the secrets of the soul too bare to declare how each hesitation to submit to what was becoming intellectually clear was followed by some moral or spiritual fall, as though the Father would allow His child to slip in miry ways, if nothing else would teach the need of guidance.

Did Charles Kegan Paul regard Horatio Bottomley, George Redway, Alfred Sinnett and Spencer Blackett as 'God's revenge?' Perhaps he did, although the temptations and 'falls' may also have presented themselves in his private life and personal relationships. Chronic pain, since the 1895 injury, must have figured largely in the sorrows and desolation of spirit.

The final moment of conversion, as he presents it in his memoir, was intellectual as much as spiritual. Paul had been translating Pascal's *Pensées*, and making a careful study of the documentation for a miraculous cure experienced by a member of the philosopher's circle. 'It is impossible to find anything of the kind better attested.' Then a friend was the beneficiary of a miracle at Lourdes. 'It was not that miracles having been declared in the Bible made these later occurrences possible, but that these, properly attested in our own days, and in times so near our own, made the Bible miracles more credible than they were before.' The conscientious and precise intellect of Eton and Sturminster Marshall, of Paternoster Square and the Savile Club, came gradually to believe in belief, and thence to believe again in God, but this time within the discipline of the Roman Catholic church.

A member of his family, probably Margaret Agnes Paul, expressed her serious misgivings about how inconsistent such a conversion would appear to anyone who knew her husband's history.[4] She was not unsympathetic with religion as such, but feared, he recorded, 'that as my opinions had been so long in a state of change, this also might be a passing phase'. In deference to her wish, he decided in the spring of 1889 to wait a year before finally making up his mind on the question. It was, as we know, an *annus horribilis* in his life; in May of 1890, while travelling in France, he became privately convinced at last, and in August he made his public submission at Fulham, London in a church of the Servite order. In the closing pages of *Memories* he expressed his absolute devotion to the Church, despite the abundance of sorrows which had come to him since his submission. And in his will he commended his soul to Almighty God and instructed his family to consult a friend, Charles Robertson, about the correct rituals of a Catholic funeral.[5]

Paul put his pen at the service of his new coreligionists, writing several pamphlets for the Catholic Truth Society, as well as his 1891 *Confessio Viatoris*, much of which is repeated word-for-word in *Memories*. He was particularly attracted to the doctrine of celibacy, but he interpreted his approval of the principle through his own experience of a long and happy marriage. A celibate priesthood, he argued, was necessary because of the fact that wives share their husband's interests. A married Catholic priest would be unable to preserve the secret of the confessional, because his wife would read his thoughts, even his thoughts about other people. 'Indeed,' he argued, 'when considered from the merely human side, it might be well that the freedom from ties of relationship should be extended beyond the priesthood. . . . To [the schoolmaster] his boys, to [the physician] his patients, should be the first care, and the principle is just as applicable to the other sex, now that the care of the sick is more and more in the hands of women, and the higher learning within the reach of girls.' And finally, facing directly the vexed question of overpopulation, and the need for checks, although not contraceptive ones, on population, 'few have considered whether it may not be well to seek the Church's remedy'.

Despite his new fascination with the theory, if not the practice, of celibacy, Paul remained at the head of a large and active family. Margaret resumed her literary career, with a new novel, *Kintail Place*, coming out in 1886.[6] Louis, their oldest son, became a telegraph engineer and worked in India. He died at the age of 41 in 1900, before either of his parents. Nancy Margaret, the eldest daughter, remained unmarried, as did Rose Mary. Nancy translated and compiled works in French history and had some connection with the nursing profession.[7] Their sister Ruth Frances was married in 1881 to Willie Rendel, a civil engineer. Paul told Oscar Browning of his satisfaction with this outcome.[8] The younger son, Eden (1865–1944) became a physician, practising in Asia; later he was a medical writer; he and his wife Cedar Paul spent the years just before the First World War in France; he also lived and worked in Japan; and he was a member and proponent of the British Sexological Society.[9] Eden and Cedar Paul were a well-known team of translators.

Friends, as always, played an important part in Charles Kegan Paul's later life. Every Easter he travelled to Europe with a group of four other men. His life-long role of mentor and tutor to younger men continued to the last. In *Memories* he noted that 'my experience has been that many young men are graciously willing to make friends of older men'. One fragment of Paul's personal correspondence that has survived, a letter to Arthur Pollard in 1887, bears out this statement. Pollard was 27, Paul 58.

> It is *such* a pleasure to me when you drop in for a talk. Some one said it was so sad when kittens grew into cats. It is almost as sad when pleasant young men who are not bored by the society of

their elders – which many of them with just reason are – grow into married men. The kittens cease to frisk, the youths no longer drop in and sit up late o'nights. For there are few in these evil days sufficiently imbued with the spirit of early Christianity to follow St Paul's rule, and having wives behave as if they had none. But you will probably retort with base and worthless minute scholarship, and say my interpretation of his words is not the right one.[10]

Paul took seriously his role as teacher, as well as parent. In an article on Shakespeare's life, he wrote: 'I am intimately persuaded that there is no such thing as gathering grapes from thorns or figs from thistles. . . . One of the most powerful motives, as it seems to me, for self-cultivation, ought not to be even our own enjoyment, but to help the generations yet unborn, our children, who so largely depend on what we are.'[11] Not only with his own sons and daughters, or with protégés like Arthur Pollard, but also with aspiring writers of his acquaintance, he made special efforts. Indeed, Paul's approach to literature, as to life, might be characterized as pastoral, in the sense that he advised and encouraged authors whose talents could flourish where his own creativity was suppressed. What is interesting is that in his own life, Paul had been drawn not to gentle and scholarly counsellor-critics, but to larger-than-life, rather flamboyant men of the world: King, Kingsley, and Bottomley. This inclination may have been shaped by Paul's troubled relationship with his own father.

It was Henry S. King's approach, that of a businessman with large amounts of ready capital at hand when the time came to invest in an International Scientific Series or a Hesba Stretton, that formed Paul's introduction to the economics of the publishing business. He renewed the contract with Tennyson in 1879, making a financial decision that may not have been altogether wise. He invested heavily in the Gordon journals in 1885, outbidding a much larger and stronger firm, Longmans. As time went on, he learned a measure of restraint, and 'the hope of authors . . . their fellow clubman' learned how to offer a commission agreement or, at best, shared profits. Possibly Alfred Trench exercised a restraining influence on his partner; or perhaps it was Margaret Agnes

Paul and the demands of a large family. Wilfrid Meynell, in his affectionate but penetrating obituary memoir, put it this way:

> Such a man, if you impersonalise him, given for the first time the opportunity of trading, will trade more closely, not more laxly, than his accustomed fellow. Now at last is his chance, he thinks; and he tightens the bargain. Moreover his timidity comes into play. Risks frighten him, and he schemes to lessen them.

But even when he grew apart from writers because of these attitudes, Paul 'always remained in general society a great favourite: a grave man, with serenity of discretion; a general lover of his race, but with a shrewdly sharp tongue for individual weaknesses; a man indeed of prejudices as well as of more agreeable prepossessions; seemingly aloof and independent, yet possessed, more than perhaps any man of his time, by the overmastering personalities of two men whose "acolyte" he was'. These, in Meynell's opinion, were Kingsley and Newman. We might, however, add the names of King and of Bottomley, whose influence in the commercial sphere was almost as strong as theirs in the spiritual.

Had Paul become a lawyer or a physician before moving into the life of a man of letters, his religious opinions would have been of little interest to contemporaries. It was because his profession was the Anglican clergy that he became interested in Unitarianism; it represented a way in which he could reconcile for a time his loss of faith with the retention of his Dorset parish. And the adherence to Comte and Positivism only seemed so dramatic and public, even scandalous, in the light of his final submission to Rome. Each step made him look, as Margaret Paul perceived, absurdly inconsistent. She may have been aware of how people like Spencer Blackett regarded her husband's opinions as irrelevant and pretentious. But Charles Kegan Paul didn't see it that way; it was so important to him to articulate his views, to argue and assert them, that he was unable to perceive that to less serious, less thoughtful contemporaries, they seemed merely ludicrous.

When Paul died on 10 July 1902, the event drew forth a variety of obituary comments. Wilfrid Meynell, writing anonymously as 'One who knew him', has already been cited extensively. Those who did not know him had less affectionate images in their minds.

The Times obituary said: 'His manner was simple, unsophisticated, but his character was more complex than it seemed.' The *Westminster Gazette* called him 'a most interesting personality, whose mental progress has been of a most adventurous order'. *The Bookman* regarded his as 'a business without any backbone', and reported that 'Mr Kegan Paul had also a knack of quarrelling with his authors. He had a sharp tongue, and used it with some freedom. The consequence was that many of them left him, and the whole position became precarious.' But despite Paul's 'mistakes and misfortunes, nobody disputed the uprightness of his character. His error was in taking up business without a sound business training.'

Some of these comments may come as a surprise to those who know Paul only by his book of memoirs published in 1899. The text of *Memories*, it is now clear, conceals more than it reveals about the nature of his cultural attitudes and business methods. Paul's memoir presents his self-created image as a gentleman publisher, a sensitive man of literature with a special interest in the best of contemporary poetry. But when his firm's history is drawn out of an analysis of its archives, resulting in a reconstruction of the publisher's list over a period of some twenty-five years, a different picture is revealed. Half the books were not financed by the publisher, but rather published on commission for the authors. Important names like Tennyson and Stevenson appear in the list, but later move on to more congenial houses. And modern secular science shares the same imprint with orthodox religion. A critical reading of the memoir has raised new questions: where did Paul's investment capital come from? How independent were his choices? And what was his identity, his personal and commercial reputation among writers and readers in the literary community of London in his time? The evidence of the obituaries and of some contemporaries, suggests that Paul was regarded as a failure, unable to resolve the tensions between commercial and literary demands in the life of a publisher. But this grim picture is tempered when we remember Paul in his prime, investing in books, courting authors, entertaining Hardy and visiting George Eliot.

The obituarists of 1902 were themselves relying on *Memories*, still in print and earning royalties after three years. That book's publishing history affected, and continues to affect, the posthumous assessment of its author. The publication of a reissue in 1971 returned the book temporarily to print, and thus made it accessible to a new generation of scholars. On the subject of Paul's self-created identity, the anonymous *Times Literary Supplement* review of the reissue is relevant: 'Written with unaffected simplicity, these memoirs form an attractive picture of a high-principled, hard-working, benevolent and successful Englishman, who might well be taken, though not altogether correctly, as a stereotype of the Victorian middle class.'[12]

II

Of publishers associated with the firm, apart from Charles Kegan Paul, the four names that stand out are King and Trench, Redway and Blackett. Henry S. King began his working life in the book trade, and made his first success there, as a quarter-share partner in the firm of Smith, Elder. And he returned to it for an important few years, from 1871 to 1877, under his own name. But King, with his banking and East India interests, was always more than a publisher. More importantly, he was never a typical publisher. He must have learned some of the skills of managing authors, marketing titles, and handling series from George Smith during their years of association. But he also learned, and built upon, the atypical side of the Smith, Elder operation, their ability to invest profits earned outside of the book trade in their publishing ventures. And as we have seen, he passed on his assumptions to his successor in the business, who scrambled to publish that way, but without benefit of the same financial backing.

Alfred Trench remains an enigma, and despite all the new evidence presented here, he still appears in the shadow of his famous father. His contribution to the firm has been so little understood that 'Trench & Co.' is sometimes described as an independent business, a firm of theological publishers.[13] It has now been established when he was born, married and died, and when he retired to Italy and later the south of France, avoiding the scandal and dreary difficulties of the firm's resurrection in the nineties. And passing references to his name in the firm's records make it clear that he was an active partner, travelling abroad, signing contracts and making decisions. However, Trench was not himself a literary man: his name does not appear on the title-pages of books, or on articles in prominent journals. When he died, still abroad, in 1938 on the eve of the Second World War, 88 years of age, there were few contemporaries in London who knew who he was, or had been.[14] And yet his counsel, his reputation and the overflow of his father's reputation, and perhaps his financial investment, may have been crucial to the Kegan Paul firm of the 1880s in ways for which no evidence survives.

All the people who managed the firm's editorial and commercial policy were men, and an analysis of its character in terms of gender roles would reveal an identity that superficially, at least, was wholly masculine. Only about a fifth of the King–Kegan Paul authors were women, working in genres that were typically restricted to women. More important, no woman secured a position anywhere near the centres of power in the firm. The same was true of other publishing houses in London at the same time.[15] And yet, a close examination of significant moments in its history suggests that the wives of publishers had a disproportionate influence on the firm's fortunes. It was marriage with Ellen Blakeway that secured Henry King's emergence from Brighton and his entrée into one of the most prestigious of London houses. George Smith sold a partnership to his fiancée's sister's husband, not to a struggling bookseller of Brighton whose grandfather had been a banker. Marriage with Harriet Eleanor Baillie-Hamilton was not quite so crucial, but it did bring to King's firm an important poet, as well as members of the Mazzini circle, notably Swinburne and his contribution to *Pleasure*. Moreover, King seems to have been highly conscious of his aristocratic Hamilton connections, the two dukes who were his wife's uncles. It is not known whether Isabella Trench, Edith Redway, or Harriet Jane Blackett exercised equivalent powers behind the scenes. But with Margaret Agnes Paul the theme of the influential wife returns in force.

When Margaret Paul died in 1905 she had £12,800 to leave, only £2,900 of which had come from her husband's estate three years earlier. The balance remained from the trust funds that had secured her marriage settlement, supplemented by capital of which she had power to dispose under the will of her brother, W.J. Colvile. Some of this wealth had already been dispersed earlier, in gifts 'by way of advancement' to her five children. It seems likely, as speculated above, that at least the interest on these funds would have been available in 1877, at the time when Charles Paul needed capital to invest in the King firm. And it might be further suggested that Margaret sensibly declined to put forward any of her wealth at the time of the Hansard Bubble, and the Kegan Paul, Trench, Trübner amalgamation.

Her novels came to the firm, and remained on the list as steady if unspectacular titles, concealed in the anonymity of 'the author of Dorothy'. She was a trusted translator, receiving several small honoraria for translations of books in French and German. Margaret Agnes Paul also created in her drawing room a literary salon where she and her husband could entertain their firm's authors and others in the London literary world. Thomas Hardy was a frequent visitor. Robert Browning was asked to dinner at least once, and he and Paul were in the habit of walking home together at night after dinner parties in other people's houses. Charles and Margaret Paul visited the Huxleys when they lived in London. And they were among George Eliot's innermost circle, visiting her and George Henry Lewes not only when they were 'at home to everybody', but on private occasions as well. Although Paul also carried on a single man's social life at his club, the Savile, Margaret made an indispensable contribution to the business by her management of the drawing room.

These observations are a reminder that the publishing fortunes of the nineteenth century were family fortunes. Leonore Davidoff and Catherine Hall have argued in *Family Fortunes* that even though women did not exercise control over the monies they brought with them into their marriages, nevertheless the way in which financial affairs were handled according to the assumptions of gender was crucial to the amassing and preserving of middle-class fortunes.[16] Ellen King, certainly, and probably Margaret Agnes Paul were each the source of funds that helped to establish or preserve the company. And as we have seen, the initial partnership between Henry S. King and Charles Kegan Paul may well have been initiated by arrangements either to review Harriet King's poetry or to publish Margaret Paul's novels. And yet the two women's contribution is not an obvious factor in the business history of the imprint. It has to be inferred and brought to the foreground, teased out of a knowledge of marriage customs in general and of this configuration of relationships in particular.

George Redway's and Spencer Blackett's contributions to the firm have required almost as much detective-work research as those of the senior publishers' wives. Redway had five years at the head of the firm (1889–94), and Blackett ten (1895–1905). But both men directed the company in a way fundamentally different from that of their predecessors, because both reported to a board of directors, and indirectly to shareholders. As a limited company, the new combined firm had purchased the Kegan Paul name and reputation along with its stock of books published in the distinguished Kegan Paul series. Both managers attempted to trade on the reputation that the Kegan Paul imprint had developed during the eighteen seventies and eighties; but neither was able either to maintain the strengths of the imprint, or to remedy its weaknesses.

George Redway's interview with *The Publishers' Circular* in 1891 gives some insight into his approach to the firm, as do his 'Reminiscences' forty years later. He was smugly pleased to show off the vast Charing Cross Road operation, five storeys of bustle and excitement. But when asked for his views on the relations between authors and publishers, he remarked 'that publishers are inclined to be too indulgent to their clients; that there is a civility in their dealings with authors which is not always appreciated. . . . I am sure I wish the Author's Society all joy of their clients, if they get some of the impracticable folk we have to deal with.' These comments were injudicious at best; they were not likely to elicit and nourish the loyalty of someone like Lady Caithness, who had bought shares in the company only to find her book dropped from the list, or Austin Dobson. A year later, Dobson would find himself struggling with the problem of how 'grasping' he should be when Redway and his colleagues wrote 'nice and agreeable letters'. Presumably he had not noticed the disagreeable interview. Redway's arrogant public remarks stand in unmistakable contrast to the much more gracious and generous tone of Charles Kegan Paul in his essay on 'The Production and Life of Books'.

In the excitement of the Bottomley years, the time when the massive Trübner list and the Paul–Trench prestige were descending on Redway's thirty-year-old shoulders, he could be ambitious as well as confident. His attempt to manage the firm in the nineties was, it transpired, the high point of his publishing career. Redway returned briefly to independent publishing in 1895 when he left the Kegan Paul firm, working from a shop in Hart Street, Bloomsbury. Then he joined the army at the outbreak of the Boer War in 1899, as a junior military officer and later an army tutor, and his subsequent career was a military one. He contributed several titles to the firm's series of Military Handbooks, and later served as First World War correspondent to *The Globe*. He continued to be a collector of books and manuscripts. But his vocation remained insecure. In 1904 Redway wrote to Richard Garnett, asking for a recommendation for a position as Secretary of the Royal United Service Institution. He reminded Garnett of their meeting twenty years earlier, 'when I found you an original edition of de Quincy's Confessions which you wanted to reprint for Kegan Paul's Parchment Series'. Redway then referred, deprecatingly, to his 'unfortunate propensity to dissipate my little fortune in producing books upon such subjects [as bibliography and archaeology]'.[17] George Redway was a person ambitious for success, without any particular skill or aptitude for the book trade, but who also happened to be a bookish dilettante. He was a very unsuccessful publisher.

As for Spencer Blackett, he seems indeed to have 'followed the life of a rolling stone to the end'. He made his way into the firm in 1895 at the age of thirty-six, impressing the board of directors with his military panache, and also with his experience for four or five years as a publisher of popular ephemeral novels, 'shilling shockers'. But when we look at Arthur Waugh's memory of his own youthful apprenticeship at the firm, in the light of our knowledge of its earlier history, it seems clear that Blackett would have been unable to function for long without a literary adviser like Waugh, and that his difficulties increased after the latter's 1902 departure. The roles of literary editor and commercial manager were no longer combined in one person, because Blackett could not handle the former and nor, for other reasons, had Redway. Blackett presided over the move in July 1903 to smaller premises in Gerrard Street. He cleverly made use of the fact that the new house had once belonged to John Dryden, renaming it Dryden House and establishing a series of Dryden House Memoirs. But his letter to *The Publishers' Circular* betrays the anxiety of a business in straitened circumstances: one hundred tons of quire stock were moved after hours, with sets of shelves dismantled one at a time, moved to the new building, and replaced. A staff whose physical labours made them look 'more like a lot of sweeps than anything else' was not a staff with the energy and outlook they would need to deal with the demands of an international publishing business.

The evocative name of 'Kegan Paul' has pushed into the background the names and personalities of the other people involved: Henry S. King, and Ellen and later Harriet King; Margaret Agnes Paul; Alfred Trench; George Redway, Spencer Blackett and their short-lived successors. Even Charles Kegan Paul himself, the idiosyncratic personality with his tenacious preoccupations, has been half-hidden behind the monolithic institution of the name he designed for himself and then imprinted on his books, and on the consciousness of his contemporaries.

III

'Kegan Paul' was regarded by the readers and writers of the late nineteenth century as a serious imprint. This identity began with Henry King's brief but dazzling entrepreneurial impact on the trade; it was solidified by Paul's own pastoral approach to editorship, and enhanced by an association with the patrician name and distinguished reputation of Trench. The Kegan Paul identity survived its treatment during the nineties, in the hands of theosophists, soldiers and sponge merchants, of lightweights and scoundrels, to emerge in the twentieth century still bearing its charge of probity and sobriety. Most of the evidence for this argument is indirect: no Edwardian market research survey survives, recording interviews with readers expressing what the Kegan Paul name meant to them. Even if such a report existed, replete with words like 'serious', 'scholarly', 'literary', 'collectable' and 'respectable', the readers sampled would have been unaware of the history and personalities behind their impressions.

Something closer to direct evidence exists in the comments of contemporary trade journals on the company's products. Both *The Publishers' Circular* and *The Bookman* routinely alluded to their admirably designed and produced, as well as authoritative and well-written books. And the book review sections of contemporary periodicals provide a rich vein of evidence that men and women of letters were inclined to take the imprint seriously, whatever their opinion of the individual title. As early as November 1874, when the *Examiner* reviewed Alice King's *A Cluster of Lives*, a very slight collection of brief biographies, they suggested it would find a place as a gift book. Later the same year the *Examiner* reviewer regarded Margaret Agnes Paul's *Vanessa* as 'unquestionable superiority to the mass of novelists whose work it is our evil fortune to encounter'. Seven years later the *St James* of April 1881 remarked that a C. Kegan Paul book by Robert W. Edis, *Decoration and Furniture of Houses*, had been 'produced in a manner worthy of the high reputation of the publishers'. And in an article in the *St James* on 'Bibliography and Bibliomania' in February 1882, Charles Kains-Jackson remarked that 'it is a matter for no small satisfaction that several of the leading publishers are men of high personal culture'. Charles Kegan Paul was among those 'whose personal influence has already done great things for literary taste'.[18]

Seriousness was a Victorian attribute like 'respectability', a personal quality that the publisher's imprint not only embodied, but also amplified. Paul himself was 'a grave man', and Henry King had evidenced 'a high and stern sense of duty for himself and others'. Beyond their personalities, one important reason for the reputation was that books other than fiction dominated their lists; another was that books were published so frequently on commission. And another was the look of the books: as physical objects, printed artefacts, King and Kegan Paul books rated very high for aesthetic appeal.

Paul was himself a very serious person, in spite of the occasional dry jest in a letter to Oscar Browning or Arthur Pollard. He cared deeply about ideas and beliefs; he conveyed his convictions to his children, his pupils and to the writers to whom he acted as mentor. He was deeply moral, and also a great moralizer. This trait is indeed a source of unintentional humour, evident to the reader in the late twentieth century and probably also to his youthful contemporaries a hundred years ago: an example might be his earnest effort to disprove theories that Shakespeare was homosexual, or rumours that the King marriage had once been on the point of breaking up. But in his own time, among his own generation, these were matters that went beyond gossip: serious people believed that it was morally wrong to allow such misrepresentations to be perpetuated.

The reputation, both Paul's own and that of his imprint, for serious application of the highest literary standards, was intensified by the tendency to publish mostly books in genres other than fiction – works on science or education, editions of the classics, volumes of poetry, and pamphlets engaging in religious controversy or reproducing particularly challenging sermons. Books of this kind, both severally and in the collective impression created by their assembly in a single list, attracted the collector, the autodidact, the parent or teacher seeking to enlighten the young, and the serious reader. Indeed, their collective *gravitas* may even have cast its serious shadow over the handful of novels beside them on the shelf.

To some extent the policy of publishing mostly non-fiction was dictated by Paul's, and presumably also Trench's, personal tastes. They regarded novels as largely ephemeral, mostly second-rate, and not very interesting. But another factor that mitigated against a practice of promoting fiction was the partners' policy of accepting large numbers of manuscripts for publishing on commission. Most novelists were in the writing business for the money, or at least so they hoped. The writer who chose to invest a couple of hundred pounds in his or her own text, rather than in a picture or a piece of jewellery, was likely to be a writer with a weighty sense of the importance of his or her message.

Finally, the air of seriousness was reinforced by the appearance of the books, as physical objects and printed artefacts. As *The Publishers' Circular* put it in December of 1871: 'No publisher can insist on securing a celebrated and successful author, but he can, and decidedly he should, do his part in making his books readable, authentic, honest, accessible, and fairly finished, with indexes and all things that a book should have. . . . Such honest attentions often redeem books from the trunk-maker, and lift them to the serene repose of the book-shelves.' King and Kegan Paul books rated very high for aesthetic appeal. They were well designed and carefully printed, on good paper with secure bindings that reflected the gravity of the material within. Books in series, in particular, conveyed this impression. A shelf laden with volumes of the International Scientific Series, or of the Parchment Library, was formidable evidence of a reader's intellectual or literary values.

When the history of an imprint, in its dual sense, is brought to the foreground, we have a rich and fruitful approach to cultural history, an entrée, by indirection, into the assumptions and approaches of a generation of readers. Publishers knew, or thought they knew, what the writer was doing, and what a reader wanted, and they stood between the two, doing their best to shape the books that would bring them into contact. The reputation for serious as well as beautiful books that King created, Paul and Trench developed, and Redway and Blackett traded upon, endured through the years when Routledge operated the firm as a separate subsidiary, and then after 1947 as Routledge and Kegan Paul. The firm's list in the twentieth century was made up of substantial works in the social sciences and humanities, and they competed with university presses for titles by academic authors. The imprint of Charles Kegan Paul's dominant personality had faded by that time, but the character which he had imparted to his books, a character that in Paul's lifetime had been associated by authors and readers with his idiosyncratic personality, remained to identify a serious imprint.

NOTES

Introduction

1. Both the interdisciplinarity of the history of the book and the burgeoning scholarly enthusiasm for it are apparent in the array of recent titles, and the wide range of disciplinary backgrounds of their authors. Several publishers and Centres for the Book have initiated series to foster scholarship and awareness of the subject: The British Library Studies in the History of the Book include *A Potencie of Life: Books in Society*, edited by Nicolas Barker (London: The British Library, 1993). Cambridge University Press publishes Cambridge Studies in Publishing and Printing History, edited by Terry Belanger and David McKitterick. The series includes such titles as Allen Reddick's *The Making of Johnson's Dictionary, 1746–1773* (1990), as well as my own *Cheap Bibles: Nineteenth Century Publishing and the British and Foreign Bible Society* (1991). Cambridge is also the publisher of *The Book Encompassed: Studies in Twentieth-Century Bibliography*, edited by Peter Davison (1992). The Penn State Series in the History of the Book, edited by James L.W. West III is projecting a list of scholarly books which employ historical, archival, biographical, critical, sociological and economic approaches. Journals publishing work in this field include *Publishing History*, as well as the journals of the several national Bibliographical Societies.

    For an introductory bibliography to older work on the period discussed in the present book see the 'Checklist for Further Reading', in Patricia J. Anderson and Jonathan Rose, eds *British Literary Publishing Houses, 1820–1880*. Vol. 106, *Dictionary of Literary Biography*. (Detroit: Gale Research Inc., 1991). This volume contains my contribution 'Kegan Paul, Trench, Trübner and Company Limited.'

2. SHARP, the Society for the History of Authorship, Reading and Publishing was founded in 1991. The Society publishes a newsletter and organizes an annual international conference.

3. For articles based on this research see Leslie Howsam, 'Sustained Literary Ventures: The Series in Victorian Book Publishing', *Publishing History* 32 (1992) and 'Forgotten Victorians: Contracts with Authors in the Publication Books of Henry S. King and of Kegan Paul, Trench 1871–1889', *Publishing History* 33 (1993).

4. Colin Franklin, 'Foreword', to Charles Kegan Paul, *Memories* (London: Routledge and Kegan Paul Ltd.; Hamden, Conn.: Archon Books, 1971). First published 1899 by Kegan Paul, Trench, Trübner & Co. Ltd.

5   See, among others, June Steffansen Hagen, *Tennyson and his Publishers* (London: Macmillan, 1979) and Jenifer Glynn *Prince of Publishers: A Biography of George Smith* (London: Allison and Busby, 1986).

6   James L.W. West III, 'Book History and Biography', *Publishing Research Quarterly* 10 (Fall 1994), 72.

7   For guides to these archives see Gillian Furlong, comp. *The Archives of Routledge & Kegan Paul Ltd. (1853–1973) Publishers* (London: University College London Library, 1978); Brian Maidment, 'Introduction', *The Archives of Kegan Paul, Trench, Trübner and Henry S. King 1858–1912* (Bishop's Stortford: Chadwyck-Healey, 1974); Sandy Merrick, *Index of Authors and Titles of Kegan Paul, Trench, Trübner & Henry S. King 1858–1912* (Bishop's Stortford: Chadwyck-Healey, 1974).

8   D.F. McKenzie defines bibliography as 'the discipline that studies texts as recorded forms, and the processes of their transmission, including their production and reception'. See *Bibliograpy and the Sociology of Texts* (London: The British Library, 1985), 4.

9   Gillian Fenwick has begun the work for a history of the *Dictionary of National Biography* with her books, *Women and the Dictionary of National Biography: A Guide to DNB Volumes 1885–1985 and Missing Persons* (Aldershot: Scolar Press, 1994); *Leslie Stephen's Life in Letters: A Bibliographical Study* (Aldershot: Scolar Press, 1993); and *The Contributors' Index to the Dictionary of National Biography, 1885–1901* (Winchester: St Paul's Bibliographies, 1989).

10 John Sutherland, *Victorian Novelists and Publishers* (University of Chicago Press, 1976), 21; 26. Robert L. Patten, *Charles Dickens and his Publishers* (Oxford University Press, 1978); Guinevere L. Griest, *Mudie's Circulating Library* (Bloomington: Indiana University Press, 1970).

11 James J. Barnes, *Free Trade in Books: A Study of the London Book Trade since 1800* (Oxford: Clarendon Press, 1964); *Authors, Publishers and Politicians: The Quest for an Anglo-American Copyright Agreement, 1815–1854* (London: Routledge & Kegan Paul, 1974); N.N. Feltes, *Modes of Production of Victorian Novels* (University of Chicago Press, 1986).

12 See *Publishing History* 29: 1991; the research fellow is Dr Alexis Weedon and programme directors are Dr S. Eliot and D.J. McKitterick. Weedon has published a *Location Register of Printers and Publishers Archives* (Cambridge: History of the Book on Demand Series, 1994); see also her articles on publishers' and printers' financial archives in the *Book Trade History Group Newsletter*, issues 12 and 13, 1990–1.

13 Other scholars have concentrated on the profession of authorship, on the man, and more recently the woman, of letters and the way they make their living. These works include Nigel Cross, *The Common Writer: Life in Nineteenth Century Grub Street* (Cambridge: Cambridge University Press, 1985); John Gross, *The Rise and Fall of the Man of Letters: Aspects of English Literary Life since 1800* (London: Weidenfeld & Nicolson, 1969); Dorothy Mermin, *Godiva's Ride: Women of Letters in England, 1830–1880* (Bloomington: Indiana University Press, 1993).

NOTES TO PAGES 10–18

14 John Feather, *A History of British Publishing* (London: Croom Helm, 1988), 140.
15 Jane Millgate, *Scott's Last Edition: A Study in Publishing History* (Edinburgh: Edinburgh University Press, 1987); Hagen, *Tennyson and his Publishers*; Robert L. Patten, *Charles Dickens and his Publishers* (1978).
16 Peter L. Shillingsburg, *Pegasus in Harness: Victorian Publishing and W.M. Thackeray* (Charlottesville: University Press of Virginia, 1992), 14.
17 R.K. Webb, *The British Working Class Reader, 1790–1848: Literacy and Social Tension* (New York: Kelley, 1971. First published 1955); Richard D. Altick, *The English Common Reader: A Social History of the Mass Reading Public 1800–1900* (University of Chicago Press, 1957); for a more recent return to the vexed question of 'readership', see Jonathan Rose 'Rereading the English Common Reader: A Preface to a History of Audiences', *Journal of the History of Ideas* (January–March 1992), 47–70.
18 Altick, 4; David Vincent, *Bread, Knowledge and Freedom: A Study of Nineteenth-century Working Class Autobiography* (London: Methuen, 1981), 111.
19 See Jonathan Rose 'Rereading the English Common Reader: A Preface to a History of Audiences', *Journal of the History of Ideas* (January–March 1992), 47–70
20 See Roger Chartier, *The Order of Books*, translation by Lydia G. Cochrane (Stanford: Stanford University Press, 1994), ch. 1, 'Communities of Readers'.
21 Royal A. Gettmann, *A Victorian Publisher: A Study of the Bentley Papers* (Cambridge: Cambridge University Press, 1960), ix.
22 Michael S. Howard, *Jonathan Cape, Publisher* (London: Jonathan Cape, 1971), 12; J.E. Morpurgo, *Allen Lane King Penguin: A Biography* (London: Hutchinson, 1979), 387.

For publishers' archives see Joanne Shattock, 'Sources for the Study of Victorian Writers and their Publishers', *Browning Institute Studies* 7 (1982), 93–113. An updated version of this article forms part of the revised edition of *Victorian Periodicals A Guide to Research* (1989).

Chapter 1

1 Obituary, *The Academy*, 23 November 1878. An abbreviated version of this memoir appears in Paul's *Memories*, 270–6.
2 Harriet Eleanor Hamilton King, *Letters and Recollections of Mazzini* (London: Longmans, Green and Co., 1912), 38.
3 Fred L. Standley, *Stopford Brooke* (New York: Twayne Publishers, 1972), 50.
4 Frederick W. Robertson *Life and Letters* (London: Smith, Elder, 1866). Paul makes a claim for what he calls King's 'one literary effort . . . [in which] his tact and literary judgement combined to produce an example of almost perfect editing', the arrangement and editing of Robertson's sermons. King worked from the preacher's own rough drafts, from notes taken by various members of the congregation, and from his own fabled memory. Paul notes that 'no editor's name was known: Mr King effaced himself for his friend' (*Memories*, 273–4). However he conceals the fact that Smith, Elder published the sermons, profitably, during King's partnership there, and that King

brought them into his own list in 1871. They first appeared in four volumes between 1855 and 1863.

5 I am grateful to Robin Alston for helping me use the British Library on-line catalogue to search for and find these obscure titles. *Redemption by the Cross of Christ* (C.D. Maitland, 1842); *Four Sermons . . . by the Rev. J.W. Buckley* (1843); *A Result of Meditations on the Bible, or an Enquiry into Truth by a Layman* (anon, 1850). The King addresses were 1, North Street and (later) 44, East Street. One of them was taken over by Treachers when he moved to London.

6 Jenifer Glynn, *Prince of Publishers: A Biography of George Smith* (London: Allison & Busby, 1986), 85.

7 The 1851 census record (HO107, 1646, 10) for 44 East Street, Brighton shows Henry S. King, 33-year-old bookseller employing seven men and three boys; his wife Ellen, then 27; his mother and sister, both named Frances King, a widow of 58 and a spinster of 28; and his younger brother, William, 26, also working as a bookseller; there were two men clerks in the household (one a cousin), and a woman house servant.

8 Ellen King's death certificate gives the cause of death as childbirth. For King as JP, see *The Homeward Mail*, 18 January 1869.

9 Paul says in his memoir that both partners were equally involved with both sides, but King's takeover of the financial side from Smith in 1868, and his return to it in 1877, suggests that his first loyalty was there. Dr Bill Bell of the University of Edinburgh confirms this supposition (private correspondence, 12 January 1994). An earlier partner, Patrick Stewart, had established the Indian agency and banking operations in the 1830s, out of personal connections in Calcutta (Glynn, 19).

10 Leonard Huxley, *The House of Smith Elder* (London, [privately printed], 1923), 9, 82–7. See also Glynn, 113–15.

11 Huxley, 87; see also Glynn, ch. 13 and J.W. Robertson Scott, *The Story of the Pall Mall Gazette* (London: Oxford University Press, 1950), 127; 139. Scott suggests that King's political sensitivity was occasioned by the fact that Harriet King's uncles, the Duke of Abercorn and Lord Aberdeen, were both Conservatives.

12 Glynn, 187.

13 George Redway, 'Some Reminiscences of Publishing Fifty Years Ago', *The Bookman* (December 1931), 186–7.

14 Born Edinburgh, 1840; died 1920.

15 Viola Meynell, *Francis Thompson and Wilfrid Meynell. A Memoir* (London: Hollis & Carte, 1952), 93.

16 William Roberts, *Prophet in Exile: Joseph Mazzini in England, 1837–1868* (New York: Peter Lang, 1989), 112.

17 *Letters and Recollections of Mazzini by Mrs Hamilton King* (London: Longmans, Green & Co., 1912). All references to Harriet King's political and personal reflections are taken from this book.

18 This was William Shaen, the barrister and social reformer who founded The People's International League ('our little group of English Mazzinians') in

NOTES TO PAGES 26–35

   1847. See M.J. Shaen, ed. *William Shaen: A Brief Sketch* (London: Longmans, Green, & Co., 1912), 17.
19 The names are family names, not those of business partners.
20 Advertisement in *The Homeward Mail*, 1 March 1869.
21 Advertisement, *The Homeward Mail*, 9 July 1870.
22 *The Week's News*, 17 February 1872.
23 Patricia Thomas Srebrnik, *Alexander Strahan Victorian Publisher* (Ann Arbor: University of Michigan Press, 1986), 127.
24 The Parker papers are held in the Longman archive among the collection of publishers' papers at the University of Reading; see Allison Ingram, comp. *Index to the Archive of the House of Longman, 1794–1914* (Cambridge: Chadwyck-Healey, 1981).
25 See Leslie Howsam, 'Sustained Literary Ventures', *Publishing History* 31 (1992), 5–26. The Cornhill Library was not numbered. It is, however, possible to deduce the order of publication from the appearance and ordering of lists of the volumes in advertisements for the series printed in King's catalogues: 1872: *Robin Gray*, Charles Gibbon; *Kitty*, Matilda Betham-Edwards; *Hirell*, John Saunders; *One of Two*, James Hain Friswell. 1873: *Ready Money Mortiboy*, J.S. Rice and Walter Besant; *God's Providence House*, Isabella Varley (Mrs G. Linnaeus Banks); *For Lack of Gold*, Charles Gibbon; *Abel Drake's Wife*, John Saunders. 1874: *Fight for Life*, W. Moy Thomas; *The House of Raby*, Jane Margaret Winnard (Mrs George Hooper). 1875: *Half a Dozen Daughters*, Victoria Baker, afterwards Rybot (J. Masterman). The lack of numbers permitted King to advertise new or forthcoming titles as 'number one', or at the top of unnumbered lists, demoting older books to make way for new ones.
26 For Appleton see Grant Martin Overton, *Portrait of a Publisher* (New York: D. Appleton, 1925) and Gerald R. Wolfe, *The House of Appleton* (Metuchen, N.J., Scarecrow Press, 1981).
27 For the International Scientific Series see Roy M. MacLeod, 'Evolutionism, Internationalism and Commercial Enterprise in Science: The International Scientific Series, 1871–1910' in *Development of Science Publishing in Europe*, A.J. Meadows, ed. (Amsterdam: Elsevier Science Publishers, 1980). A bibliography of the International Scientific Series, by Michael Collie and myself, to be published by Scolar Press, is in preparation.
28 'Memorandum of Agreement', filed in the Kegan Paul Contracts under 'Anglo-American Series'. Agreements with the French, Italian and Russian publishers (Baillière, Dumolard and Znanie).
29 E.L. Youmans in his 'American preface' to Tyndall's, *Forms of Water* viii–ix.
30 See Linda Marie Fritschner, 'Publishers' Readers, Publishers and their Authors', *Publishing History* 7 (1980), 45–100.
31 The first evidence for the 1874 date is a letter of Paul to Tennyson dated August. This and other letters to Alfred and Emily Tennyson are preserved in the Tennyson Research Centre, Lincolnshire County Library, Lincoln. Tennyson's letters are published as *The Letters of Alfred Lord Tennyson*, ed. by Cecil Y. Lang and Edgar F. Shannon, Jr. (Oxford: Clarendon Press, 1990).

32 Margaret Nancy Cutt, *Ministering Angels: A Study of Nineteenth-Century Evangelical Writing for Children* (Wormley: Five Owls Press, 1979), 142.
33 'On English Prose Style', *Faith and Unfaith*. For Hesba Stretton see Cutt, *Ministering Angels* and J.S. Bratton, *The Impact of Victorian Children's Fiction* (London: Croom Helm, 1981). Bratton characterizes King as a cut-rate publisher. A brief essay by Leslie Howsam is found in the *Dictionary of Literary Biography, British Children's Writers II–1800–1880*, ed. Meena G. Khorana (Charleston, S.C.: Bruccoli, Clark, Layman, 1996).
34 June Steffansan Hagen, *Tennyson and His Publishers* (London: Macmillan, 1979).
35 Srebrnik, ch. 1.
36 Srebrnik, 116; 130.
37 Srebrnik, 165.
38 'Introduction, *The Nineteenth Century*, 1877–1900', *The Wellesley Index to Victorian Periodicals, 1824–1900*, vol. II (Toronto: University of Toronto Press, 1972), 621–5.
39 Alexander Strahan, 'Strahan and Co., Versus King'. 11-page printed circular dated 30 August 1877. British Library Add. Mss. 44454, fol. 364–9. See also *Publishers' Circular* (2 August 1877) and Srebrnik, 166–76.
40 Joseph R. Dunlap, 'Two Victorian Voices Advocating Good Book Design. II. Charles Kegan Paul, Perceptive Publisher', *Printing History* 2, 1 (1980), 20–7; Lorie Roth, 'A British Publisher [C.K. Paul] on Galley Proofs', *The Library* 6th series, 6 (1984), 381–3.
41 *The Publishers' Circular* (1 September 1884), 822.
42 *Who Was Who, 1929–1940* (London: A. & C. Black, 1941).

Chapter 2
1 Paul, 'George Eliot', in *Biographical Sketches*; 'On English Prose Style', in *Faith and Unfaith and other Essays*.
2 'Charles Kegan Paul. By One who Knew Him', *The Academy and Literature* (26 July 1902). Meynell is identified as the obituarist in J.A. Hammerton, ed., *Stevensoniana* (Edinburgh: John Grant, 1907), 81. See Charmazel Dudt, 'Wilfrid Meynell: Editor, Publisher & Friend', *Victorian Periodicals Review* 16 (1983), 104–9. His journal *Merry England*, which 'became . . . the vehicle for the literary renaissance of Catholic England during the last years of Victoria's reign', contains essays by Charles Kegan Paul.
3 For 'paraphernalia of gentility' see J.A. Banks, *Prosperity and Parenthood: a Study of Family Planning among the Victorian Middle Classes* (London: Routledge & Kegan Paul, 1954); for 'liberal of the liberals' see Paul, 'John Henry, Cardinal Newman', in *Biographical Sketches*. Paul identifies himself with 'the extreme left' in both politics and religion in 'The Condition of the Agricultural Labourer', *Theological Review* (January 1868, 107). For Stevenson see chapter 3. The following account of Paul's life is taken from his own narrative in *Memories*.
4 George Eliot, *The Mill on the Floss* (Oxford: Oxford University Press, 1980), ch. II, 1. First published 1860.

5   Paul, 'John Henry Newman' *Biographical Sketches*.
6   Paul, *The Communion of Saints: a Sermon preached in the parish church S. Mary, Bloxham . . . All Saints Day, 1853* (London: J. Whitaker, 1853).
7   At the time of the possible appointment to Bloxham, the senior Rev. Mr Paul travelled from London to visit the Provost of Eton to intercede for his son.
8   Most people in the *lower* middle class regarded £150 as a minimum. These matters are discussed in detail by J.M. Robson in *Marriage or Celibacy?* (Toronto: University of Toronto Press, 1995).
9   Their marriage certificate shows that the ceremony took place at St Paul's Church [Knightsbridge], in the registration district of St George's Hanover Square. The bride was attended by her brother Eden (the eldest, William, was in India) and her sister Georgina Mary, wife of Frederick Rogers; Paul's best man was Richard Francis Bowles (see also *Memories*) and he was also supported by another friend, Robert Liddell.
10 Alexander Wedderburn, *The Wedderburn Book*, 2 vol. (Printed for private circulation, 1898). As an example of the complexity of the family history, it may be noted that the descendants in male line of Sir John Wedderburn, 5th Baronet of Blackness were as follows: (I) Sir John Wedderburn of Balindean and his descendants; (II) James Wedderburn of Inveresk and his descendants, (a) the Wedderburn-Colviles of Ochiltree [Margaret's forbears]; (b) the Wedderburn-Ogilvies of Ruthven; and (c) the Wedderburn-Maxwells of Middlebie. For the Edens see *The Journal and Correspondence of William, Lord Auckland*, 4 vol. (London: Richard Bentley, 1861–2).
11 For James Colvile (1810–80) see *Dictionary of National Biography*; for Eden Colvile (1819–93) see *Dictionary of Canadian Biography*.
12 This is referred to in her will, where the capital sum was still intact in a trust fund to be used 'by way of advancement' to give her own children a start in life. No evidence has survived of how much it amounted to, except that she had over £12,000 to leave when she died in 1905.
13 Paul to Oscar Browning, 22 March 1876, Browning papers, Library of King's College, Cambridge.
14 Robert Bernard Martin, *The Dust of Combat: A Life of Charles Kingsley* (London: Faber and Faber, 1959), 208–9.
15 *Tracts for Priests and People*. No. V, 'On terms of Communion': I. 'The Boundaries of the Church', by the Rev. C.K.P. [*sic*]; II. 'The Message of the Church', by J.N. Langley (Cambridge: Macmillan & Co., 1861).
16 The Dorset County Museum (Dorchester) holds copies of the Sturminster Marshall *Parish Magazine*. Paul's successor James Cross took a great interest in parish history; manuscript notes on the value of the living are to be found pasted in the back of his own volume of the magazine, as 'Report to Eton Coll. 1 Feb. 1877 by G.R. Dupuis: Sturminster-Marshall Income & Outgoings'. The income from tithes (£120) and rental of the glebe and farm (£256) was offset by rates, fees to Eton, insurance, taxes, a small fee to an agent, and payments on a loan to Queen Anne's Bounty, all amounting to £90. On top of this the rector would have collected a few pounds each year in fees for marriages and funerals.

Also in the Museum is an excerpt from the *Parish Magazine* of about 1877 that corroborates Paul's description. Finally destroyed by the thatch catching fire in 1893, Bailie House was 'old, part of it very old'; built on the ground, damp and cold in winter, with a thatched roof. The rooms were rather low but of fair size; the offices (sanitary arrangements) damp and not good. The ground floor included drawing room, dining room, study, storeroom, pantry, kitchen, scullery, servants hall, and small bedrooms. On the first floor were three good bedrooms, two smaller ones, and three others (used for schoolrooms and bedrooms), as well as two bedrooms for maidservants and a water closet. In the attics were two more large rooms, appropriate for night nurseries, and another large one, good for a day nursery, plus another water closet. The gardens were pleasant, a lawn with flower garden and fine trees, as well as 'capital kitchen garden' for vegetables, all surrounded by a mud wall all round. A garden house, coal house and stable (two horses and a pony) completed the arrangements, along with a new coach house (the loan for which accounted for the debt to Queen Anne's bounty.

17   The squire was Charles Joseph Parke. The Dorset *Post Office Directory* for 1867 states that the value of Paul's living was £303 annually; in 1861 the population had ben 850; in 1875 it was 847 and in 1877 about 830. Like rural people everywhere in England, Paul's parishioners were migrating to the cities and abroad.

18   Most of the children's names, along with Margaret's and Charles's later appear in the firm's records as translators, and both Nancy and Maurice translated other books as well.

19   Paul's letters to Lady Tennyson about her sons are housed in the Tennyson Research Centre in Lincoln.

20   Paul to J.M. Ludlow, 4 December 1869, Cambridge University Library Add Mss. 7348. The annual fee might have been more than £100: 'I have three pupils instead of six from Septr. till Christmas, making a difference of £200 in my receipts for this [?] time.'

21   King also published Paul's verse translation of Goethe's *Faust* in 1873. The Godwin essays were *The Genius of Christianity Unveiled* (1873).

22   See the introductory essay in the *Wellesley Index to Victorian Periodicals*, (III: 505–11), on the *Theological Review*, edited by Charles Beard.

23   See Brian Harrison, *Drink and the Victorians: the Temperance Question in England, 1815–1872* (London: Faber and Faber, 1971) and Lilian Shiman, *The Crusade against Drink in Victorian England* (Basingstoke: Macmillan Press, 1988).

24   Sturminster Marshall *Parish Magazine* (December 1905); see also obituary of Paul, August 1902: 'He never shrank from upholding a cause if he thought it right, however unpopular it might make him.'

25   1871 Census; when the census-takers came to Bailie House only Paul and the servants were at home; Margaret and the children were presumably away on a visit.

26   *Two Sermons Preached at the First Anniversary of the Free Christian Union, 1st June, 1869, by the Rev. Athanase Coquerel, fils, Pastor of the Reformed Church of France;*

and the Rev. C. Kegan Paul, M.A. Vicar of Sturminster Marshall, Dorset (London: Williams & Norgate, [1869]).

27 Paul to J.M. Ludlow, 4 December 1869, Cambridge University Library, Add Mss. 7348.

28 The first known London address (October 1875) is the Grove, Clapham Common; from at least 1879 to the end of 1883 the Pauls lived in west London at 16 Kensington Square, then at 38 Ashburn Place (also known as Kensington Vestry). In 1890 or 1891 they moved to 9 Avonmore Road, West Kensington.

29 Paul, 'George Eliot', in *Biographical Sketches*, 158.

30 For Browning see letter of 16 April 1879, Browning to Paul, declining (at Harry Ransom Humanities Research Center, The University of Texas at Austin), and *Memories*, 333–4; 338; for George Eliot see *Memories*, 335–8 and his essay about her in *Biographical Sketches*.

31 Christopher Kent, *Brains and Numbers: Elitism, Comtism, and Democracy in Mid-Victorian England* (Toronto: University of Toronto Press, 1978), xiii; 63.

32 Charles Robert Ashbee, Ashbee journals, Entries 27 December 1885 and 27 June 1886. See also letter 9 January 1888, Paul to Ashbee, Ashbee Letters, King's College Library, Cambridge. For Ashbee's career see Alan Crawford, *C.R. Ashbee: Architect, Designer and Romantic Socialist* (New Haven: Yale University Press, 1985).

33 Paul to Richard Congreve, 1 June 1887, Positivist Papers, British Library Add Mss 45240, f. 226. Kent provides a sidelight on the publication of the sermon when he notes that Comte disapproved of journalism, and 'declared that privately printed broadsheets and pamphlets appearing at irregular intervals were the only means of public communication which avoided the corrupting influence of journalism'. Congreve acquiesced in this injunction (Kent, *Brains and Numbers*, 68).

34 The evidence for Paul's enthusiasm is not in *Memories* but in letters to authors, especially the Tennyson correspondence. See below, for example, his attempt to persuade Francis Galton to contribute to the International Scientific Series. For King's linguistic limitations see Paul's obituary in the *Academy*. For the assurance of the translation's quality, see *Memories*, 283.

35 [Maria Trench], *Richard Chenevix Trench, Archbishop: Letters and Memorials* (London: Kegan Paul, Trench & Co., 1888). See also John Bromley, *The Man of Ten Talents: A Portrait of Richard Chenevix Trench 1807–86: Philologist, Poet, Theologian, Archbishop* (London: SPCK, 1959). The *DNB* article on the Archbishop credits him with six sons, but Maria Trench's memoir mentions eight. Alfred Trench was born 4 November 1849; attended Eton from 1863 to 1866 and matriculated at University College, Oxford, in January 1868; he was married 27 November 1873 to Isabella Moore, daughter of James Moore of Dalchoolin and they had no children; he died 13 March 1938.

36 F.A. Mumby, *The House of Routledge 1834–1934, with a History of Kegan Paul, Trench, Trübner and other Associated Firms* (London: George Routledge & Sons, Ltd., 1934). Mumby depends heavily on Paul's *Memories* for his chapter on the firm. It is interesting that in the 'interview' Trench takes responsibility for

what Paul claims in *Memories* that he accomplished, the acquisition of the Gordon diaries.

37 *The Nineteenth Century* switched over between June and July of 1881.
38 I have consulted the Trench family correspondence held by the Representative Church Body Library, in Dublin (MS327). There is no reference to financial or other support for Alfred's publishing venture.
39 Paul to Hallam Tennyson, 12 May 1866, Tennyson Research Centre. The context was advice about Marlborough School: 'I wrote to Philip Trench about you, and I hope he has spoken to you. It is little of course that an elder lad can do for a younger one at a great school, but he is a good boy, and it is well to have an elder friend . . . to whom you can streak in case of troubles.' Marlborough School records include Philip Francis Chenevix Trench, son of P.C. Chenevix Trench, born 1849.
40 J.S. Exell to Kegan Paul, Trench, Trübner & Co., 18 January 1894. Kegan Paul Archives, contracts: Exell.
41 Arthur Waugh, *One Man's Road* (London: Chapman & Hall, 1931), 278.
42 The lands of Mounteagle, otherwise Ballyeagle, were appointed by deed poll to Alfred 19 November 1873, at the time of his marriage. This property was occupied by about twenty-five tenants, and worth about £390. (Sources are the Archbishop's will at Somerset House, and a letter from Archbishop Trench to T.C. Trench, 24 April 1860 in the Trench papers, Representative Church Body Library, Dublin.)
43 Paul to E.H. Coleridge, 9 April 1885, Harry Ransom Humanities Research Center, The University of Texas at Austin.
44 Her will (dated 20 October 1902 after Paul's death) refers to sums raised earlier from trust funds comprised in her marriage settlement to 'advance' her sons and to appoint a marriage settlement to her married daughter Ruth. But this does not preclude the raising of a sum to finance her husband's investment.
45 Paul to Dobson, 19 May 1877; 25 November 1879, Dobson papers, University College London Library.
46 Kegan Paul, Trench & Co. to Martin Conway (in Paul's hand, dated from the Savile Club), 18 April 1882, Cambridge University Library Add Mss 7676 P/41.
47 Paul to Garnett, 20 December 1878, Harry Ransom Humanities Research Center, The University of Texas at Austin.
48 Michael Millgate, *Thomas Hardy: A Biography* (Oxford: Oxford University Press, 1982), 203; 207; 219.

Chapter 3
1 Hagen, 150–4.
2 Quotations here are from the book version.
3 The commission was paid initially to the Archbishop's widow and later to his son Alfred, who inherited the copyrights.
4 These comments were found useful as evidence of contemporary practice by Lorie Roth, 'A British Publisher on Galley Proofs', *The Library* 6th series, 6 (1984), 381–3.

5   Paul says in *Memories* that he got to know Morris through membership in the Society for the Protection of Ancient Buildings. For an article stressing Paul's comments on printing see Joseph R. Dunlap, 'Two Victorian Voices Advocating Good Book Design. II. Charles Kegan Paul, Perceptive Publisher', *Printing History* II, 1 (1980).

6   See Guinevere L. Griest, *Mudie's Circulating Library and the Victorian Novel* (Bloomington: Indiana University Press, 1970).

7   For book trade statistics throughout the nineteenth century, see Eliot, *Some Patterns and Trends*. The figures he provides for 'Subject Classification 1870–1919', (pp. 46–53), while not directly comparable with the Kegan Paul output, indicate that the 1871 figures may safely be used throughout the seventies and eighties.

8   Eric J. Evans, *The Forging of the Modern State: Early Industrial Britain 1783–1870* (London: Longman, 1983) 295. Paul says he never knew Dawson, whose works were negotiated by King [*Memories*, 287].

9   *Publishers' Circular* (15 September 1890); the bookseller was R.D. Dickinson, who specialized in theological books.

10 A.W. Pollard and Gwendolen Murphy, *A Select Bibliography of the Writings of Alfred W. Pollard* (Oxford: Oxford University Press, 1938), 6–7, 23; Paul, *Memories*, 290.

11 Pfeiffer's verse was published by the firm on commission, beginning in 1877. For Paul's criticism see his letter to Austin Dobson, 7 August 1877 (Austin Dobson papers, University of London, 810/III/76): 'It seems to me however it hit the criticism of a paper [the *Spectator*] which refuses the Song of Four Seasons, and admits Mrs Pfeiffer's Sonnets is neither to be dreaded nor valued.'

12 Eleanor de Selms Langstaff, *Andrew Lang* (Boston: Twayne Publishers, 1978), 149.

13 J.M. Dent, *The House of Dent, 1888–1938* third edition (London, J.M. Dent, 1938), 105. Dent remembered this 'bon mot' being said at a Toynbee Hall lecture by Paul on 'the making of books'.

14 'On English Prose Style', in *Faith and Unfaith and Other Essays*. Also on Paul's list was Cardinal Newman; although Paul didn't think of him as a novelist, Newman was the author of *Calista: A Sketch of the Third Century* (1856).

15 Michael Millgate, *Thomas Hardy a biography* (New York: Random House, 1982), 169.

16 Mumby, 190.

17 Roger G. Swearingen, *The Prose Writings of Robert Louis Stevenson: a Guide* (Hamden, Conn.: Archon Books, 1980), 29–31, 43–5, 56–7, 70. A recent study of Stevenson by Frank McLynn, *Robert Louis Stevenson a biography* (London: Hutchinson, 1993) does not refer to Paul or Meynell. For McLynn, clues to Stevenson's 'divided self' are nuanced literary references, not pinned down to a single individual.

18 Michael Collie, *George Meredith a Bibliography* (Toronto: University of Toronto Press, 1974), 43–4.

19 T.W. Heyck, *The Transformation of Intellectual Life in Victorian England* (London: Croom Helm; Chicago: Lyceum Books, Inc., 1982), 122.
20 Cited in Sydney Spokes, *Gideon Algernon Mantell* (London: John Bale, Sons & Danielsson, Ltd., 1927), v–vi.
21 Adrian Johns, 'History, Science, and the History of the Book: The Making of Natural Philosophy in Early Modern England', *Publishing History* 35 (1994), 3. Recent and forthcoming scholarship by James Secord and Jonathan Topham also contribute to the juxtaposition of the history of science with the history of the book.
22 *The Publishers' Circular* November 1880, 918–19; June 1882, 532.
23 Michael Collie, *Henry Maudsley: Victorian Psychiatrist a bibliographical study* (Winchester: St Paul's Bibliographies, 1988), 25; 91–2; 101–2.
24 The full history of the International Scientific Series is dealt with in Collie and Howsam's forthcoming *Bibliography*. Paul also made a point of having consulted Archbishop Trench about 'What attitude we should take with regard to books against religion, such as some of the works in the "International Scientific Series" and others of a free-thinking or agnostic nature.' The Archbishop is supposed to have graciously remarked that these questions must now be discussed, as long as it was done in a 'reverent and serious spirit . . . but that we should sternly reject any that were merely flippant and written for the sake of destruction'. In his anxiety to demonstrate that he was on consultation terms with the Archbishop, Paul seems to have forgotten that his own religious views at the time were free-thinking and agnostic.
25 2 November 1877, Kegan Paul & Co. to Galton: typescript of Galton's note dated 6 November; 7 November 1877, Kegan Paul & Co. to Galton; Kegan Paul & Co. to Galton, 23 and 24 October 1879, Pearson Papers, University College London, Mss Add 589.
26 Dent, *House of Dent*, 53.
27 In the case of Wise, this interest extended to forgery, to the practice of creating and selling faked editions of real poems. See John Carter and Graham Pollard, *An Enquiry into the Nature of Certain Nineteenth-Century Pamphlets* (London: Constable, 1934).
28 Appleton to Trench, 16 February 1880, Kegan Paul Archives, contracts, Appleton.
29 2 January 1884, Browning papers, King's College, Cambridge.
30 Paul to Dobson 11 December 1882, Dobson papers, University of London.
31 Paul to Pollard, 31 January 1887, Harry Ransom Humanities Research Center, The University of Texas at Austin.
32 Australia Report (by Spencer Blackett), Kegan Paul archives, contracts.
33 A photographic reprint edition of the Pulpit Commentary in 23 volumes remains available, from Christian Book Distributors. I am grateful to the Rev. Eric Griffin for this information.
34 The Browning papers are in the library of King's College, Cambridge.
35 Frank Foden, *Philip Magnus: Victorian Educational Pioneer* (London: Valentine, Mitchell, 1970).
36 16 March 1899, Browning papers, King's College, Cambridge.

37　Paul to Browning, 16 March 1876, King's College Library.
38　Anstruther, *Oscar Browning*, 9.
39　Paul to Browning, 8 March 1881. The remark about the medieval curriculum is unchanged in the printed book, but other emendations proposed by Paul, such as [Sir Thomas] More for Moore, were made.
40　Unpublished titles, advertised as 'in preparation', were *Home Training and School Teaching* (Rev. Dr Abbott, City of London School); *Art Teaching in Schools* (F. Edward Hulme, Marlborough College); *The Teaching of Geography and History* (F.S. Pulling Exeter College, Oxford); *The Kindergarten System* (Emily Shirreff, President of the Froebel Society); *Psychology in its Bearings on Education* (James Sully, University of London); *Science Teaching in Schools* (Dr Wormell, City Corporation Schools and Prof. Tilden, Mason's College, Birmingham).
41　Richard D. Altick, 'From Aldine to Everyman: Cheap Reprint Series of the English Classics 1830–1906', *Studies in Bibliography* 1958: 3–24; William B. Todd, 'Books in Series', in *Collectable Books: Some New Paths* ed. Jean Peters (New York: R.R. Bowker Co., 1979); John L. Kijinski, 'John Morley's "English Men of Letters" Series and the Politics of Reading', *Victorian Studies* Winter 1991, 205–25.
42　See Simon Eliot, 'The Three-decker Novel and its First Cheap Reprint, 1862–1894', *The Library* Sixth Series, vol. 7, no. 2 (March 1985).
43　Paul to Gladstone, 24 June 1887, Gladstone Papers, British Library Add Mss 44501, f. 94.
44　See C.E. Frazer Clark, *Nathaniel Hawthorne: a descriptive bibliography* (Pittsburgh: University of Pittsburgh Press, 1978). Kegan Paul archives, contracts, Houghton, Mifflin & Co. to Trench, 9 February 1883.
45　Kegan Paul Archives, contracts: Conder. For James Edward Thorold Rogers (1823–90) and Conder see *Dictionary of National Biography*. See the *National Union Catalogue of Pre-1956 Imprints* for attributions to Rogers. The *British Library Catalogue* lists these books under Jesus Christ, Bible Selections and Saint Paul.
46　The percentage of women authors declined in the Kegan Paul, Trench period, after 1881. The figures are: King 75.5% men, 19.4% women, 5.2% unidentified; C. Kegan Paul 78.1%, 19.4%, 2.5%; Kegan Paul, Trench 83.0%, 13.5%, 3.5%.

Chapter 4
1　Paul's testimony reported in *The Times* (2 December 1891).
2　The Prospectus is on file in the Guildhall Library, which also holds a complete run of the *Stock Exchange Year Book*. Annual reports for the firm are also held at the Guildhall Library.
3　See *Dictionary of National Biography*; see also Alan Hyman, *The Rise and Fall of Horatio Bottomley: The Biography of a Swindler* (London: Cassell, 1972).
4　Feather, *History of British Publishing*, 144–8; N.N. Feltes, *Modes of Production of Victorian Novels* (Chicago: University of Chicago Press, 1986), 76–81.
5　Waugh, *A Hundred Years of Publishing: Being the Story of Chapman & Hall Ltd.* (London: Chapman & Hall, [1930]), 96.

6   N.N. Feltes, *Literary Capital and the Late Victorian Novel* (Madison: The University of Wisconsin Press, 1993), 28.
7   This account of Trübner is taken from my entry in the *Dictionary of Literary Biography* volume *British Literary Publishing Houses, 1820–1880*, which in turn is based primarily on F.A. Mumby's *The House of Routledge*.
8   Coincidentally the building at 12 Paternoster Row was to become the home of Henry S. King and Company when it was initiated in 1871.
9   William Heinemann, *The Bibliographer* cited in Mumby, *House of Routledge*, 166–7.
10 Henry Festing Jones, *Samuel Butler Author of Erewhon (1835–1902) A Memoir* (London: Macmillan, 1919), I: 148; 294.
11 'Publishers of Today', interview with Redway in *The Publishers' Circular*, 10 October 1891; George Redway, 'Some Reminiscences of Publishing Fifty Years Ago', *The Bookman*, December 1931, 186–7.
12 Redway was born 9 October 1859 in the Paddington district of London; his parents were Charles Redway (footman) and Mary Ann Redway, née Richardson; he died 26 April 1934. These data appear in his birth certificate and in the Somerset House registry of his estate.
13 Redway claims to have 'moved' George Moore to write his important anti-censorship pamphlet *Literature at Nurse; or, Circulating Morals* (London: Vizetelly, 1885).
14 See Thomas J. Wise, *A Bibliography of the Writings in Prose and Verse of Algernon Charles Swinburne* (London: Printed for Private Circulation, 1919, I: 369–78) for a discussion of the rather sordid transaction by which Redway is supposed to have acquired some 'indecent' letters of Swinburne's and traded them back to the poet in exchange for the copyright of the poem, which he published in 1887. The letters in question are among the British Library Ashley Manuscripts (Ashely MSS 5081). In a letter to Wise of 18 May 1920, Redway objected to being 'treated badly' by Wise's accusations in the *Bibliography*, and claimed that he had been 'the victim of a piece of roguery' at the time of the 1885–6 transaction (Harry Ransom Humanities Research Center).
15 This was Richard Le Gallienne in *The Bookbills of Narcissus: an account rendered* (Derbey: F. Murray, 1892).
16 *Who Was Who, 1916–1928* (London: A. & C. Black, 1929). Sinnett was born 1840 and died 1921.
17 'Publishers of Today. Messrs Kegan Paul, Trench, Trübner & Co., Limited', *The Publisher's Circular* (10 October 1891), 424–5.
18 The prospectus, and reports in the *Stock Exchange Year Book* are housed in the Guildhall Library.
19 Horatio Bottomley, *Bottomley's Book* (London: Odhams Limited, 1909), 149–50.
20 *The Times*, 2 December 1891; for the 1893 hearing see Hyman, *Rise & Fall*, 40–1.
21 *Bottomley's Book*, 151; *The Publishers' Circular* (28 November 1991). A related matter was the Anglo-Austrian Printing and Publishing Union, in which Bottomley extended the Hansard Union principle to dealings in Vienna.

NOTES TO PAGES 149-71

22   Kegan Paul Archives, Contracts: Caithness. Caithness to Redway, 14 November 1889 and 19 February 1890.
23   *The Times*, 13 March 1890.
24   The prospectus had announced they would be consolidated at Trübner's Ludgate Hill office. In his memoir in *The Bookman*, Redway relates how Nicholas Trübner's vast archive of correspondence survived in that building until the new company sold it by the ton as waste paper. The Charing Cross building was later occupied by the Royal National Lifeboat Institution and currently houses a retail business.
25   Louise Chandler Moulton to Roberts Brothers, 26 August 1892, cited by James G. Nelson, *The Early Nineties: A View from the Bodley Head* (Cambridge, Mass.: Harvard University Press, 1971), 343.
26   The Index to the Kegan Paul Archives prepared by Sandy Merrick includes books published up to the end in 1911.
27   A.W. Pollard and Gwendolen Murphy, *A Select Bibliography of the Writings of Alfred W. Pollard* (Oxford: Oxford University Press, 1938), 11–12.
28   Essex Cholmondeley, *The Story of Charlotte Mason (1842–1923)* (London: J.M. Dent & Sons, 1960), 17.
29   Redway to Hazlitt, 23 April 189[7], British Library, Add. Mss. 38907.
30   Frederic Whyte, *William Heinemann. A Memoir* (New York: Doubleday Doran & Co., 1929), 78–9. Another of the 'cheerful souls in whose society Heinemann loved to frolic' was Gerald Duckworth, now best known as Virginia Woolf's step-brother. Blackett was born in Ealing, a suburb of London, on 28 November 1858; he died 20 September 1920.
31   Arthur Waugh, *One Man's Road: Being a Picture of Life in a Passing Generation* (London: Chapman & Hall, 1931), 275–80; 285–8.
32   Information from birth certificate and army lists. See also portrait of Hurst and Blackett in the *Sketch* (26 February 1896). In that article two of Henry Blackett's sons are described as having entered the business, Arthur Henry in 1870 and Herbert Walter in 1880. There is no mention of their brother, then in his first year at Kegan Paul. See also B.Q. Schmidt, 'Hurst and Blackett' in Anderson and Rose, eds. *British Literary Publishing Houses 1820–1880*.
33   See N.N. Feltes, *Literary Capital and the Late Victorian Novel* (Madison: University of Wisconsin Press, 1993).
34   Kegan Paul Archives, contracts: Australia Report.
35   A letter from Wolseley to James, dated 19 April 1897, was included in several of the books. Wolseley wrote: 'I hope the officers of her Majesty's army may never degenerate into bookworms. There is happily at present no tendency in that direction, for I am glad to say that this generation is as fond of danger, adventure, and all manly out-of-door sports as its forefathers were. At the same time, all now recognize that the officer who has not studied war as an applied science, and who is ignorant of modern military history, is of little use beyond the rank of Captain.'
36   Advertisement in Annie Fields, *Nathaniel Hawthorne* (London: Kegan Paul, Trench, Trübner & Co. Ltd., 1899).
37   Kegan Paul Archives, Contracts: Small, Maynard.

206   NOTES TO PAGES 171–8

38   Noel's remark is cited in J.W. Lambert and Michael Ratcliffe, *The Bodley Head 1887–1987* (London: Bodley Head, 1987), 39; Richard Le Gallienne wrote to Mathews about fluid verse, cited in James G. Nelson, *The Early Nineties: A View from the Bodley Head* (Cambridge, Mass: Harvard University Press, 1971), 154.
39   Lambert and Ratcliffe, *The Bodley Head*, 161.
40   Goerge Routledge, publisher in London since 1836, had died in 1888. The following year, his firm became a limited company, and was itself in trouble in 1902. Routledge's equivalent of J.H. Schmitz was the banker Arthur E. Franklin, who recruited a new board of directors and revived the firm. William Swan Sonnenschein was a small publisher, and Laurie Magnus, son of Philip Magnus (editor of Kegan Paul's Education Library) had published educational books with John Murray. Magnus and Sonnenschein became joint managing directors. Franklin was chairman of the board, and the fourth director was Sir William Crookes, who had been a member of the Kegan Paul board since Bottomley's and Redway's time. James J. Barnes and Patience P. Barnes, 'George Routledge and Sons', in Anderson and Rose, eds *British Literary Publishing Houses 1820–1880* (*DLB* 106), 1991.
41   Kegan Paul Archives, contracts: Brooke.

Chapter 5
1   Paul, *On the Way Side: Verses and Translations* (London: Kegan Paul, Trench, Trübner & Co. Ltd., 1899), 33.
2   See the anonymous obituary in the *Athenaeum* (26 July 1902).
3   Paul, 'Faith and Unfaith', *The Nineteenth Century* (12 October 1882), 505–6.
4   He refers to 'one of my own family, having a right to speak'. The children's objections would presumably have been accorded less weight than that of his wife.
5   Paul's will is at Somerset House. It is dated 27 May, 1900; he left only £2,900, all to his wife, who was to control its disposition.
6   *Kintail Place: A Tale of Revolution* (by the author of 'Dorothy, An Autobiography') was published by Swan Sonnenschein, Lowrey & Co., in 1886; it is a historical novel. Kintail Place was the name of the house in Jersey where several generations of a family had lived. The subject is La Vendée, and the novel is a quasi-scholarly narrative of events during that upheaval, embedded within a conventional romance of a wilful, spoiled girl who creates confusion for good people by insisting she get her own way.
7   She compiled *True Stories from French History* (London: Griffith, Farran, Okenden & Welsh, 1890) and later produced other editions and translations. In an article on nursing, she declared herself not a nurse, but one who 'has unusual opportunities of hearing all sides of the question' ('Modern Nurses, A Reply', *National Review* (January 1897)). This was two years after Charles Kegan Paul's disabling accident; Nancy expressed her admiration for the new trend to visiting nurses who come in twice daily to wash patients and dress their wounds. They were less likely to get into mischief than others. In July 1906 she wrote a letter headed from The Nurses Hostel in Francis Street, London W.C. concerning the prospect of a central nursing board and an

independent examination. (Nancy Paul to Alice Zimmern, 4 July 1906; Fawcett Library correspondence collection.)

8   Paul to Oscar Browning, 30 May 1881, King's College Library, Cambridge.
9   See *Who Was Who, 1941–1950* (London: A. & C. Black, 1952); See also Stanley Unwin, *The Truth About a Publisher* (London: George Allen and Unwin, 1960), 142–4: Eden and Cedar Paul returned to England in August of 1914 recounting their escape, 'penniless and starving', from France, 'where they had been living a nomadic existence with all their belongings in a little hand-cart'.
10 Paul to Pollard, 31 January 1887. The Harry Ransom Humanities Research Center, the University of Texas at Austin.
11 'What We Know of Shakspere,' *Faith and Unfaith and Other Essays* (London: Kegan Paul, Trench, Trübner & Co. Ltd., 1891), 172–3.
12 (2 April 1971); see also reviews in *Books and Bookmen* 17 (April 1971), 40; *Papers of the Bibliographical Society of America* 66 (April 1972), 227.
13 Brian Maidment, 'Introduction', *The Archives of Kegan Paul, Trench, Trübner & Henry S. King 1858–1912*, (Bishop's Stortford: Chadwyck-Healey, 1974); a brochure advertising the Chadwyck-Healey edition of the publishers' archives on microfilm perpetuates this error.
14 Trench's will was dated New Club, Menton; he left £6,783 (Isabella had died in 1934, in France, leaving her husband nearly £3,000); his beneficiaries were friends, a godchild, and a servant.
15 The exception was the Victoria Press, a productive and successful business established by Emily Faithfull for the purpose of demonstrating that women could work as compositors. See also my article 'Women in Publishing and the Book Trades in Britain, 1830–1914', *Leipziger Jahrbuch zur Buchgeschichte* 6 (1996), 67–79.
16 Leonore Davidoff and Catherine Hall, *Family Fortunes: Men and Women of the English Middle Class 1780–1850* (Chicago: University of Chicago Press, 1987).
17 Redway to Garnett, 16 January 1904, The Harry Ransom Humanities Research Center, The University of Texas at Austin.
18 The present study has not included a systematic analysis of reviews of the King–Kegan Paul publications that appeared in the Victorian periodicals. I would welcome the appearance of such a study, which would, I expect, serve to supplement my more bibliographical approach to a study of the publishers' imprint.

CHRONOLOGY OF EVENTS

1871 (MAY)–1877 (OCTOBER)

Imprint: H.S. King & Co. 65 Cornhill and 12, Paternoster Row.
1871: founding meeting of International Scientific Series (ISS) (August).
1872: launch of ISS and Cornhill Library of Fiction; 'alliance' with Strahan from March 1872 to December 1873; publication of the *Contemporary Review* (edited by Strahan and Knowles) June 1872–November 1873.
1873: Paul starts as reader (February) and his Faust and Godwin essays published; contract with Hesba Stretton.
1874: first five-year contract with Tennyson (January 1874–December 1879); Paul joins firm (August at the latest).
1875: King's illness begins.
1876: publication of *Contemporary Review* (June–November 1876); King goes to Italy.
1877: publication of *Nineteenth Century* (from March); court case Strahan vs. King (August); Paul takes over (October).

1877 (OCTOBER)–1881 (OCTOBER)

Imprint: C. Kegan Paul & Co. 1 Paternoster Square.
1878: publication of Stevenson; new contract with Tennyson for 1879–1883; beginning of Military Handbooks; Trench involved from at least August.
1879: publication of Meredith; publication of *New Quarterly Magazine* (Paul editor; January 1879–April 1880).
1880: beginning of Parchment Library and Pulpit Commentary.

1881 (OCTOBER)–1888 (DECEMBER)

Imprint: Kegan Paul, Trench & Co. 1 Paternoster Square.
1881: Trench's name appears (June); Trench goes to USA; beginning of Education Library; publication of Henry George *Progress and Poverty*.
1882: Dobson edits *Eighteenth-Century Essays* and John Gay for Parchment Library.

CHRONOLOGY OF EVENTS

1883: fire destroys warehouse; Paul's *Fortnightly Review* article (April); Trench goes to USA; loss of Tennyson; Huxley resigns ISS committee.
1884: loss of Stevenson.
1885: publication of Gordon journals; Trench to Australia.
1886: death of Archbishop Trench and firm starts publishing his works; involvement of Pollard; beginning of Home Education Series; Berne convention on copyright.
1887: launch of Colonial Library; Trench to Australia.
1888: agreement for incorporation of firm in Kegan Paul, Trench, Trübner & Co. (31 December).

1889 (JANUARY)–1911

Imprint: Kegan Paul, Trench, Trübner & Co. Ltd. [from 1891:] Paternoster House, Charing Cross Road; [from 1903:] 43 Gerrard Street, W.
1889: informal amalgamation of three firms (from January); George Redway (Manager), Paul (Literary Manager), Sinnett and Düffing (of Trübner) involved; beginning of Hansard Union (April); Trench retires to Italy; formal sale of Kegan Paul, Trench to Kegan Paul, Trench, Trübner & Co. Ltd., 14 November 1889.
1890: firm pays 7% dividend on first 18 months (June); Paul joins Roman Catholic church (August); beginning of Eminent Actors Series.
1891: collapse of Hansard Union (May); move to new headquarters Paternoster House, Charing Cross Road (July); loss of *Nineteenth Century* to Sampson Low; Modern Science Series (edited by Lubbock); US copyright Act.
1892: no Stock Exchange Report; newspapers say debit £313.
1893: no Stock Exchange Report; Pollard edits Books about Books 1893–4.
1894: debit £313; end of Parchment Library; end of three-volume novel.
1895: fall in profits and capital written down to 10%; resignation of Redway and directors and new board chaired by John Hubert Schmitz (February 1895); Spencer Blackett takes over management (June); Paul's accident and retirement (October).
1896: Arthur Waugh joins firm as assistant to Blackett (January); profit £251.
1897: Blackett goes to North America (February); beginning of Pamphlet Library, Out of Door Library, Wolseley Military Series; debit £3,577.
1898: debit £2,357; Blackett goes to Australia and North America (October).
1899: Paul's *Memories* published (October); debit £3,913; Net Book Agreement.
1900: debit £5,247.
1901: debit £5,903.
1902: Waugh leaves firm for Chapman & Hall; debit £5,519.
1903: move to Dryden House, 43 Gerrard Street, W., Soho (July); debit £5,161.
1904: beginning of Dryden House Memoirs; debit £4,703.
1905: debit £4,634.
1906: H. Wingfield becomes manager; debit £5,049.
1907: Basil W. Willett becomes manager; debit £5,675.
1908: debit £5,685.
1909: debit £5,611.

1910: no accounts.
1911: last book published in ISS; management and control taken over by George Routledge & Sons Ltd. (September); managers Laurie Magnus and William Swann Sonnenschein.

WHO'S WHO

Blackett, Spencer Collinson: b. 28 Nov. 1858 Ealing, London; at the Charterhouse School 1873–6; Royal Military College, Sandhurst; 21st Hussars 1879–82; m. about 1882 Harriet Jane [surname unknown]; d. 20 Sept. 1920, Brookwood Railway Station, Hampshire.

King, Henry Samuel: b. 15 November 1817, Lewes, Sussex; m. 1850 Ellen Blakeway; m. 22 September 1863, H.E. Baillie Hamilton; d. 17 November 1878, 45 Pall Mall, London.

King, Ellen (née Blakeway): b. about 1824; m. 1850 H.S. King; d. in childbirth 1860.

King, Harriet Eleanor (née Baillie Hamilton): b. 10 February 1840; m. 22 September 1863 H.S. King; d. 1920.

King children: Ellen's: Henry Seymour, b. 1852; Harold R., b. 1854; Ellen T., b. 1858. Harriet's: Violet, b. 16 August 1864; Arthur H., b. 1866; Margaret F., b. 1868; Katherine D., b. 17 January 1869; Honoria L., b. 1870; Samuel, b. 1871.

Paul, Charles Kegan: b. 8 March 1828, Ilminster, Somerset; BA Oxon. 1849; m. 11 December 1856 M.A. Colvile; d. 19 July 1902 9 Avonmore Road, Kensington, London.

Paul, Margaret Agnes (née Colvile): b. 18 July 1829; m. 11 December 1856 C.K. Paul; d. 30 March 1905.

Paul children: Andrew Louis, b. Berks (Eton) 1858; d. Canary Islands, 15 April 1900; Nancy Margaret, b. *c.*, 1860, Eton, Berks; Ruth Frances, b. 1862 Eton, Berks, m. Willie Rendel, 1881; Rose Mary, b. 1863., Sturminster Marshall, Dorset; Maurice Eden, b. 1865 Sturminster Marshall; m. Cedar [surname unknown; date unknown, but before October 1902].

Redway, George William: b. 9 October 1859, Paddington; m. Edith Rowden (3 sons 1 daughter); d. 26 April 1934.

Trench, Alfred Chenevix: b. 4 November 1849, Itchenstoke, Hampshire; Eton 1863–6; Oxford (University College matriculated January 1868); m. 27 November 1873 Isabella Moore ('Ella'; d. of James Moore of Dalchoolin, Ireland); d. 13 March 1938, Menton, France.

INDEX

Adcock, St John 102
Adelaide, Queen 18
Allen, Rev. John 51
Altick, Richard 10–11
Amos, Sheldon 129–31
Appleton, D. & Co. 30, 32–3, 47, 76, 106, 111, 113
Archer, William 157
archives of Kegan Paul firms 5–7, 13–14, 91
Ashbee, C.R. 75–6, 149
Associated Book Publishers 173
Athenaeum 14, 29

Bagehot, Walter 5, 130
Barnes, William 82
Beacon Biographies *see* Series
Beauclerc, Marie 94
Beeton, Isabella and Samuel 13
belles-lettres. See Genres
Bibliographica 157
Blackett, Harriet Jane 160, 183
Blackett, Henry 159
Blackett, Spencer Collinson 1–4, 158–72 *passim*, 174, 185–7
Blackett & Hallam 160
Blackwood, John 13
Blakeway, Ellen. *See* King, Ellen Blakeway
Blunt, Wilfrid Scawen 74, 96, 97
Bodley Head, The 171–2
Bookman, The 117, 131, 143, 181, 187
Bogue, David 143
Books About Books. *See* Series
Bottomley, Horatio 1, 2, 56, 138–40,

144–8, 150, 152, 154, 175–6, 179, 180, 185
Brackenbury, Charles Booth 123–4
Bradley, F.H. 130–1
Brontë, Charlotte 18, 29, 110
Brooke, Stopford 17–18, 21, 28, 31, 34, 56, 73, 128, 172
Browning, Oscar 115, 120–3, 178, 188
Browning, Robert 18, 21, 55, 74, 88, 117, 170, 184
Buchanan, Robert 40–1, 116
Burn & Co. (bookbinders) 44, 113, 115
Burton, Sir Richard and Lady Isabel 106–7, 129
Butler, Josephine 142–3
Butler, Samuel 142–3

C. Kegan Paul & Co. (imprint) 2, 39, 45, 79, 84, 97, 109, 128
Caithness, Countess of 149, 150, 185
Cambridge University Press 9, 122
Carlyle, Thomas 101
Catholicism (CKP's) 53, 75, 76, 114, 175
Chace Act 140
Chapman & Hall 10, 101, 142, 160, 171
Chatto & Windus 100, 137
Chiswick Press 113, 115
Colonial Library. *See* Series
Colvile, Margaret Agnes. *See* Paul, Margaret Agnes
commission agreements. *See* Contracts
Comte, Auguste 74–5, 114, 149, 180
Conder, Claude Reignier 133–4, 136
Congreve, Richard 74–6, 80, 95

Contemporary Review 40–2, 208
Contracts with authors; commission 6, 30, 81–2, 88–9, 125, 131–7, 189; purchase of copyright 15, 29–30, 88, 125–8, 148; royalty 88–9, 125, 128–31; shared profits 88–9, 125, 128–31
Conway, Martin 81
copyright, international legislation 9, 32, 121, 140–1
copyright, purchase of. *See* Contracts
Cornhill Library of Fiction. *See* Series
Cornhill Magazine 19, 23, 31
Cornish, Frank 115
Crawfurd, Oswald 82, 117
Crookes, Sir William 147

Dante 115–17
Darnton, Robert 8
Darwin, Charles 32
database of authors and titles 5–7, 92–3
Davidoff, Leonore and Catherine Hall 184
Dawson, George 94, 129
Day of Rest, The 41–2
de Vere, Aubrey 97
Dent, J.M. 112
Dickens, Charles 8, 10, 68, 110
Dobson, Austin 74, 81, 91, 96–7, 116–17, 155–6, 185, 208
Dowden, Edward 114–15
Dryden House 167, 171, 186, 209
Dryden House Memoirs. *See* Series
Duff, E. Gordon 157
Düffing, Frederick 143–4, 148, 152, 209

Education Library. *See* Series
education, philosophy and classics; law and jurisprudence. *See* Genres
Edwards (Trübner manager) 143
Eliot, George 10, 13, 51, 69, 74, 77–8, 88, 98, 110, 114, 170, 181, 184
Eliot, Simon 9

Examiner 34, 188
Exell, Rev. J.S. 95, 118–20, 124, 131

Faithfull, Emily 13
Feather, John 10
Feltes, N.N. 141
fiction. *See* Genres
Fortnightly Review 86, 89, 209
Franklin, Cecil 172
Free Christian Union 72–3
Funk & Wagnall 165

Galton, Francis 111–12
Gardiner, Samuel 102
Garibaldi, Giuseppe 22, 29
Garnett, Richard 82, 114, 186
gender 5–8, 91, 135–7, 183–4
Genres published by the Kegan Paul firms: *belles-lettres* 92, 107; education, philosophy and classics; law and jurisprudence 92, 107–9; fiction 6, 31, 92, 98–101; history and biography 92, 101–4; juvenile works 92, 108–9; poetry 6, 91–2, 96–8; political and social economy 92, 105–6; religion/theology 6, 92, 94–6, 105; science; medicine and surgery 92, 104–5, 108. *See also* Series. International Scientific Series; travel and geographical research 92, 106–7
George, Henry 5, 106, 208
Gettman, Royal S. 12
Gilbert & Rivington 143, 152
Gladstone, William Ewart 21, 40, 42, 79, 103, 127
Godwin, William 35, 68, 208
Good Words 36, 40
Goodford, C.O. 52, 54, 59, 60
Gordon, Major-Gen. C. George 103, 110, 126, 179, 209
Gosse, Edmund 114, 129
Gough, Edward 131–3
Greenwood, Frederick 20

Greg, William R. 142
Griffith & Farran 44, 160

H.S. King & Co. (imprint) 2, 15, 28, 41, 45, 172
Hackney Hansard 145
half profits. *See* Contracts
Hallam, Percy 160
Hansard Union 2, 139, 140, 145, 147, 175, 209
Hanson, Edward 143
Hardy, Thomas 5, 36, 69, 78, 82–3, 85, 98–9, 128, 181, 184
Harper & Brothers 102, 121
Haweis, Hugh Reginald 34, 94
Hawtrey, Stephen 66
Heinemann, William 142, 158–60, 163, 165
history and biography. *See* Genres
history of the book, method and theory 1, 3–14, 91–3, 187–8
Hollings, Frank (William Redway) 143
Holt, Henry 102
Home Education Series. *See* Series
Hopkins, Peter 173
Howard, Michael S. 12
Hueffer, Francis 82
Hurst & Blackett 159
Huxley, Leonard 20
Huxley, Thomas H. 5, 32–3, 75, 111, 124, 184, 209
Hyndman, H.M. 130

Ilminster 49, 51, 52, 58, 211
Ingelow, Jean 40–1, 109, 125
International Scientific Series. *See* Series
Isaacs, Sir Henry 148

Jenkins, Edward 40, 42
Jowett, Benjamin 17
juvenile works. *See* Genres

Kains-Jackson, Charles 114, 188
Kegan Paul International 3, 173
Kegan Paul, Trench & Co. (imprint) 2, 84, 128, 137, 139
Kegan Paul, Trench, Trübner & Co. Ltd. (imprint) 2–3, 140–5, 167, 172–3, 185
Kennard, Coleridge 147–8, 152
King, Daniel 16
King, Ellen Blakeway 18–20, 183–4
King, Harriet Eleanor (Hamilton) 1, 4, 16, 21–6, 28–30, 34, 46, 183–4
King, Henry Samuel 16–18, 44–6, 54; publishing and banking 1–2, 4, 6, 15–47 *passim*, 73, 78, 179, 182, 190
King, Henry Seymour 18, 24, 46
King, Richard 17, 46
Kingsley, Charles 17, 29, 35, 55–60, 65, 69, 73, 78, 94, 179, 180
Knowles, James T. 37, 40, 42, 208

Lake, Reginald 152
Lane, John 171
Lang, Andrew 96–7, 114
Laurie, Simon 122–3, 172, 210
Lethbridge, Sir Roper 148
Lindsay, William 148, 154
Little, Brown 109
Lives of English Popular Leaders. *See* Series
Longman 31, 43, 68, 71, 103, 141, 143, 179
Lubbock, Sir John 104, 156, 209
Ludlow, J.M. 72, 78

MacDonald, George 40–1, 125–6
Macmillan 46, 79, 108
Macrae, Curtice and Co. 138, 145, 146
Magnus, Laurie 172
Magnus, Sir Philip 108, 121–4, 157, 210
Marindin, Isabella 60, 61, 64
Mason, Charlotte Maria Shaw 108, 157
Mathews, Charles Elkin 171
Maurice, Frederick D. 17

INDEX

Mazzini, Giuseppe 4, 21–9 *passim*, 41, 183
Meredith, George 5, 85, 100–1, 175, 208
Meynell, Wilfrid 48, 86, 99, 100, 180
Military Handbooks. *See* Series
Millgate, Michael 82
Modern Science Series. *See* Series
Morris, Lewis 30
Morris, William 90
Mudie (Circulating Library) 9, 90
Mumby, F.A. 12, 79
Murray, John 136

Net Book Agreement 140, 209
New Quarterly Magazine 82, 208
Newman, John Henry (Cardinal) 36, 53–4, 82, 114, 171, 176, 180
Nineteenth Century 42–3, 71, 208–9

Out of Door Library. *See* Series

Pall Mall Gazette 19, 72
Pamphlet Library. *See* Series
Parchment Library. *See* Series
Parker, John W. & Son 31, 61, 64, 95
Parry, Edward Abbott 157
Pascal, Blaise 117, 176
Paternoster House 151, 167, 209
Paul, Andrew Louis 63–4, 77–8, 178
Paul, Charles (father of CKP) 49–52, 54–6, 59
Paul, Charles Kegan 17, 34–5, 49–57, 57–78, 80, 161, 174–8, 180–2; publishing 1–4, 15, 37–40, 43–5, 48–9, 74–83, 84–137 *passim*, 138–61 *passim*, 179–80, 188–90; Works. *William Godwin* (1876) 35; 'The Production and Life of Books' (1883) 86, 91, 110, 126, 185; *Confessio Viatoris* (1891) 177; *Faith and Unfaith* (1891) 86, 175; *Memories* (1899) 3–4; *On the Way Side* (1899) 174

Paul, Frances (Horne) 49, 52, 55, 59
Paul, Margaret Agnes 1, 31, 34, 60–5, 71–3, 76–7, 80–1, 178, 180, 183–5
Pleasure xxi, 29–30, 41, 183
poetry. *See* Genres
political and social economy. *See* Genres
Pollard, Arthur 95–6, 117, 127, 149, 156–7, 160, 167, 178–9, 188, 209
Publishers' Circular 9, 15, 28–9, 32, 45, 77, 84, 86, 94, 114–15, 126, 144, 147, 151, 153, 156, 185, 187, 189
Pulpit Commentary. *See* Series.

Rayment, Arthur 154, 162
Redway, Charles 143–4
Redway, Edith (Rowden) 183
Redway, George William 1–6, 143–4, 148–54, 175, 185–7
religion/theology. *See* Genres
Religious Tract Society 35, 98, 108
Rendel, Willie 178, 211
Robertson, Charles 177
Robertson, Frederick W. 17, 19, 34, 56, 88
Rossetti, Dante Gabriel 41, 116
Routledge, George & Son 3, 12, 124, 172–3, 190
Routledge & Kegan Paul 1–3, 172, 173, 190
royalty. *See* Contracts

Saint Paul's Magazine 40
St James 32, 33, 114, 188
St James's Gazette 157
Savile Club 74, 177, 184
Schmitz, J. Hubert 150, 153–4, 160, 162, 209
science; medicine and surgery. *See* Genres
Scott, Sir Walter 10, 22, 50
Series published by the Kegan Paul firms: Beacon Biographies 157, 164, 169–71; Books About Books 156, 157, 209; Colonial Library 41, 109,

INDEX

124–6, 156, 209; Cornhill Library of Fiction 31, 34, 44, 208; Dryden House Memoirs 167, 186, 209; Education Library 108, 115, 120–4, 157, 208; Home Education Series 108, 155, 157, 209; International Scientific Series 31–4, 44, 76, 84, 104–5, 111–13, 121, 124, 156, 160, 173, 208; Lives of English Popular Leaders 31; Military Handbooks 123, 124, 154–6, 168, 169, 186, 208; Modern Science Series 155–6, 209; Out of Door Library 168, 209; Pamphlet Library 167, 209; Parchment Library 49, 97, 107, 112–15, 117–18, 120, 124, 137, 156, 165, 190, 208–9; Pulpit Commentary 80, 95, 118–20, 124, 131, 155–6, 164, 165, 208; Westminster Biographies 155, 157, 164, 169–71; Wolseley Military Series 168, 209
series as a publishing form 6, 31
Sewell, William 55
Shakespeare, William 50, 68, 94, 107, 114–15, 164, 165, 188
shared profits agreements. *See* Contracts
Shaw, George Bernard 106
Shelley, Percy 35, 68, 114
Shillingsburg, Peter 10
Shorter, Clement 113
Sinnett, Arthur 1, 143–5, 147–9, 152–4, 175–6, 209
Small, Maynard & Co 164, 169, 170
Smith, Elder & Co. 18–21, 23–4, 26, 28–9, 34, 43, 99, 117, 182
Smith, George 18–20, 117, 141, 182–3
Society of Authors 89, 140
Sonnenschein, William Swan 172, 210
Spence, H.D.M. 118–19
Spencer, Herbert 5, 32–3, 122, 124
Spottiswoode (printers) 44
Stevenson, Robert Louis 49, 85, 99–101, 137, 175, 181, 208–9
Strachey, Jane Maria 117
Strachey, Sir Richard 72, 148, 154

Strahan, Alexander 34, 37, 40–4, 47, 88, 109, 208
Stretton, Hesba 34–6, 47, 98, 108, 179, 208
Srebrnik, Patricia 40
Sutherland, John 8–11
Swinburne, Algernon 21, 29, 41, 115–16, 183

Tennyson, Alfred 2, 10, 15, 36–46 *passim*, 52, 67, 74, 79–80, 85, 96, 101, 106, 113, 116–17, 160, 175, 179, 181, 208–9
Thackeray, William M. 10, 18–19, 29
Theological Review 49, 68–9
Times, The 22, 34, 53, 85, 123, 150, 171, 181
Thompson, Hugh 155–6
travel and geographical research. *See* Genres
Trench, Alfred Chenevix 1–4, 78–81, 84–137 *passim*, 140, 182–3, 190
Trench, Frederick Chenevix 124
Trench, Isabella (Moore) 183
Trench, Maria 103
Trench, Philip 80
Trench, Richard Chenevix (Archbishop) 79, 89, 95, 97, 131
Trollope, Anthony 10, 40
Trübner, Marie 141, 143
Trübner, Nicholas 1–2, 106, 140–3, 149
Trübner & Co. 2–3, 139, 145, 148, 151–2, 173, 185
Tyndall, John 32–3, 124
typography and design 90, 189–90

Venturi, Emilie Ashurst 24, 29, 41
Vincent, David 11
Vizetelly, Henry 143–4

Wallace, Alfred Russel 106
Waugh, Arthur 80, 141, 158–61, 167, 170–1, 186, 209

Webb, Robert K. 10–11
West, James L.W. 4
Westminster Biographies. *See* Series.
Wilberforce, Samuel (Bishop) 58, 66, 94
Willett, Basil W. 123, 172
Wingfield, H. 171, 209
Wise, Thomas J. 113, 115, 179

wives of publishers 4, 183–5
Wollstonecraft, Mary 35, 68
Wolseley Military Series. *See* Series
Wordsworth, William 117

Youmans, Edward L. 32–3, 111–12

For Product Safety Concerns and Information please contact our EU
representative GPSR@taylorandfrancis.com
Taylor & Francis Verlag GmbH, Kaufingerstraße 24, 80331 München, Germany

www.ingramcontent.com/pod-product-compliance
Lightning Source LLC
Chambersburg PA
CBHW062143300426
44115CB00012BA/2026